CRUISING: A GUIDE TO THE CRUISE LINE INDUSTRY

CRUISING: A GUIDE TO THE CRUISE LINE INDUSTRY

Marc Mancini, Ph.D.
Professor of Travel
West Los Angeles College

Africa • Australia • Canada • Denmark • Japan • Mexico • New Zealand • Phillippines
Puerto Rico • Singapore • Spain • United Kingdom • United States

Notice to the Reader

Publisher does not warrant or guarantee any of the products described herein or perform any independent analysis in connection with any of the product information contained herein. Publisher does not assume, and expressly disclaims, any obligation to obtain and include information other than that provided to it by the manufacturer.

The reader is expressly warned to consider and adopt all safety precautions that might be indicated by the activities herein and to avoid all potential hazards. By following the instructions contained herein, the reader willingly assumes all risks in connections with such instructions.

The Publisher makes no representation or warranties of any kind, including but not limited to, the warranties of fitness for particular purpose or merchantability, nor are any such representations implied with respect to the material set forth herein, and the publisher takes no responsibility with respect to such material. The publisher shall not be liable for any special, consequential, or exemplary damages resulting, in whole or part, from the readers' use of, or reliance upon, this material.

Delmar Staff:
Business Unit Director: Susan Simpfenderfer
Executive Editor: Marlene McHugh Pratt
Editorial Assistant: Judy Roberts
Executive Marketing Manager: Donna Lewis
Executive Production Manager: Wendy A. Troeger
Production Editor: Elaine Scull
Cover Design: Joseph Villanova
Cover Image: Commodore Cruise Line

COPYRIGHT © 2000

Delmar is a division of Thomson Learning. The Thomson Learning logo is a registered trademark used herein under license.

Printed in Canada

1 2 3 4 5 6 7 8 9 10 XXX 05 04 03 02 01 00 99

For more information, contact Delmar, 3 Columbia Circle, PO Box 15015, Albany, NY 12212-0515; or find us on the World Wide Web at http://www.delmar.com

Library of Congress Cataloging-in-Publication Data
Mancini, Marc, 1946–
    Cruising: a guide to the cruise line industry / Marc Mancini.
       p. cm.
    Includes bibliographical references and index.
    ISBN: 0-7668-0971-4
    1. Ocean travel   2. Cruise ships   I. Title
G550.M19   1999
910.4′5—dc21   99-33793
                                CIP

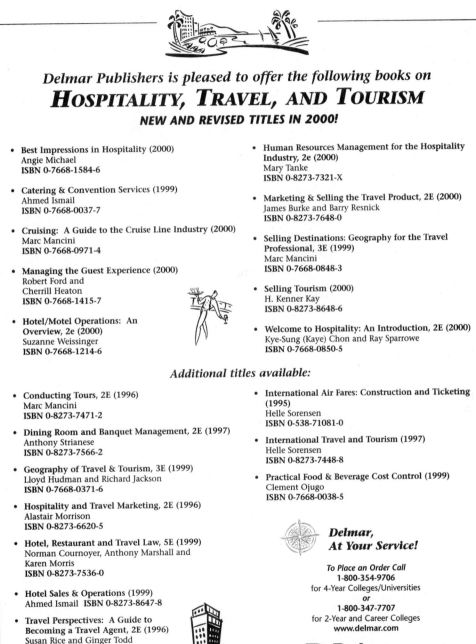

Delmar Publishers is pleased to offer the following books on
HOSPITALITY, TRAVEL, AND TOURISM
NEW AND REVISED TITLES IN 2000!

- **Best Impressions in Hospitality (2000)**
  Angie Michael
  ISBN 0-7668-1584-6

- **Catering & Convention Services (1999)**
  Ahmed Ismail
  ISBN 0-7668-0037-7

- **Cruising: A Guide to the Cruise Line Industry (2000)**
  Marc Mancini
  ISBN 0-7668-0971-4

- **Managing the Guest Experience (2000)**
  Robert Ford and
  Cherrill Heaton
  ISBN 0-7668-1415-7

- **Hotel/Motel Operations: An Overview, 2e (2000)**
  Suzanne Weissinger
  ISBN 0-7668-1214-6

- **Human Resources Management for the Hospitality Industry, 2e (2000)**
  Mary Tanke
  ISBN 0-8273-7321-X

- **Marketing & Selling the Travel Product, 2E (2000)**
  James Burke and Barry Resnick
  ISBN 0-8273-7648-0

- **Selling Destinations: Geography for the Travel Professional, 3E (1999)**
  Marc Mancini
  ISBN 0-7668-0848-3

- **Selling Tourism (2000)**
  H. Kenner Kay
  ISBN 0-8273-8648-6

- **Welcome to Hospitality: An Introduction, 2E (2000)**
  Kye-Sung (Kaye) Chon and Ray Sparrowe
  ISBN 0-7668-0850-5

Additional titles available:

- **Conducting Tours, 2E (1996)**
  Marc Mancini
  ISBN 0-8273-7471-2

- **Dining Room and Banquet Management, 2E (1997)**
  Anthony Strianese
  ISBN 0-8273-7566-2

- **Geography of Travel & Tourism, 3E (1999)**
  Lloyd Hudman and Richard Jackson
  ISBN 0-7668-0371-6

- **Hospitality and Travel Marketing, 2E (1996)**
  Alastair Morrison
  ISBN 0-8273-6620-5

- **Hotel, Restaurant and Travel Law, 5E (1999)**
  Norman Cournoyer, Anthony Marshall and Karen Morris
  ISBN 0-8273-7536-0

- **Hotel Sales & Operations (1999)**
  Ahmed Ismail **ISBN 0-8273-8647-8**

- **Travel Perspectives: A Guide to Becoming a Travel Agent, 2E (1996)**
  Susan Rice and Ginger Todd
  ISBN 0-8273-6533-0

- **International Air Fares: Construction and Ticketing (1995)**
  Helle Sorensen
  ISBN 0-538-71081-0

- **International Travel and Tourism (1997)**
  Helle Sorensen
  ISBN 0-8273-7448-8

- **Practical Food & Beverage Cost Control (1999)**
  Clement Ojugo
  ISBN 0-7668-0038-5

Delmar,
At Your Service!

To Place an Order Call
1-800-354-9706
for 4-Year Colleges/Universities
or
1-800-347-7707
for 2-Year and Career Colleges
www.delmar.com

Delmar
Thomson Learning™

CONTENTS

PREFACE

Ask 100 people what makes a vacation getaway perfect, and you'll get 100 answers: relaxation, comfort, exploration, learning, great experiences in great places, plenty to do and plenty to see, great shopping, fabulous meals, constant pampering, and more.

Some travel products feature *some* of these things. Cruises provide them *all*.

Cruising has become one of the most significant phenomena of our age. For that reason, it's something that almost certainly intrigues you. And if it does, then *Cruising: A Guide to the Cruise Line Industry* is surely the right book for you.

Cruising is written for two kinds of readers:

- *Industry professionals,* such as travel agents and potential cruise line employees, who want to know more about the cruise experience
- *Students of travel* who are contemplating careers as travel agents, cruise line employees or other cruise-related professionals

If you fit either of these categories, then *Cruising* is written with you in mind.

How This Book is Unique

Cruising is a unique sort of textbook:

- **It approaches its topic from the perspective of a working professional.** You'll get a true insider's look on how cruise sales, marketing, and operations unfold.
- **It makes reading about cruising fun.** Cruising *is* fun. A book—even a textbook—on cruises should be the same. *Cruising* uses a breezy, magazine-like prose to make learning an enjoyable experience for you.
- **It uses many educational strategies to help you remember and understand what you read.** Highlighting, bullet points, headings, graphs, tables, photos, and application activities serve to clarify, magnify, and reinforce information. The result: You absorb a far greater percentage of what you read.

How This Book is Organized

Cruising features ten chapters. Each blends definitions, statistics, anecdotes, insights, and examples into what we hope is a definitive look at the cruise business.

- Each chapter begins with a list of *objectives.* They describe what you'll know and should be able to do by chapter's end.
- **Key terms** and **phrases** are boldfaced in the text to underscore their importance.
- *Photos, graphs,* and *sidebars* expand each chapter's content.
- *Questions for discussion* permit you to test your understanding of the material in that chapter.
- *Activities* close each chapter and challenge you to take a hypothetical situation and apply it into a creative solution.
- The book concludes with *appendices* (key addresses and a bibliography), a *glossary* of cruise-related terms, and an *index.*

About CLIA Certification

If you're already a travel agent enrolled in the CLIA certification program, studying this book and passing a test available from CLIA and specific to this text will yield you 25 credits. You may order your test via CLIA's fax-on-demand service at (800) 372-CLIA or by calling (212) 921-0066. If you would like to know more about CLIA certification, call CLIA's fax-on-demand service or visit its Web site at www.cruising.org.

To the Instructor or Trainer

Cruising has been created with your pragmatic needs in mind. It can serve as your primary textbook in a course on cruising, or it may be used as a supplement to other courses.

Its content was determined through a questionnaire sent to college and industry educators across North America. Ninety-three surveys were completed and returned to us, so we feel confident that our text reflects the needs of the educational community. The book was also thoroughly reviewed by the CLIA Marketing Committee, which is comprised of senior cruise line executives. For this reason, the content should be accurate and timely.

An *Instructor's Manual* amplifies the book and will make your teaching much easier. Among its content:

- Thematic outlines for all chapters
- Suggested answers to the Questions for Discussion
- Suggested solutions to the Activities
- A bank of quizzes, with answers, for each chapter

Acknowledgments

The author wishes to acknowledge the following educators for serving as reviewers: Barbara Gallup, Parks Junior College, Denver, Colorado, and Sherry A. Hine, Mid Florida Technical Institute, Orlando, Florida.

We would also like to thank the CLIA member lines and their representatives to the marketing committee, as well as the CLIA staff, for their assistance, input, and support.

And special thanks to Jim Godsman, CLIA's president; Bob Kwortnik, CLIA's director of training; and to my assistants, Karen Fukushima and Ramani Durvasula, for their efficient, thorough, and enthusiastic support throughout this project.

About the Author

Marc Mancini, Ph.D., is one of the travel industry's most famous consultants and speakers. Over 60,000 people have attended seminars he's presented or designed, and nearly 100 companies and organizations—including CLIA—have benefited from his consulting skills.

He has written two other textbooks (*Selling Destinations* and *Conducting Tours*), published over 200 articles, and appeared on CNN and *Good Morning America*. He has a B.A. from Providence College and an M.A., M.S., and Ph.D. from the University of Southern California. He was named Teacher of the Year by the International Society of Travel and Tourism Educators. He lives in Brentwood, California.

CHAPTER ONE

INTRODUCTION

After reading this chapter, you'll be able to

- Define the term *cruise*

- Explain the history of cruising and how it affects today's cruise vacation experience

- Describe the contemporary cruise experience

- Distinguish among different types of itineraries

W hen historians of the future look back to the way people of our time traveled, they'll almost certainly zero in on one remarkable phenomenon—the success of cruising.

They'll cite the fact that the number of people who took a cruise vacation increased by almost 10% each year—a growth unmatched by any other segment of the travel industry. They'll note that over 95% of all cruisers said that they were very to highly satisfied with the cruise experience. They'll marvel at the great, graceful vessels—both large and small—that carried just about every kind of person—married, single, young, old, wealthy or just getting by—to virtually every place on the globe. And, most of all, they'll be astonished by the level of service and spectrum of activities—both on and off the ship—that these passengers enjoyed. No wonder consumers are highly satisfied with the cruise experience, rating it higher than any other vacation choices. (See Figure 1-1.)

We live in exciting times, when more and more people discover how truly wonderful a cruise vacation can be. And as a member—or a potential member—of the vast travel community that makes such cruise dreams come true, you should justifiably be proud.

As important as the present and future of cruising is, however, you should also know a little about its past. The cruise industry's genealogy is important. And it's a fascinating tale indeed.

Definitions and Beginnings

Before exploring cruising's ancestry, how about the definition of cruising? *A cruise is a vacation trip by ship.* It's that simple. This definition excludes traveling by water for purely business purposes (e.g., cargo ships), sailing on one's own small pleasure craft,

FIGURE 1-1 Satisfaction comparison of cruises with other vacations
Source: *Cruising Dynamics Study*

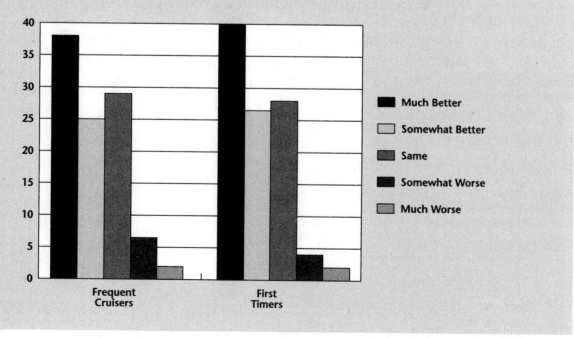

Not only are consumers highly satisfied with their cruise experiences; they rate them higher than other vacation choices.

or travel on a vessel for primarily transportational purposes (e.g., a short ferry ride). A cruise is primarily a leisure vacation experience, with the ship's staff doing all the work. Some cruise ships also transport cargo, and all of them carry people from place to place. But at the core of cruising—from the perspective of the traveler—is the desire to relax, to get away from it all, to experience, to learn, to be pampered, and to have fun. Today that almost always takes place on a vessel custom-built to satisfy these goals, though it can also take place on a freighter, a ferry-like ship, or during a transatlantic sailing. So long as the emphasis is on the passenger's desire to have a great time, it's cruising.

And that's exactly what was going on in ancient times, to a limited extent, in the Mediterranean. Of course, ships sailed this legendary sea mostly for practical purposes: exploration, commerce, migration, and warfare. But there were always a few hardy souls who came aboard just to experience the far-flung ports that these vessels visited. The most famous: Herodotus, who during his sailing compiled a list of the most interesting manmade things he saw. Today we call them the Seven Ancient Wonders of the World (see Figure 1-2). And there's a reason he did it: to provide other pleasure travelers of his time with a sort of guidebook to where to go and what to see. And like him, most of them did it by boat.

After about 500 A.D., "leisure" travel virtually disappeared. Certainly, some awesome seagoing trips took place (e.g., people from Tahiti sailed 2,000 miles to Hawaii, the Vikings reached North America, and controversial evidence exists that the ancient Chinese crossed the Pacific all the way to California). But these and other sailings were to explore, to trade, to conquer, or to settle. "Tourists" aboard these ships were a rarity. Pleasure was only an afterthought.

The Arrival of Leisure Sailing

In the 1800s, shipping companies rediscovered that they could increase their profits by booking passengers aboard their merchant ships. A few of these travelers were wealthy patrons looking for adventure in faraway lands. Most of the others were relatively poor people looking for a new place to live.

Eventually shipping companies began building vessels whose primary purpose wasn't to transport cargo, but to transport people. Technology helped make it possible,

FIGURE 1-2   The Seven Ancient Wonders of the World

- The Pyramids (Giza, Egypt)

- The Hanging Gardens of Babylon (near Baghdad, Iraq)

- The Statue of Zeus at Olympia (Greece)

- The Temple of Diana at Ephesus (Turkey)

- The Mausoleum (Helicarnassus, Turkey)

- The Colossus (Rhodes)

- The Pharos Lighthouse (Alexandria, Egypt)

as wooden ships with sails were replaced by steel-hulled vessels that were driven by coal, oil, and steam—not wind. (The early steel ships also had sail riggings, which were only there to reassure passengers.) These transports became larger and larger, with names like *Aquitania, Leviathan,* and, yes, *Titanic.* Surprisingly, a few of the "steamship" companies that built the great turn-of-the-century vessels are still around today: Cunard, P&O, and Holland America.

Ocean liners were among the most astonishing creations to appear in the early 1900s. Their exteriors were majestic and boastful, their interiors as lavish as the great hotels of Europe. Or at least parts of them were.

The major purpose of the ocean liner of those times was to carry immigrants, not the well-to-do. That was where most of the money was made. Ships were usually divided into two or three "classes." In first class were the wealthy; second class accommodated people of modest but sufficient means; third class, or "steerage," was for the masses. On any given sailing, there might be 100 passengers in first, 100 in second, and 2,000 in third.

The contrast between first class and steerage was striking. In first class, passengers dined in elegant surroundings, were entertained by tuxedoed musicians, and slept in the poshest of staterooms. (Though there's controversy about this, the word *posh* is said to come from the words *Port Out, Starboard Home,* which described the best side of the ship to to have your cabin on when sailing between England and India.) In steerage, passengers ate soup and boiled potatoes, were entertained by their fellow passengers, and slept in vast dormitories on cots bunked two or three high. Nowhere on the ship were the two groups allowed to mix.

Yet these steerage passengers were so important to profitability that steamship lines actually designed their ship exteriors to appeal to immigrant beliefs. For example, steerage passengers would arrive at a port, dragging their ample baggage along, with no idea which ship they would take. They believed, naively, that the quality of a vessel could be judged by its number of smokestacks. So the steamship lines would often put extra funnels atop their ships—funnels that had absolutely no function except to attract passengers.

This sort of travel seems alien to us today. But consider this: About one out of four North Americans has at least one ancestor who arrived via one of these ships. There's a good chance, then, that you wouldn't be here if it weren't for an ocean liner.

The Luxury Palaces

During World War I most ocean-crossing vessels were converted into troop transport ships. After the war they were joined by a new generation of ships: bigger, sleeker, and, above all, faster. Speed became the most important goal. Indeed, something called the *Blue Riband* was awarded regularly to whichever ship could cross the North Atlantic in the least amount of time. Transportation, not "cruising," continued to be what passenger ships were mostly about.

During the 1920s and 1930s, though, ocean liners did begin to provide more entertainment, attract more of the middle class, and provide much of the pampering we associate today with cruising. Even the Depression failed to dent the business. A key reason: During Prohibition, just about the only place for an American to drink liquor was on the high seas. (Onboard casinos, however, were still a rarity.) Being on an ocean liner became a fashionable thing. Newspapers regularly touted the names of celebrities who were sailing on ships.

Ships continued to become larger, with their costs often subsidized by governments. Nations used ocean liners as symbols of their prosperity, taste, and might. The

On July 5, 1961, seven luxury liners all happened to be in New York City at the same time. The vessel arriving is the *Queen Elizabeth*. Docked, from bottom to top, are the *Independence, America, United States, Olympia, Mauretania* and *Sylvania*. Also in the shot: The aircraft carrier *USS Intrepid*.
Courtesy of CLIA

Queen Mary—now an attraction in Long Beach, California—was Britain's pride, while the *France*—now the *Norway*—was everything Gallic achievement could be. These ships were huge, floating cities, every bit as big as many of today's cruise vessels.

The Birth of Contemporary Cruising

Though plenty might be going on aboard ship, it would be wrong to call transoceanic crossings "cruising," as we know of cruising today. The primary purpose was transportation, with no intermediate stops to see what was along the way. But even in the early 1900s, a few (usually smaller) steamship lines devised a product that was closer to a "cruise." During winter (when ocean crossings were least popular), they would concede the transatlantic business to their bigger competitors and "reposition" their ships to warmer places, like the Caribbean. (It was a nice way to avoid icebergs, too.) The experience—often called an *excursion*—became purely leisure. People would book a cruise to visit a series of exotic ports and to do interesting things while onboard. Even a few around-the-world cruises appeared.

This vacation cruise business was a minor one—crossoceanic transportation still dominated—until June 1958. During that month, airlines started the first commercial

The Norway is one of the few classic cruise ships remaining (it was originally called *The France*).
Courtesy of Norwegian Cruise Line

jet service across the Atlantic. Ocean crossings became a matter of hours, not days. And the cruise lines were instantly in trouble.

People bound for another continent suddenly found ships to be a slow, boring choice. Within one year, more people were crossing the Atlantic by air than by sea. Only those who feared air travel or were looking for a very leisurely, away-from-the-ordinary experience continued to book transoceanic crossings. The joke was that ocean liners were only for "the newly wed and the nearly dead." Though they continued to sell their ships as transocean transportation, steamship lines—or at least some of them—concluded that they had to rethink their business dramatically. Crossings diminished, and cruising was in.

Modern Cruising Develops

Those smaller ships cruising the Caribbean became the business model nearly every company pursued. Let's think of ships as floating resorts, they said, that offer pleasurable activities, great food, superb service, and—yes—convenient,

A shift to Caribbean destinations marked the rebirth of contemporary cruising.
Courtesy of Carnival Cruise Lines

no-packing-and-unpacking transportation from place to place. The Blue Riband no longer resonated in the minds of consumers—the fun ships and love boats did.

A few new liners, built primarily for ocean crossings, appeared in the 1960s. There were still enough passengers to justify them, and it was believed that more "modern" vessels would bring the passengers back.

But the emphasis on leisure cruising led to the rapid conversion of many existing ships into cruise vessels. The cruise lines tore out the bulkheads separating the classes, installed air conditioning, expanded pool areas, put in casinos, and converted staid function rooms into discos. Cruising became a major phenomenon, with cruise companies building new ships in the 1970s designed specifically for cruising.

Cruising gained even greater momentum in the 1980s and especially the 1990s. "Megaships" appeared that far exceeded the size and scope of the biggest ocean liners, while smaller super-luxury vessels targeted people who sought the very highest of experiences. There were high-tech masted sailing ships, too, and small expedition vessels that provided "soft" adventures. Massive paddlewheelers once again plied the Mississippi, and one ship, a super-sized catamaran-like vessel, carried over 300 passengers. Soon there was a cruise experience for just about everyone.

Cruising Today

Each year millions of travelers choose to cruise. And far more intend to do so soon. One Cruise Lines International Association (CLIA) survey determined that 56% of all people in Canada and in the U.S. who are over 25 and who have a household income of at least $20,000 would like to cruise. That represents over 74 million potential cruisers.

Cruise factoids
Source: *Selling the Sea,* Bob Dickinson and Andy Vladimir

- A cruise company typically purchases over $600 million of food and beverages each year.

- Mass-market cruise lines spend about $10 per day per passenger for raw food stuffs. For the most expensive lines, the average is about $40.

- On a week-long cruise aboard a large vessel, about 5,000 cases of wine and champagne are used.

- Many ship gyms use air-resistance exercise machines. The kind that incorporate actual weights would be too heavy.

- A fully equipped ship-based gym and spa costs about a half million dollars.

- One-third to one-half of the people onboard a ship are crew members.

- Large cruise ships typically carry $3 million of spare parts.

- The typical dining room server makes $25,000 to 30,000 a year in salary and tips (and crew members have few onboard living expenses).

- On most cruise lines, the number one source of revenue onboard is beverage sales (so many places and opportunities to buy).

- People who gamble on a ship spend about $10 a day.

- In Bermuda, the typical cruise passenger spends $90 while in port.

What are their choices? Many people try out cruising by selecting a short itinerary, such as a three-day Bahamas cruise out of Florida or a four-day journey from Los Angeles to Catalina and Ensenada, Mexico. Some may even sample a one-day "party cruise" before actually taking a multi-day sailing.

Among the more popular itineraries, however, are five- to twelve-day cruises, with seven days being the most common. (In cruise terminology, a Saturday-to-Saturday sailing is called a seven-day cruise, even though eight days are involved in the itinerary. Even more confusing: Since the ship probably leaves Saturday evening and arrives the following Saturday morning, passengers are actually sailing on the ship for six and a half days!)

The ship's agenda can be a **round-trip** or **circle itinerary,** with the vessel leaving from and returning to the same port. For example, a ship could sail from Vancouver, head northward through the Alaskan Inside Passage, turn back at, say, Skagway, and return to Vancouver (stopping, of course, at interesting ports along the way).

In other situations, the cruise might start at one port, but finish at another. A ship could leave Vancouver, but finish its trip in Anchorage. This is called a **one-way itinerary**. In all probability, the vessel would take on a whole new set of passengers in Anchorage and repeat the same itinerary, in reverse, to Vancouver. (For an example of each, see Figure 1-3.)

During the cruise, passengers experience a wealth of onboard activities (e.g., meals, shows, contests, lounging at the pool), which take place primarily on **at-sea days** (when the ship is traveling a long distance). On **port days** (usually the ship docks early

Cruising today satisfies virtually every type of cruiser.
Courtesy of Cunard Line

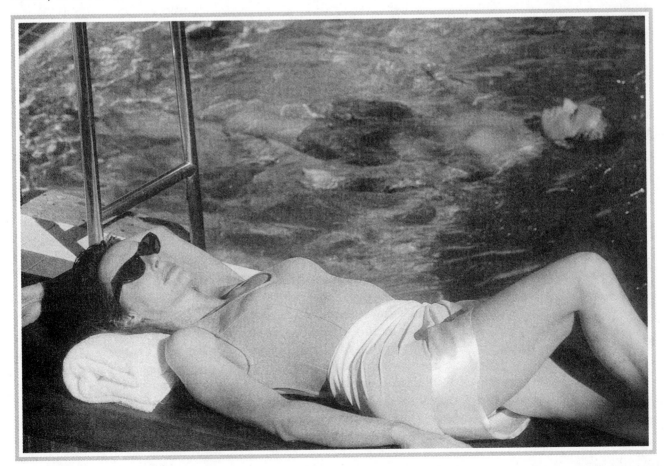

Round-Trip		Arrive	Depart
Sun	Vancouver		5:30 P.M.
Mon	Inside Passage Cruising		
Tue	Juneau	1:00 P.M.	11:00 P.M.
Wed	Skagway	7:00 A.M.	7:30 P.M.
Thu	Glacier Bay Cruising	6:00 A.M.	4:00 P.M.
Fri	Sitka	7:00 A.M.	1:00 P.M.
Sat	Inside Passage Cruising		
Sun	Vancouver	Disembark A.M.	
One-Way (Northbound)		**Arrive**	**Depart**
Sat	Vancouver		5:30 P.M.
Sun	Inside Passage Cruising		
Mon	Ketchikan	6:30 A.M.	2:00 P.M.
Tue	Juneau	6:30 A.M.	11:00 P.M.
Wed	Skagway	7:00 A.M.	7:30 P.M.
Thu	Glacier Bay Cruising	6:00 A.M.	3:00 P.M.
Fri	College Fjord Cruising	3:00 P.M.	6:00 P.M.
Sat	Anchorage (Seward)	Disembark A.M.	

FIGURE 1-3   Two Possible Alaska Itineraries
Source: *Princess Cruises*

in the morning and leaves in the early evening), passengers have the option of going ashore (most do) or staying on the ship. During most itineraries, port days far outnumber at-sea days.

The cruise experience can extend well beyond the cruise itself. Cruise clients sometimes arrive at the cruise departure port a day or two early and/or stay at the port afterward. Their lodging can be purchased from the cruise line or booked separately. (These are called **pre-** and **post-cruise packages.**) In a few cases the cruise line may even bundle and sell the hotel stays for one price, as part of a larger cruise experience. For instance, a family could purchase a package that includes, among other things, a three-night stay at an Orlando hotel, several theme park admissions, transfer to Port Canaveral, and a three-day cruise to the Bahamas, with transfer back to Orlando.

And what of flights? Here are three possibilities. Let's say a couple from New York City wishes to take a cruise that follows a circle itinerary, departing and returning from New Orleans. Their travel agent could book a flight for them to and from New Orleans. (In airline terminology, a flight to and from the same city is called a **round-trip** or **closed-jaw itinerary**.) Or the agent could purchase the flight directly from the cruise line. (The cruise lines contract with the airlines for space and resell that space to passengers.) In a few cases, the flight might even be included in the cruise price, but this is becoming less common.

What if this New York City couple wants to visit the Eastern Mediterranean? They would fly into, say, Venice, Italy. From there, their ship would sail eastward and finish a week later in Istanbul, Turkey. The couple would then fly home from Istanbul. (They could also continue on an extended land vacation in the Middle East.) When an air itinerary features a return from a different city than to the one first flown, it's called an **open-jaw itinerary**.

There's a third possible scenario. A couple who resides in New York City decides to take a cruise to and from Bermuda. The cruise begins and ends in New York City, so there's no need for air at all. (This would be booked as a **cruise-only trip**.)

This discussion of the various shapes a cruise experience can take may have triggered other questions in your mind: What other places do cruises go? How does a typical cruise unfold? What kind of people actually take cruises? All these, and more, will be answered in chapters to come.

Questions for Discussion

1. How did a transoceanic sea voyage differ from a modern cruise?

2. Explain why a seven-day cruise might be viewed as either six, seven, or eight days long.

3. Define the following:

   - at-sea day

   - port day

   - circle itinerary

   - one-way itinerary

   - closed-jaw itinerary

   - open-jaw itinerary

Activity

Obtain a brochure from one cruise line. Study it carefully, then answer the questions below:

Cruise line: For which year?
Title of the brochure:

1. Are there any cruises of four days or less? If yes, briefly describe one itinerary.

2. Are there any cruises of seven days or more? If yes, briefly describe one itinerary.

3. Does the cruise line offer pre- or post-cruise packages? If yes, give a brief description of one of them.

4. Does the cruise line offer air? If yes, describe how it is offered (e.g., as part of the cruise price? As an "extra" that can be booked separately? Anything else?).

CHAPTER TWO

WHO CRUISES— AND WHY

After reading this chapter, you'll be able to

■ Describe the typical clients onboard cruises of different lengths

■ Explain 14 reasons why people are drawn to cruising

■ Identify what is typically included on a cruise, and what isn't

■ Explain how cruises are priced

■ Recognize the 14 most common roadblocks to cruise purchase

Imagine a huge wall map in an imaginary "Museum of Cruising." On that map, little lights mark the spots where every cruise ship currently is located. The first surprise: There are lights just about everywhere there's water, hundreds of them—on the South China Sea, up the Amazon, around Hawaii, even along the coast of Antarctica.

Now press a button. Those lights disappear and are replaced by a new set of lights. These indicate the location of the cruise lines' headquarters. Fewer lights now, but again they're spread across the map—Athens, Miami, Tokyo, and more. Press one more button. This time you'll see where cruise passengers come from. Just about the whole map lights up.

Cruising is indeed a global phenomenon. People from everywhere take cruises to everywhere. One important statistic: Currently only about 11% of all North American adults who can afford to take a cruise have done so, but over five times more say they would someday like to do so.

Here are a few facts, based on research studies done by CLIA and other researchers:

- Twenty-seven percent of all cruisers are under 40 years old, 45% are between 40 and 59, and 28% are over 60. This clearly punctures the myth that "cruises are for old people."
- On average, about 40% of the people onboard are taking their first cruise.
- Three out of every four cruisers are married.
- People who take cruises earn about 20% more money in household income per year than do non-cruisers. They also travel more, in general.
- About 10% of all cruisers bring a child or children along.
- Only 1% travel alone.

Does this give you a clearer picture as to who cruises? Good. You should remember, though, that these statistics define the *average* cruiser. A wide variety of types make up each "average" statistic. The kind of cruise has a powerful bearing on which type within these statistics will be cruising.

There are also many categories of cruisers (e.g., families, singles, and the physically challenged). We'll examine these in more detail later. Just remember for now that the category you fit in very much affects why you cruise.

For example, on a short cruise, passengers tend to

- Be younger
- Have more modest incomes
- Have less education
- Be more likely to work full-time
- Be new to cruising

Conversely, on a longer cruise, the passengers tend to

- Be older
- Have higher incomes
- Be more educated
- Be more likely to be retired or semi-retired
- Have already experienced cruising

Why People Cruise

It often seems that there are as many motives to cruise as there are people. Sometimes the reason is pure curiosity. Other times it's because of a travel agent's recommendation or, very often, positive word-of-mouth from a friend. Perhaps it's simply to fulfill a fantasy. Or maybe it's just to get away from a cold winter.

The cruise industry has intensely studied why people take cruises. Here are the 14 motives that seem to predominate:

1. **A cruise is a hassle-free vacation.** On a cruise, you pack and unpack only once. There's no driving around, looking for your hotel, or wondering where you should eat next. The cruise experience minimizes your concerns, melts away your stress and maximizes your actual vacation time.

2. **A cruise takes you away from it all.** "It's different out there . . ." So went one cruise line's promotional slogan. Smog, pollution, stress, traffic, alarm clocks, beepers, ringing telephones, blinking computers, chattering fax machines—these are *not* what a cruise is all about. Cruises are instead about water, sea, sky, and landscape—the simple things that touch us so deeply.

3. **You're pampered like nowhere else.** Breakfast in bed. Lounging on deck. Soaking in a hot tub. Afternoon tea. Perhaps champagne and caviar. And the most ever-present and gracious service you're ever likely to experience. These are rare in our everyday life but commonplace on a cruise.

4. **You can do it all—or nothing at all.** Most cruises provide a vast series of choices, the kind that enable you to pick, choose, or pass up as you wish. Your day might start

Pampering is a major selling point for cruises.
Courtesy of Norwegian Cruise Line

with morning exercises on deck, yoga in the gym, or dance lessons in the lounge, followed by breakfast. After eating, maybe it's a cooking class or a port lecture. You might choose to watch a new movie or learn a new sport . . . and all this before lunch. But no one will pressure you. You can sleep in until noon or snooze in a deck chair. It's all up to you.

The level of planned activities also varies from ship to ship and from cruise line to cruise line. People who like plenty of things going on can certainly find a cruise that fits the bill. On the other hand, more independent types can select a cruise that features a very relaxed experience with very little structure.

5. **You can sample a broad geographic area.** A cruise usually covers a vast area, stopping at the most interesting places along the way. This is why over 80% of cruisers, according to a CLIA study, consider a cruise vacation to be a good way to sample vacation spots that they may want to return to later for a resort vacation. A number of destinations are in fact *best* visited via a ship. Some examples: Alaska, the Caribbean, the Mediterranean, Indonesia, and the fjords of Norway.

6. **Cruises offer a huge variety of events, activities, and meals.** See a show. Snooze lazily by the pool. Jog. Learn. Swim. Shop. Dine indoors or out, casual or elegant, seven times a day if you want. Explore a port or stay onboard. Cruises these days are about *choice*. Of course the size and "personality" of the ship determine what choices you'll have, but almost surely you'll find it impossible to be bored on a cruise.

7. **It's easy to make friends on a cruise.** Meeting new people on a cruise is simple. Opportunities to socialize seemingly are endless. Many of the people you meet will share your interests—that you chose the same ship, cruise, and destinations assures it. And some of these friendships may endure well beyond the cruise.

8. **A cruise is a romantic experience.** It's amazing how many films, plays, songs, and books use cruises as the setting for romance. Cruises have a way of breathing new energy into an old relationship, or of setting the stage for a new one. (A *Cosmopolitan* survey concluded that 80% of cruisers feel more amorous at sea. It concluded many other things that we will not go into here . . ..)

9. **A cruise is a learning experience.** Even if your goal is merely to have a good time, you're almost sure to learn something new about the ports you visit. On many cruises, expert lecturers onboard give "enrichment" presentations that help you understand more fully the history and culture of places on the itinerary. Indeed, some specialty cruise lines make passenger learning their primary goal (and that's precisely why their passengers select them). A few merge "soft" adventure experiences with education, offering what is called an "expedition" cruise product.

10. **There's a cruise that can satisfy virtually anyone.** As you've no doubt concluded by now, just about everyone—families, singles, clubs, church groups, young people, old people, lovers of sports, lovers of knowledge, and more—can find a cruise to be fulfilling. Few other vacation experiences can make that claim. And it doesn't even have to be a vacation. Many companies hold their meetings, retreats, or incentive events on ships. Some charter the whole vessel.

11. **Everybody's talking about how wondeful cruises are.** Cruising is an "in" thing. Everyone seems to talk about cruises—and that's being reinforced by many TV shows and movies. Several studies indicate that word-of-mouth from relatives, friends, and acquaintances is a prime reason consumers choose to cruise. And several experts argue that a "hidden" reason for people to go on cruises is so they can brag about it when they get back.

12. **Cruises represent a safe travel experience.** In an age when crime or terrorism happens far too easily, a cruise represents one of the safest vacation choices available.

Tweety Bird tucks in a young cruiser.
Courtesy of Premier Cruises

The ship's environment is highly managed. Anything out of the ordinary is swiftly noted. Passage onto and off the ship is strictly controlled. And vessels have safety devices and construction features that make problems very unlikely.

13. **It's a fabulous value for the money.** When you compare what you get for your cruise dollar to what you'd pay for a similar land–based vacation, you discover quickly that a cruise is a remarkable bargain. Since consumers regularly rate cruises higher than other vacation choices, a cruise's value becomes keenly apparent.

14. **You know what you're paying in advance.** A cruise generally is an inclusive vacation. When people pay for their cruise experience, they know up front what the majority of their vacation will cost. Rarely is this so for other sorts of trips. For example, a family driving through southern Europe will probably know what their air, hotel, and car rental costs will be. But the cost for food, drinks, gas, tolls, and entertainment is quite unpredictable. These items could easily add 50% to the cost of the trip.

The degree of cruise "inclusiveness," however, varies from cruise line to cruise line, from ship to ship, and even from itinerary to itinerary:

- *Always or almost always included* are stateroom accommodations, stateroom amenities (e.g., shampoo), meals, certain beverages, entertainment, onboard activities, supervised children's programs, access to the exercise facility, and, of course, the ship transportation. In a few cases, room service or dining at a special alternative onboard restaurant entails a modest add-on charge.

- *Sometimes included, sometimes not* are airfares, port charges (what ports charge cruise lines to dock), government fees and taxes, and transfers between the airport and the dock.

- *Usually not included* are shore excursions, gratuities to ship and shore-side personnel, alcoholic beverages and soft drinks (but they cost less than at a hotel), optional activities, transfers when the air isn't purchased from the cruise line, laundry, certain special offerings (e.g., gourmet desserts at an onboard sweets shop), and pre-, post-, and/or land packages. As mentioned in Chapter 1, some cruise lines bundle pre- and/or post-cruise experiences, at one price, into a single package. Also noteworthy: Very upscale lines tend to include almost everything in their packages. Clients on such cruises get almost all drinks and maybe some shore excursions for the price they pay. Also, on such luxury cruises the crew is not allowed to accept tips.

- *Never included* are the cost for meals ashore, parking at the departure port, shopping, gambling, photos, medical services, babysitting services, personal services (e.g., a massage or hairstyling), and insurance. (The cruise line usually does offer trip cancellation, interruption, and lost/damaged luggage insurance for a reasonable fee.)

The same reasons that account for the popularity of cruising among consumers also apply to travel agents, who account for the vast majority of cruise sales. They, too, like the idea of a hassle-free, pampering, safe, diversified, and immensely satisfying vacation that can be offered to their clients—and that also represents a value. Moreover, cruise vacations are easy to book, they reinforce client loyalty, and are one of the most profitable products an agent can recommend.

Cruise Prices

Every cruise brochure spells out the exact price for each sailing, as well as what's included and what's not. The price is **basis two** or **double occupancy**—it's *per person*, based on two passengers to a room. Price depends upon where the desired stateroom "category" is located on the ship. (The industry prefers the word "stateroom" to "cabin," though consumers tend to use the words interchangeably.) In general:

- The higher the deck your stateroom is on, the higher price.
- **Outside staterooms** (which have windows) are generally more expensive than **inside** or **interior staterooms** (generally without windows). Often, the industry calls an outside stateroom an "ocean-view" stateroom.
- Larger staterooms on a given ship are usually more expensive than smaller ones.
- Outside staterooms whose views are obstructed (e.g., by a lifeboat) often cost less.

On certain ships, it's possible to have three or four different stateroom price categories on a single deck: The smaller outside staterooms toward the front might be one price, larger outside staterooms another, inside ones another, a suite on that deck still another, etc.

Many other factors can affect price.

- Booking six to nine months or more in advance usually yields a savings.
- A last-minute "sale" when the ship isn't fully booked also results in lower prices.
- To encourage early bookings or to energize slow sales, cruise lines often offer special promotional fares, such as two-for-one prices, 50% off the second passenger, and the like.
- If there's a third or fourth person in your stateroom, their per-person price is often much less than for the first and second persons. (Conversely, a **single occupancy**—one person in a stateroom designed for two or more—usually costs much more.)

"Seasonality" is a factor, too. Cruise lines almost always price their itinerary according to seasonal demand. For example, summer is **high season** in the Mediterranean; that's when cruises there are most costly. Spring and fall are **shoulder seasons**, when prices are somewhat lower. Winter is **low season**. Prices for a Mediterranean cruise then are usually the lowest. (The weather is windier and rainier.) **Repositioning cruises**, when vessels are moving from one general cruise area to another, are almost always a bargain. (More about repositioning cruises in Chapter 7.)

Other factors that can reduce the cost of a cruise are special **alumni** or **past passenger rates** (rates given to people who have sailed on that cruise line before), group rates (for groups of about 10 or more), and whether the cruise is bought through a travel agency that has specially negotiated prices. On occasion, cruise lines will discount their brochure rates substantially to increase slow bookings. (The practice of adjusting price to supply and demand is called **yield management**.)

Since cruise pricing is such an "elastic" thing, you should not consider the rate given in the brochure as set in stone. Think of it, instead, as something more akin to a "suggested retail price."

Roadblocks to Purchase

You would think, with so many things *good* about cruising, that just about everyone would be ready to buy one! Not so. When average persons think about a cruise (especially if they've never been on one), they sometimes feel reluctant to commit. After all, it's hard to decide on something unknown. Their reasons are often based on misconceptions (though in some cases—e.g., extreme sensitivity to motion—their feelings may be valid).

		Typical land-based vacation vs. cruise vacation	
		Land-based resort package 7 Nights	Cruise 8 days/7 nights 3 ports
Fixed	Base price	$680 ($97/day)	$1,475 ($210/day)
	Air	$400	Included
	Transfers	Included	Included
	Meals	$350	Included
	Service charges	$93	—
	Tips	—	$60
	Taxes	$76	$89
Variable	Sightseeing	$35	$40
	Entertainment	$55	Included
	Beverages	$150	$100
	Total	$1,839	$1,764
	Per diem	$263	$252

FIGURE 2-1 Cost comparison
Source: *CLIA travel agency estimate for mid-range vacation*

Here are the 14 most commonly heard objections to cruising:

1. **Cruises are too expensive.** In most polls, this is the number one obstacle to purchasing a cruise. One reason: Consumers aren't accustomed to paying for their whole vacation experience at once, well in advance of departure. They forget that since a cruise is inclusive, it will *seem* to have a high price tag. This is why CLIA urges travel agents to do an analysis for clients that compares the cost of a cruise to a conventional land–based trip. When the clients see their costs spelled out, they realize that a cruise represents a remarkable value. (See Figure 2-1.)

2. **Cruises are boring.** This objection comes from the days of transatlantic crossings, when the most some passengers did was sit on a deck chair bundled up in a blanket. Cruises are a different experience today. The problem isn't that there's too little to do, but that there's often too much . . . .

3. **Cruises are only for older people.** Here's another objection with roots in old-time cruising. A few cruise experiences do indeed skew toward a more *mature* passenger profile, but brochure descriptions make this bias very clear. Others tend toward *younger* passengers. The majority of cruises, however, feature passengers from just about every age group, with the *average* age becoming lower and lower. (It's currently 43 years.)

Formal: Tuxedo (alternatively a dark suit) for men. Evening gown or other formal attire for women. In a two-week cruise there will usually be three or four formal evenings.

Informal: Jacket and tie for men. Cocktail dress, dressy pantsuit, or the like for women.

Casual: For men, slacks and a jacket over sweater or shirt. For women, a blouse with skirt, slacks, or similar attire is appropriate.

Resort Casual: For men, slacks and a sweater or shirt. For women, skirt or slacks with a sweater or blouse.

FIGURE 2-2 Dress code (after 6 P.M.) for an upscale cruise line
Source: *Seabourn Cruise Line*

4. **Cruises are stuffy and too formal.** A cruise is largely an informal and relaxed experience. On certain ships, a dress code does prevail in the main dining room, sometimes for lunch, often for dinner. Formality is somewhat *more* frequent on upscale cruises, much *less* likely or even non-existent on a budget cruise, a sailing ship, or an adventure/education cruise. (See Figure 2-2 for a typical dress code requirement on an upscale cruise.)

5. **Cruises are too regimented.** To achieve the efficient flow of hundreds to thousands of passengers, cruise lines do try to organize things as best they can. But organization on a ship is far from rigid—there's plenty of freedom. Routines are especially relaxed on upscale cruises, sailing ships, and adventure/education cruises.

6. **There's not enough time in ports.** It's true that cruise ships rarely stay in a port for more than twelve hours. At minor ports, this (or less time) may be all that's needed. And as we said earlier, one of the major purposes of a cruise client is to *sample a region.*

    For example, a traveler might wish to visit the major ports of the Western Mexican Coast, then return a few years later for a resort stay in the city that was most impressionable. Moreover, it *is* possible—through a pre- or post-cruise package—to spend extended time at the departure and/or arrival port. And to satisfy those clients who want a more extended port experience, some cruise lines are now spending more than a day in certain intermediate ports or building faster ships that will get from place to place more quickly, thus permitting a longer port stay.

7. **The ship environment is too confining.** Cruise ship designers have become increasingly adept at creating a sense of spaciousness aboard ship. Vast windows in public spaces, pale colors, and other tricks of the architectural trade "expand" the environment. The actual space that each client has is fairly well-expressed by something called *space ratio.* More about that in Chapter 3.

8. **Aren't you forced to socialize with people?** As mentioned earlier, meeting interesting fellow passengers aboard ship is perceived as a *benefit* by many cruisers.

    The likelihood that you'll meet people you have plenty in common with is great. Some people, though, find socializing uncomfortable. To address this, cruise lines organize all sorts of optional events to make mixing comfortable and easy. In theory, though, someone who wants to be alone could very well do that aboard a ship. Reading while in a deck chair, dining in one's stateroom, watching the scenery go by from a private verandah—these and more can enable someone to enjoy a cruise without a whole lot of socializing.

Up-close destination experiences attract many people to cruising.
Courtesy of Holland America Line

9. **I was in the Navy, and the last thing I want to do is take my vacation on a ship.** You'd be surprised how often this one comes up. But a pleasure cruise is dramatically different from the Navy experience. Virtually everyone who cites this objection discovers quite rapidly that this is a silly preconception.

10. **Are ships really safe?** The *Titanic* still looms large in the minds of the public—witness the immense box office success this 1998 film achieved. But a *Titanic*-like catastrophe is virtually impossible today. Modern safety regulation requirements and radar have seen to that. Fires aboard ships have occurred, but they're rare and easily contained.

11. **I'll eat too much and put on weight.** Cruise veterans jokingly refer to "five-pound cruises" and "ten-pound cruises." The reality today is this: Low-calorie, healthy dining choices are increasingly available on ships, plus exercise opportunities allow you to work off all those calories. Or at least some of them . . . .

12. **It's too far to fly to the port.** This is a problem voiced by those who live far inland (e.g., North Dakota or Saskatchewan) and whose ship is leaving from, say, San Juan. Make them realize it's worth it for such a great experience (e.g., "It's only a half-day to one of the greatest vacations of your life"), or sell them on a closer port destination—one that requires less flying time and/or fewer connections.

13. **I'm worried about seasickness.** Some people are especially vulnerable to motion discomfort. But ship **stabilizers** (underwater wing-like devices that reduce a ship's roll) and other design features have minimized this problem. Cruise vessels also tend to sail in protected waters, where motion is less likely to occur. Many cruisers use Sea Bands®, wrist bracelets that, through accupressure, apparently reduce the effect of ship motion. Physicians can also prescribe pills or skin patches that, for most people, relieve motion sickness. Alcohol and lack of sleep can worsen seasickness. People who are prone to motion discomfort should avoid drinking too much or sleeping too little.

   A question allied to this: What happens if I get ill while onboard? Health professionals are right there aboard ship to deal with problems. No hotel can offer that.

14. I don't know enough about cruises. Though this objection is not commonly voiced, it's behind almost all the others. Many people are afraid to try something they've never experienced. More information usually resolves their reluctance, since this objection often implies that the client wants to know more . . . . Your job: to make them visualize themselves on a ship and feel—in advance—how wonderful it will be.

In sum, the reasons to take a cruise vacation are many. The reasons *not* to take a cruise are often bogus. The key to cruise client satisfaction: A person must take the right cruise, on the right ship, and to the right destination for them. That's why travel agents—familiar with both cruises and their clients—are so critical to the cruise-buying process. When the personalities of the traveler and the cruise match, then all the objections a client may conceive will probably, and simply, melt away.

Questions for Discussion

1. You're going on a three-day cruise out of Florida. What can you predict about the passengers?

2. You've "graduated" to a ten-day cruise of Northern Europe. What can you anticipate about the passengers this time?

3. Give the six most important reasons why, in *your* opinion, the cruise experience is so successful.

4. What's typically included on a cruise? What isn't?

5. List at least six objections that people might have about a cruise vacation.

Activity

Do you know at least one person who has taken a cruise? Interview that person by using the questions below. Summarize that person's answers in the spaces given. It doesn't matter whether you've cruised or not. The purpose of this exercise is to explore *someone else's* perceptions.

1. What cruise or cruises have you taken?

2. What was the most important reason you decided to try out cruising?

3. What were the other motives you had for cruising?

4. Were you reluctant in any way about taking a cruise? What caused this reluctance? Did the actual cruise change your mind?

5. Now that you've tried out cruising, what's the best thing about it?

6. Do you plan to take another cruise? If yes, what kind of cruise will it be? (Destination, cruise line, number of days.)

CHAPTER THREE

THE ANATOMY OF A CRUISE SHIP

After reading this chapter, you'll be able to

■ Classify ships according to their "style"

■ Compare older ship styles to newer ones

■ Explain how ship size and space are measured

■ List the facilities found on most cruise vessels

■ Interpret a deck plan

T hink of a cruise ship. What have you pictured in your mind? A great ocean liner slicing through the Atlantic? A floating resort–like palace sliding from tropical isle to tropical isle? Did you think of a ship with sails? A Mississippi paddlewheeler? An overgrown yacht? All these and more can be found in the cruise industry.

Styles of Ships

The kinds of ships that offer a cruise experience are far more diverse than you probably ever imagined. Let's take a quick look at the types of vessels that cruisers can choose from.

- *The classic ocean liner.* These ships—some of which are still in service today—epitomize the first Golden Age of cruising. Primarily used for transatlantic crossings or world voyages, and mostly built before 1970, they're sleek, streamlined, and built to knife their way through open ocean waves. Most are rather small by today's cruise standards, but several vintage liners are as big as some of the larger contemporary ships.

- *The contemporary cruise ship.* In the 1970s, ship designers began to redefine what a cruise ship should be. Speed was no longer of prime consideration. Tapered, knife-like hulls gave way to broader, boxier, still attractive vessels built to accommodate uniformly sized staterooms and the numerous activity venues that the modern cruise vacation experience requires. These ships have grown larger and larger, eventually surpassing the size and capacity of the mid-twentieth century behemoths, like the *Queen Mary* and *Queen Elizabeth*. The industry generally calls these new giant-sized ships **megaships**. They can accommodate 2,000 passengers or more and have 12 or more decks (a **deck** is the equivalent of a story in a building).

- *Small ships.* In contrast to megaships are much smaller vessels, most of which accommodate fewer than 200 passengers. Here the emphasis is on an up-close, more intimate cruise vacation. The cruise lines that rely on small-ship cruising often stress education, soft adventure, and/or luxury experiences. Their ships often look like cruise ships in miniature or oversized yachts.

- *Masted sailing ships.* Yes, there are still cruise ships that have masts and sails, and are partly or almost entirely powered by the wind. In some cases, these vessels are technologically sophisticated, with computers controlling the sails. In other instances, the crew and even passenger volunteers rig the sails. The ships have motors, just in case the wind dies down. People who sail on such ships want an experience rooted in other times, when billowing cloth and the romance of the sea were what sailing was all about.

- *Riverboats.* Another time machine to the past is the riverboat. Often modeled after the great steamboats of the nineteenth century, these vessels permit passengers to experience America's great rivers in a style memorialized in the works of Mark Twain. Modern-style riverboats, too, are popular vehicles for experiencing such legendary rivers as the Rhine, the Danube, and the Nile.

- *Barges.* Whether it's a twelve-passenger barge drifting along a French canal or a much larger vessel floating down the Mississippi, barge travel is far less spartan than you might think. In fact, it's usually quite the opposite. Passenger barges are usually luxurious, affording a pampered and leisurely discovery of the countryside.

- *Ferries.* Usually we don't think of a ferry trip as a cruise. Yet in Europe (especially in Northern Europe), many ferries provide an overnight or even multi-day, cruise-like experience, with private staterooms, glitzy entertainment, and bountiful dining.

Masted sailing ships provide an intriguing alternative to conventional vessels.
Courtesy of Windstar Cruises

- *Multi-purpose ships.* Some vessels, like those that sail the fjord-lined west coast of Norway serve many functions. They carry cargo, transport passengers between close-by villages and–yes–serve as cruise ships for leisure travelers too.
- *Tenders.* Tenders aren't cruise ships, per se. They're the small vessels that shuttle passengers between the port and the cruise ship. (Tenders are used when the ship is too large or has too deep a **draft** to dock at a particular port.)
- *Miscellaneous.* Many unusual forms of water transportation provide cruise-like vacations. It's possible, for example, for a leisure traveler to book passage on a freighter. The itineraries are unpredictable and the entertainment non-existent (except for videotapes), but the food is usually excellent and the staterooms are oversized. It's also possible to charter your own yacht, either with a crew or without. (The latter is called a **bare boat charter**.)

Figure 3-1 gives a comparison between older and newer ships.

Sizing Ships

How does the cruise industry measure its ships? One way is by the number of staterooms. Another is by how many passengers the ship accommodates. (The cruise business often uses the word "guests" instead of "passengers.") For example, any vessel that carries 2,000 passengers or more is usually considered a megaship.

A third way to measure is by something called **gross registered tonnage**, or **GRT**. Gross registered tonnage is determined by a formula that gauges the volume of the public spaces on a ship. It measures only enclosed space available to passengers. It doesn't factor in open areas, like the promenade decks, or private spaces used only by the crew (e.g., the engine room). Since it deals only with parts of the vessel, the actual

The era when a ship was built has a direct impact on the cruise experience. The table below compares older with newer ships. Remember: Some clients prefer older vessels, others newer ones. It's just a matter of taste. Also: The descriptions given are *generally* true. Exceptions do exist.

Older, or "classic," ships	Newer "modern" ships
• Much use of wood, brass, and other natural materials	• Synthetic materials more common
• Modest-sized public areas	• Large public areas (especially atriums, showrooms, and casinos)
• Can travel up to 30 knots	• Travel at 20–25 knots
• Nostalgic appearance	• Modern appearance
• Hulls have deep drafts; some ports are therefore inaccessible and/or require tendering	• Hulls have shallow drafts; ports more accessible (except for truly huge ships)
• Small windows or portholes	• Larger windows
• More obstructed stateroom views	• Fewer obstructed stateroom views
• "Pedestrian" flow through ship sometimes awkward	• Easy "pedestrian" flow through ship
• Stateroom verandahs more rare	• Stateroom verandahs more likely
• Smaller swimming pools	• Larger swimming pools
• "Promenade" decks common	• "Promenade" decks less common
• Many different-sized staterooms; staterooms are relatively large	• More standardized stateroom size; staterooms can be small

FIGURE 3-1 Comparing older with newer ships

ship's weight is probably much more than the GRT. And, no, there are no huge scales to test it out.

How the formula works is unimportant. What the resulting number *means*, however, *is* important. Here's how the industry generally interprets GRT, with a rough idea of how many passengers each ship size accommodates. (**Pax** is an industry abbreviation for "passengers.")

- *Very small:* Under 10,000 GRT; under 200 pax
- *Small:* 10,000–20,000 GRT; 200–500 pax
- *Medium:* 20,000–50,000 GRT; 500–1,200 pax
- *Large:* 50,000–70,000 GRT; 1,200–2,000 pax
- *Megaship:* 70,000 GRT or more; 2,000 pax or more

As the cruise industry continues to grow, more 100,000 to 150,000 GRT ships will appear. This could lead to a whole new category beyond megaship, or it might mean that ships in the 70,000 GRT will be categorized as medium-sized, while megaships will refer to anything that exceeds 100,000 GRT.

Once unimaginable, 100,000-ton ships now offer a wide variety of onboard options.
Courtesy of Princess Cruises

Some cruisers like smaller ships, others prefer larger ones. What are the benefits of each?

Larger ships . . .

- Offer many more facilities, activities, choices, and options
- Are often more dramatic-looking
- Are able to serve a wider spectrum of guest types
- Easily accommodate groups
- Are generally quite stable in the water

On the other hand, smaller ships . . .

- Offer a more intimate atmosphere
- Can sail into smaller places
- Permit easier **embarkation** and **debarkation**
- Make it simple for passengers to get to know the ship and others onboard

One other function of ship size is something called the **space ratio**. The space ratio of a vessel is determined by dividing the GRT by passenger capacity. For instance, if a vessel has a 30,000 GRT and can carry 1,000 passengers, its space ratio is 30.

The space ratio number conveys the "space" or "elbow room" each person will have. The higher the space ratio, the more passengers will have a sense of the ship's "roominess": the less crowded the hallways and stairs will be, the more space there will be between tables in the dining room.

A few things about space ratio:

■ Most ships have a space ratio of about 20 to 35. The lowest is about 8, the highest is about 60.

■ The space ratio doesn't necessarily correlate to size. Small ships can have high space ratios, while megaships can have low space ratios. It all depends on how many passengers a certain-size ship carries.

■ A ship's space ratio isn't the only thing that conveys roominess. Light colors and ample windows can make a ship with a low space ratio seem more spacious.

■ If a vessel with a low space ratio isn't full (say, 80% of the staterooms are occupied), the passengers will probably feel less crowded than they would if it were fully booked.

■ Space ratio doesn't necessarily correlate to stateroom size. A ship with small staterooms may have huge public areas, yielding a higher space ratio number. Remember: The space ratio is derived from the *entire* ship's non-crew volume, or GRT.

■ The more expensive a cruise is per day, the more likely the ship will have a high space ratio. One of the features that an upscale cruise offers is roominess.

How can you find out a ship's space ratio? Most reference sources and many brochures give passenger capacity and tonnage. Just plug them into the formula and you'll have the space ratio. Indeed, some references actually give you the space ratio, already calculated, for every ship afloat.

One final point: A high space ratio isn't necessarily critical to the enjoyment of the cruise experience. Some people prefer the cozy feeling that ships with low space ratios convey. Others feel that if they've saved money by booking a vessel with a low space ratio, then the tradeoff was worth it. The bottom line: If the passengers see interesting ports, experience wonderful food and entertainment, meet interesting people, and have a great time, then the space ratio will probably be a minor consideration.

Ship Facilities

Space on a ship can be divided into three types: stateroom space, private (or crew) space, and public space.

Passengers almost never see the spaces that serve the ship's crew. (They're usually on decks below those of the passengers.) These include crew cabins, dining areas, and recreational facilities. Other private spaces are the **bridge** (where the vessel is controlled), the **galley** or kitchen (where food is prepared), and mechanical areas (such as the engine room). On certain cruises, passengers are permitted to visit the bridge and/or the galley on a special, "behind-the-scenes" tour.

Public spaces are those where passengers mingle. Here are the most common:

■ *The reception area.* All ships have a lobby-like area where the **purser's office** (also known as the **front desk, hotel desk, reception desk,** or **information desk**) is located. The purser's office is the direct equivalent of a hotel's front desk (though, unlike hotels, cruise passengers do *not* need to check in at this desk to get their rooms). Nearby is usually the shore excursion office or tour desk, where passengers can inquire about and/or book port tours and activities. On newer ships, the reception area may be in a multi-story space called an **atrium**.

■ *The dining room.* Guests eat dinner here, and, often, breakfast and lunch as well. Larger ships typically feature several main dining rooms.

First introduced in hotels, atriums have now become common on cruise ships.
Courtesy of Royal Caribbean International

- *Alternate dining areas.* Informal, buffet-like dining usually takes place on the pool deck for some or all meals. Guests can dine indoors or, in good weather, outdoors. (This area is often called the **Lido deck** or cafe.) Some ships also have alternate restaurants—such as pizzerias or specialty cafes—that are open part or even all of the day. Small facilities dispensing fast food (e.g., hot dogs and hamburgers) are often located on the pool deck.

- *The showroom.* Entertainment events usually take place here each night. During the day, the showroom may host orientation meetings, port lectures, games (e.g., bingo), movies, or other special events. Most ships usually feature one or more additional entertainment areas, bars, and discos.

- *The pool area.* The majority of ships today have one or more swimming pools, perhaps with Jacuzzis nearby. These pools aren't usually very big, however. Imagine how much such a volume of water weighs! Since the pool is usually on the top deck, a massive pool would destabilize the ship. A deck with many lounge chairs and (perhaps) tables usually surrounds the pool. There may be a shallow wading pool for kids. On some ships, a glass skylight—sometimes called a **magrodome**—can cover the pool area. In warm weather it slides away, permitting passengers to feel the cool sea breeze in an open environment. In cold or rainy weather, it slides shut.

- *The health club.* Most cruise vessels provide an area for guests to exercise, with an aerobics area, stationary bicycles, treadmills, and weight machines. The health club frequently adjoins a **spa** that offers massages, facials, saunas, whirlpools, aromatherapy, and other beauty or relaxation-related services. Ships may also have jogging tracks, basketball courts, and other exercise-related facilities.

- *The gift shop.* On some ships it's just a little store where you can buy sundries. On many others it's a more extensive place that sells souvenirs, duty-free goods, tee-shirts, and the like—often themed to the ship. Some vessels feature many places to buy things, arranged in mini-mall–like fashion.

- *The medical facility.* Maritime law requires any vessel that carries more than 100 passengers to have a physician onboard, often assisted by one or more nurses. These health care professionals work out of a small, hospital-like facility.

- *The movie theater.* Many ships feature screenings of recent movies in a theater. These theaters often serve double-duty as meeting spaces. In-cabin video, however, is—on some ships—eliminating the need for an onboard movie theater.

- *The photo gallery.* At key moments and picturesque spots, professional photographers take photos of passengers. These photos are then displayed in a photo gallery on the ship. Passengers can purchase the ones they like for a reasonable price.

- *The casino.* Since gambling is usually legal on ships, most cruise vessels boast casinos where clients can play blackjack, roulette, slot machines, and other games. (Gambling *is* prohibited on ships calling only on U.S. ports.) The casino—either for legal reasons or so as not to compete with shoreside facilities—is usually closed when the ship is in port.

The above list represents the most common and important public spaces found on a ship. Figure 3-2 lists other facilities—some common, some unusual—that a guest will find on some of today's cruise ships.

Cruise Staterooms

A **stateroom**—also called a **cabin**—is to a ship what a guest room is to a hotel. There's one big difference: Ship staterooms are usually extremely compact. Author Douglas

babysitting play areas	drugstore	miniature golf course
bars	entertainment lounges	observation area
card rooms	function rooms	climbing wall
cigar/smoking lounges	game/videogame rooms	teen facilities
discos/dance facilities	golf simulation areas	water slide
launderette	libraries (books and/or videos)	watersport platforms
chapel (for non-denominational services and weddings)		ice skating rink

FIGURE 3-2 Other possible shipboard facilities

Ward has an evocative name for them: "hotel rooms in miniature." The average hotel room in America today is about 350 to 450 square feet. Some staterooms are as small as 100 square feet, and only a few exceed 250 square feet.

However, staterooms are astonishingly efficient. Ship designers manage to fit all manner of cabinets, drawers, and shelves into the typical stateroom, making it often as functional as a hotel room twice the size.

Three types of ship staterooms exist:

- *Outside staterooms* have windows. Because you can look outside, these ocean-view accommodations feel more open. They're ideal for clients who worry about feeling cramped. Older ships have portholes. Newer ships have larger windows. Some staterooms feature a full-wall sliding glass door that leads to a verandah. (Believe it or not, some first-time cruisers conclude that outside accommodations must be out on deck or even off the ship!)

- *Inside staterooms* are in the ship's interior. Usually they have no windows, but often use mirrors, pastel colors, bright lighting, and even false window drapes to make the room feel more open (a few ships do have inside staterooms that look out onto an interior atrium). Many cruisers prefer inside staterooms because these rooms usually are the least expensive on the ship. They also may feel that a stateroom "is only a place to sleep." Late sleepers like inside staterooms because early daylight won't disturb them.

- *Suites* are the most expensive accommodations on a ship. Some vessels have only a few, others boast an entire upper, concierge-like deck made up of larger staterooms and/or suites. By the traditional definition, a suite should feature a living room, a sleeping room, and a bathroom. This is not so on a ship. Except for the very largest—which resemble a room in a luxury hotel—shipboard suites typically feature, in the same rectangular space, a sitting area and a sleeping area, often divided by a curtain. Suites can usually accommodate more than two people, making such accommodations popular for families (the sofa often converts into a bed).

Here's what you find in a typical stateroom:

- Two single **lower beds**, either parallel to each other or at right angles. Beds can be pushed together to create a double or queen-sized bed. Larger staterooms boast double, queen, or even king-size beds. Staterooms with **upper beds** can accommodate three or four passengers; these uppers are recessed into the wall or ceiling

Suites are the ultimate in shipboard accommodations.
Courtesy of Silversea Cruises

during the day. In cruise jargon, a bed is often called a **berth**. (*Berth* also can refer to the docking space of a ship.)

- A bedstand between the beds or on each side.
- A vanity, often with a chair, along with built-in drawers, cabinets, and the like.
- A closet, perhaps with multiple levels and storage places.
- A television that feeds live or repeated broadcasts of shipboard events, movies, port talks, and satellite transmission of regular TV programming.
- Extensive lighting, wall-to-wall carpeting, and everything else you'd associate with a hotel.

For examples of stateroom floor plans, see the diagrams given in Figure 3-3.

A stateroom on today's ships almost always has a connecting bathroom. It's usually very compact but, again, well-conceived, with a sink, toilet, and shower. Larger staterooms may have a full tub and shower, while suites sometimes have a little vanity area between the stateroom and its bathroom. Some staterooms feature balconies or verandahs that permit guests to go outside and experience the environment in a direct and private way.

Reading A Deck Plan

Every cruise brochure and many reference resources (such as the *CLIA Cruise Manual*) reproduce the plans of ships. A ship plan usually consists of two elements: the **deck plan** (or floor plan) and a cross-section of the ship, with each "layer" shown (only those

CP ■ *Crystal Penthouse with Verandah*

DECK TEN/982 SQUARE FEET (WITH VERANDAH)

• Spacious living room • Dining area • Private verandah • Well-stocked service bar • CD player
• 25-inch color television • Cordless phone • Guest bathroom • Large bedroom • King-size bed or twin
beds • Remote TV & VCR • Master bath with Jacuzzi® & ocean view • Separate shower • Bidet
• Walk-in closet • Refrigerator • Security safe

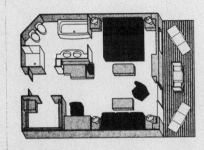

PS ■

Penthouse Suite with Verandah

DECK TEN
491 SQUARE FEET (WITH VERANDAH)

• Sizable living area • Large private verandah
• Well-stocked bar • Remote TV & VCR
• Picture window view from bedroom • Large
bedroom • Queen-size bed or twin beds • Full
Jacuzzi® bathtub • Separate shower • Bidet
• Walk-in closet • Refrigerator • Security safe

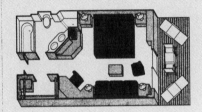

PH ■

Penthouse with Verandah

DECK TEN
367 SQUARE FEET (WITH VERANDAH)

• Spacious living area • Private verandah • Large
bedroom • Well-stocked bar • Queen-size bed or
twin beds • Remote TV & VCR • Full Jacuzzi®
bathtub • Separate shower • Walk-in closet
• Refrigerator • Security safe

A ■ B ■

Deluxe Stateroom with Verandah

DECKS EIGHT & NINE
246 SQUARE FEET (WITH VERANDAH)

• Private verandah • Queen-size bed or twin
beds • Seating area • Mini-bar • Remote TV
& VCR • Full bathtub/shower combination
• Refrigerator • Security safe

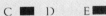

C ■ D ■ E ■

Deluxe Stateroom

DECKS FIVE, SEVEN & EIGHT
202 SQUARE FEET

• Large picture window • Queen-size bed or twin
beds • Seating area • Mini-bar • Remote TV &
VCR • Full bathtub/shower combination • C & D
have sweeping views, E has a view that is limited or
extremely limited • Refrigerator • Security safe

FIGURE 3-3   Stateroom floor plans
Source: *Courtesy of Crystal Cruises*

Outside staterooms are like hotel rooms in miniature.
Courtesy of Royal Olympic Cruises

decks that are "public" are indicated). Sometimes accompanying the deck plan are floor plans of various kinds of staterooms.

Here are a few things you need to know about ships' plans.

- **Deck plans are important.** Unlike at hotels, guests can often select the exact staterooms they want when the cruise is booked. But there are exceptions. These will be explained in Chapter 9.

- **In brochures, color coding makes a deck plan easy to read.** Colors help indicate which price categories apply to which staterooms. (A **stateroom category** is the price that a certain kind or level of stateroom represents). Other reference resources usually reproduce deck plans in black and white, however.

- **Usually, the higher the deck is on the ship, the higher the category and price.** Suites and larger staterooms are generally located on the highest decks. There are, however, many exceptions.

- **Deck plans often note certain special stateroom circumstances.** Examples include obstructed views from windows (a lifeboat may be in the way), staterooms specially equipped for the physically challenged, or those that can accommodate three or four passengers.

- **Deck plans are also posted aboard ship.** They're usually located in the elevator/staircase areas. These deck plans help guests orient themselves onboard. (For the record, the front of the ship is called the **bow**, the back is called the **stern**. Facing forward, the left side is labeled the **port** side, the right side **starboard**.) To further help passengers find their way around, each deck usually has a name and/or number.

Location	Potential Advantage(s)	Potential Disadvantage(s)
Near elevators	Not far to walk to elevators	Pedestrian "traffic" and noise in hallway
Near bow or stern	Usually less expensive; possibly dramatic views; quiet	Far from everything; greater feeling of ship motion
Near public spaces	Close to where things are happening	Potential noise (e.g., if the public space is below or above the stateroom)
Lower deck	Less expensive; less motion felt	Possibly far from public spaces; may be smaller staterooms
Higher deck	Possibly closer to public areas; closer to "sun" deck and pool; feels more prestigious; often larger staterooms	More expensive; possibly more "traffic"; potential to feel more ship motion

FIGURE 3-4 Location, location, location!

When cruise clients and travel agents study a deck plan, they should carefully examine the relationship of a stateroom to the ship's public spaces. See Figure 3-4 to learn how a location can be an asset or a drawback, depending on the client's needs.

Miscellaneous Considerations

What else should you know about cruise ships? Here are two important thoughts:

■ **A ship's "registry" usually has nothing to do with where the line is headquartered.** Financial, legal, and routing concerns tend to dictate the ship's registry. The name of the country where the ship is registered is usually painted on the exterior of the vessel's stern and the ship flies that country's flag. (This is called its *flag of convenience*.)

■ **On some ships smoking is permitted almost everywhere onboard.** On most it's limited to certain officially designated places. One or two ships are smoke-free.

Questions for Discussion

1. Give at least five ways in which a "classic" ship differs from a "modern" ship.

2. Explain GRT and space ratio.

3. List at least four advantages of larger ships; of smaller ships.

4. Name eight public facilities that typically are found on cruise ships.

5. Define or describe the following:

   - magrodome

   - atrium

   - Lido deck

   - purser's office

   - spa

   - inside stateroom

   - suite

   - stateroom category

   - bow

   - stern

   - port side

   - starboard

   - galley

   - bridge

⚓ Activity

Examine Figure 3-5, the deck plan for Cunard's *Seabourn Goddess* vessels. Then answer the following questions:

1. Which is the only deck that has no staterooms?

2. How many inside staterooms are there?

3. How many dining facilities are there onboard? What are they and on which decks?

4. How many elevators does this vessel have? Why?

5. Deck 1 is not indicated. What could be a possible reason?

6. Which two staterooms are the closest to the ship's bow?

7. A potential passenger is worried about the ship's motion. In which two staterooms would she probably sense the least motion?

8. Do any staterooms have obstructed views? Why?

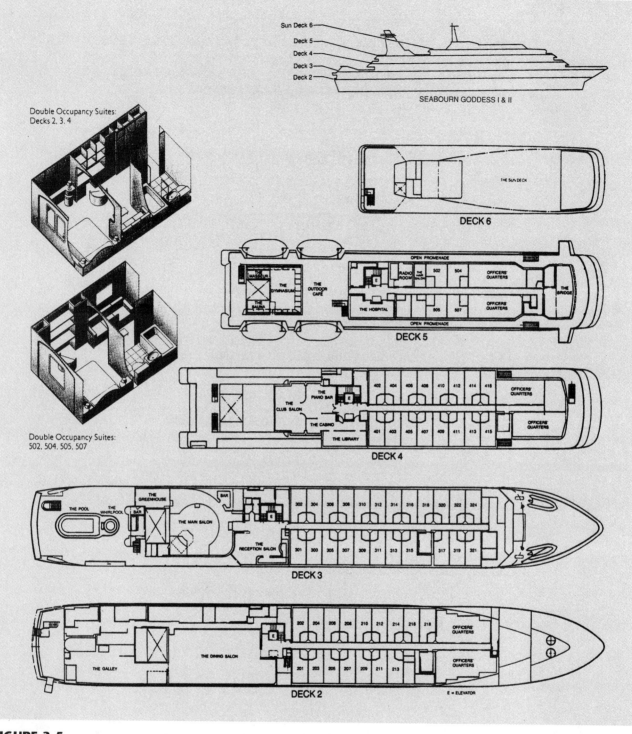

Sun Deck 6
Deck 5
Deck 4
Deck 3
Deck 2

SEABOURN GODDESS I & II

Double Occupancy Suites:
Decks 2, 3, 4

Double Occupancy Suites:
502, 504, 505, 507

THE SUN DECK

DECK 6

OPEN PROMENADE

THE MASSEUR | THE GYMNASIUM | THE OUTDOOR CAFÉ | RADIO ROOM | THE MAIN SALON | 502 | 504 | OFFICERS' QUARTERS | THE BRIDGE
THE SAUNA | THE HOSPITAL | 505 | 507 | OFFICERS' QUARTERS

OPEN PROMENADE

DECK 5

THE CLUB SALON | THE PIANO BAR | 402 | 404 | 406 | 408 | 410 | 412 | 414 | 416 | OFFICERS' QUARTERS
THE CASINO | 401 | 403 | 405 | 407 | 409 | 411 | 413 | 415 | OFFICERS' QUARTERS
THE LIBRARY

DECK 4

THE POOL | THE WHIRLPOOL | BAR | THE GREENHOUSE | BAR | THE MAIN SALON | 302 | 304 | 306 | 308 | 310 | 312 | 314 | 316 | 318 | 320 | 322 | 324
THE RECEPTION SALON | 301 | 303 | 305 | 307 | 309 | 311 | 313 | 315 | 317 | 319 | 321

DECK 3

THE GALLEY | THE DINING SALON | 202 | 204 | 206 | 208 | 210 | 212 | 214 | 216 | 218 | OFFICERS' QUARTERS
201 | 203 | 205 | 207 | 209 | 211 | 213 | OFFICERS' QUARTERS

DECK 2   E = ELEVATOR

FIGURE 3-5

CHAPTER FOUR

THE CRUISE EXPERIENCE

After reading this chapter, you'll be able to

■ Describe what occurs before a passenger actually sails

■ Explain dining patterns and options

■ Relate what typically takes place on a day at sea and a day at port

I f only we could take you on a cruise, right now! So much of what this book covers would become apparent, immediately, in a direct and compelling way.

But, sorry. We don't have that luxury. So let's take an imaginary, first-time cruise vacation, instead. Let's say it's to the Bahamas and the Caribbean. If you've never been on a cruise, much of this will be fresh and new. If you're a cruise veteran, our imaginary trip will bring back pleasant memories. Remember: It portrays a *typical* cruise. (About half of all cruises are to the Bahamas and the Caribbean.) All sorts of variations —both minor and major—are possible on the scenario that you're about to read.

Before You Buy

Almost surely you found out about cruising from ads, commercials, or a friend. Your interest ignited, you probably contacted a travel agent. This is, after all, an important decision—the kind that requires the insight, analysis, and opinions of someone who knows cruising well. (To see how far in advance cruise clients plan their vacation, see Figure 4-1.)

The travel agent asks you a series of questions to discover your needs. He or she understands that many types of cruises are available, and, to be satisfied, it's critical that you travel on the ship, itinerary, and line that's right for you. The recommendation of a Caribbean cruise sounds great. "Go ahead. Let's do it," you say. You give your deposit, with the balance due later. (This whole process will be explored in detail in Chapter 9.)

FIGURE 4-1 Planning ahead for a cruise
Source: *Newspaper Association of America*

HOW FAR IN ADVANCE CRUISE WAS PLANNED

Less than two weeks	8%
Between two and four weeks	19%
Between one and three months	52%
Between four and six months	12%
Six or more months	9%

Source: New York-based Newspaper Association of America. Based on survey of 908 Americans who had taken at least one cruise in the past three years.

A few weeks before departure, your travel agent calls. Your cruise documents have arrived. You pick them up. You'll find *some* or *all* of the following in the documents folder:

- An invoice, confirmation, ticket, or voucher that verifies you're on the trip, probably also listing such information as embarkation date and hours, pier location, cabin number, which dining room seating you have, your booking ID number, and the terms and conditions of your voyage
- A booklet summarizing important information on such topics as dress requirements, onboard credit policies, and what clothes to bring
- A list of the documents you'll need (e.g., passport)
- An identification button
- A document on tuxedo rentals
- A gift order form (e.g., for champagne available in your cabin upon arrival)
- Color-coded luggage tags (usually two for each person)
- Immigration and customs forms, if needed
- An explanation/sign-up form for travel insurance (not necessary if you've already purchased insurance from your travel agent)
- An itinerary
- Air tickets and hotel information (if arranged through the cruise line)
- Embarkation port information (the cruise line or your travel agent may also have given you a map of your embarkation port—see Figure 4-2 for an example)
- A leaflet on how ship-to-shore communication works, which may also list important telephone and fax numbers (make a copy of this document for friends or family in case there's an emergency back home)
- A list of shore excursions and how to sign up for them
- A card that will serve as your identification throughout the trip in order to charge things, to get on the ship, etc. (you might not get this card until you get to the ship)

On the Way to Your Cruise

On the day of your cruise, you fly to Miami. (If you live in or near Miami, you can drive to the port.) You could have flown in a day or two before to take advantage of a pre-trip package. However, you've visited the Miami area several times, so you passed on that option.

Since the flight was booked through the cruise line, a company representative meets you at the gate, along with others bound for the same ship. (If you had booked your flight separately, no **meet-and-greet** person from the cruise line would be there for you, and the cruise line transfer service wouldn't be part of your package.)

With your fellow passengers, you board a motorcoach for the transfer to the port of Miami. Your luggage is placed in the bus, too, or on another vehicle. You probably won't see it again until you get to your stateroom. The cruise line will take care of everything. It's the first of many hassle-saving benefits of a cruise.

Your bus arrives at the port terminal. Embarkation began at 2 P.M. and it's now 3:30 P.M. So you check in with a cruise line representative, who reviews your documents and gives you any materials you need. (This is the equivalent of checking in at a hotel front desk.) You make your way up the **gangway**—the walkway that connects the ship with the dock. Perhaps the ship's photographer takes your picture. It will be the first of

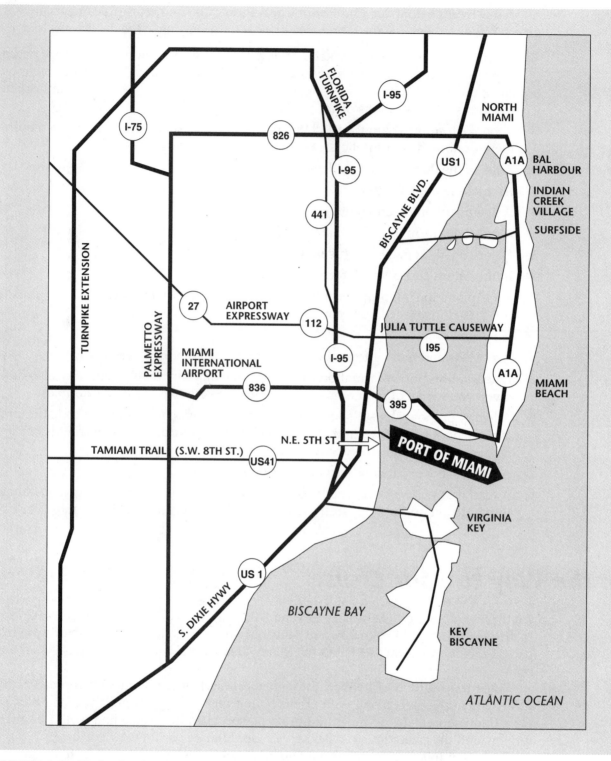

FIGURE 4-2 Embarkation port map of Miami
Source: *Courtesy of CLIA*

many photo opportunities. (The pictures will be available for your inspection and purchase later, if you like, at the ship's photo gallery or via a computer screen.)

As you enter the ship, you pass through a security screening checkpoint, similar to those at airports. As you enter, several smiling ship's staff members greet you. A trio of musicians may be playing, too. You're finally finding out what others have told you: Once you're on a cruise ship, boredom is left behind on the dock.

Onboard the Ship

You now find your way to your stateroom, escorted by a crew member. The stateroom door is open. You settle in and review any in-room literature, such as the daily activities log, to find out what happens next. (Some cruise lines even provide daily "children-only" activities logs in addition to the regular one.) You're eager to explore the ship, too, maybe stopping by the dining room to confirm your seating. You also may go to the purser's desk to register your credit card. Most ships today operate on a "cashless" basis. You sign to your account all onboard expenses not included in the cruise price. On the last day, they'll be charged to your credit card. (Some cruise lines do this credit card registration when you first check in at the port.)

Gaming is one of many onboard activities on most ships.
Courtesy of Royal Caribbean International

Upon return to your stateroom, you find that your luggage has arrived. At this time your **cabin steward**—the person who maintains your stateroom—introduces himself or herself to you. You sense already that the level of service on a ship exceeds what hotels provide. The last time you stayed at a hotel, was the maid there to say hello?

On every ship, a lifeboat drill must take place within 24 hours of departure. It often happens before you even set sail. You knew it was going to happen: The ship's activities log gave you the time and details. Now a public address announcement reminds you it's about to occur. You put on the orange life vest you found in your stateroom—*fumble with* are better words. Like most people, you have to figure out how it goes on. (Of course, that's the point!) You then report to the lifeboat station that was preassigned to you. The ship's crew members inspect you and your fellow passengers, explain procedures, then dismiss you. It's back to your stateroom to prepare for the upcoming festivities.

Departure

A ship's departure is one of the most energetic moments on a cruise. You notice it's 6 P.M.—departure time—so you head for the pool deck, where a Caribbean steel drum band performs, staff members serve you tropical beverages with hors d'oeuvres, and everyone watches as the ship dramatically glides from its dock. The sky is blue, the breeze is warm and wonderful, and the sense of fun and excitement is everywhere.

After enjoying some activities, you return to your stateroom. A cocktail reception is next. But the big departure-day event is your first dinner at sea.

When you booked your cruise, your travel agent asked you which "seating" you wanted for the voyage. **First seating** is the earlier of two meal times; **second seating** is the later one. You opted for first. The maitre d' escorts you to your assigned table—it happens to be a table for eight. There you meet your companions for this meal and for subsequent dining-room meals. They certainly seem congenial. (For other dining formats, see Figure 4-3.)

Your table captain, waiter, and other dining staff introduce themselves. You order wine. (This cost isn't included in the cruise price.) The waiter presents the menu. It's extensive. And there will be a different menu at each meal. (For a sample, see Figure 4-4.) You order the lobster. Each course is served with a flourish. Yes, you can get used to this.

Dinner on most ships is followed by entertainment in the main showroom. Tonight it's a Las Vegas-style revue. And there are plenty of choices, now or later: a drink at the lounge, a little shopping perhaps, a try at the casino slot machines. And this is only the first night . . . .

FIGURE 4-3   Dining formats

The first seating/second seating dinner format at tables assigned for the entire cruise is common. But others exist. Smaller ships may have only one seating. Some have **open seating**—passengers sit where they wish during extended times, much like a restaurant. One cruise line has three dining rooms, each themed uniquely. Guests eat in a different one each night, but with the same fellow guests, at a similarly placed table, with the same waiters. Passengers, though, have other choices. Most ships today also feature alternate dining facilities, like pizzerias and Lido-deck buffets, which offer extended hours and open seating. Some have smaller upscale restaurants which require reservations (passengers book them when they board the ship). And there's always room service.

Dinner Menu

Appetizers

Escargot Classic in Garlic Lemon Herb Butter

Chilled Artichoke Stack with Tiger Prawns, Vegetable Spaghetti
and a Tomato Coulis

Array of Tropical Fruits & Fresh Mint

Soups

Traditional French Onion Soup with a Gruyere Crouton

Chilled Papaya Soup with Spicy Relish

Salads

Belgian Endive Salad with Croutons, Crisp Bacon Bits and
a Champagne Vinaigrette

Wind Star House Salad with a Yogurt Dressing

Additional Salad Dressings:
French, Italian, Thousand Island, Blue Cheese, and Hot Honey Mustard

Entrees

Grilled Salmon with Slivered Potatoes and Horseradish Nage

Country-Style Poussin with Braised Cabbage, Glazed Shallots
and Apple-Smoked Bacon

Roasted Tenderloin of Beef with Herb Mashed Potatoes,
Julienne Vegetables and a Peppercorn Gravy

Rack of Lamb Provencale with Roasted Potatoes, Sautéed Vegetables
and a Savory Lamb Jus

Homemade Spinach Ravioli with a Herb Mouseline Sauce

Vegetarian Sail Light

Grilled Mushroom Quesadilla

Calories: 421   Fat Grams: 13.0

Baked Potato and Vegetables of the Day available upon request

Special thanks to Chef Joachim Splichal of Patina and Jeanne Jones
for taking us in New Culinary Directions "180° from Ordinary."

FIGURE 4-4   A sample menu
Source: *Courtesy of Windstar Cruises*

A Day at Sea

Basically, cruise days come in two varieties: *days at sea* and *days in port*. Except when a ship is doing an ocean crossing, days in port far outnumber days at sea. Let's assume, though, that your first full day is at sea.

Your wake-up call—which you set up the night before—reminds you it's time to get going. A condensed, faxed news summary was slid under your door overnight. You read it to catch up on what's going on in the world (which seems so far removed).

Breakfast may be on the Lido deck or in the main dining room. It's your choice. In either place, there's almost too much to choose from. The cuisine quality, you note, is high, the presentation refined. Seating this time is open. (Assigned seating usually applies only to dinner in the main dining room.) You decide that tomorrow you'll order room service and have breakfast in bed instead.

Alternative cruising dining venues—often outdoors—have become increasingly common.
Courtesy of Seabourn Cruise Line

What to do now? Again, the choices seem endless. You attend an orientation lecture that explains all you need to know about this cruise. You then decide that you want to read a book and work on a tan. So you change and head for the pool.

Before you know it, it's time for lunch! You opt again for the Lido cafe and its seemingly endless buffet. You feel guilty. So much food! It's time to burn off some of those calories, so you jog for about 20 minutes on a track that encircles the ship, finishing off with a workout at the health club. Next door, an aerobics class is going through the paces. You remind yourself to do that tomorrow.

Down now to your stateroom. It's already been spiffed up by your cabin steward. You shower, change, then attend a "port talk" that will prepare you for tomorrow's stop at St. Thomas. The cruise director describes St. Thomas, the **shore excursions** (port-based tours) available, and what you might wish to buy while there. The cruise line even gives you a list of approved shops. If you buy from one of these, you'll get a discount and a guarantee that if anything goes wrong, the cruise line will help resolve the problem. You decide to sign up for some of the shore excursions. Then back to your stateroom for a snooze—it's been freshened up *again* by your steward. How does he know when you come and go? It's one of the great mysteries of the cruise experience.

Tonight it's formal night. You dress well, head for the dining room's first seating and dine by candlelight. Then it's off to see a spectacular magic show, followed by a few drinks with newly made friends. And some people think a cruise is boring!

A Day in Port

You're up early. The ship docks at Charlotte Amalie, the capital city, at 8 A.M. You want to take the 9 A.M. shore excursion—a two-hour tour of St. Thomas. (See Figure 4-5 for an example of the possible shore excursions in St. Thomas.) You spend the afternoon strolling Main Street to do some shopping. Then it's back to the ship for—yes—dinner. But this time you're a bit tired from all that sun. You decide to have dinner in your stateroom, selecting from the room service menu. You feel reenergized, so you head down to the ship's theater to watch a movie. Then you realize: There's a midnight buffet tonight! And it's a grand one, too. You sample a few things as a late snack, then return to your stateroom. The sound of the sea outside lulls you into a perfect night's rest.

FIGURE 4-5   St. Thomas shore excursion options
Source: *Royal Caribbean International*

• St. Thomas Sightseeing Tour	• Scuba Adventure
• St. John Island Tour	• Scenic St. John Sea & Snorkel
• St. John Beach Tour	• Virgin Island Seaplane Adventure
• Atlantis Submarine Tour	• St. Thomas Helicopter Tour
• Kon Tiki Party Boat	• Kayak Marine Sanctuary Tour
• Buck Island Sail & Snorkel Tour	• Island Bike Adventure
• Catamaran Sail & Snorkel Tour	• Paradise Point Tramway
• Champagne Catamaran Sailaway	• Golf Ahoy!—Mahogany Run

The Last Night and the Following Day

After several more ports, countless events, and some genuinely memorable meals (during one, the waiters—dressed in red, white, and blue—marched out to a tune of John Philip Sousa while carrying Baked Alaska lit with sparklers), it's time for your great vacation to draw to a close. Dinner, a pleasant show, and back to the stateroom to do some packing. As per directions, you keep a few overnight things with you and put all the rest in your luggage. You place the suitcase outside your stateroom door. A staff member will pick it up and store it for the night.

You've already left a gratuity for your cabin steward and presented your table staff with tips, too. The cruise line gives a guideline for what those gratuities generally are. (See Figure 4-6 for an example.)

You fill out a customs form and a comment card. (See Figure 4-7.) You then settle your outstanding bills at the purser's office.

The next day there's an early breakfast. You head with your overnight things to a public area, where you await the announcement of your turn to **disembark** (exit the ship). As with most events on a ship, disembarkation runs like clockwork. Luggage tags are color coded. Twenty percent of the passengers have red tags, 20 percent yellow, and so forth. Each color is called sequentially. You leave the ship, claim your luggage (it's in one big room), go through immigration and customs, and board your motorcoach to Miami International Airport. Your cruise has been all you had hoped for, and more. And the only thought going through your mind is this: "Why didn't I do this sooner?"

Miscellaneous Thoughts

Yes, that's the typical cruise vacation experience. But as we've noted all along, *all manner of variations are possible*. Small ships may offer a more intimate experience, with only a few, well-selected options. Cruises on sailing ships, ferry-like vessels, riverboats, and barges will certainly stray from the scenario we've portrayed. So, too, will cruises that strongly emphasize education, adventure, or exploration.

The cruise scenario we've described was flawless. But nothing is ever entirely perfect. Sometimes a few things do go wrong. Yet on a cruise, these glitches are rare.

A few miscellaneous bits of information about the cruise experience:

- When ships are in exotic or adventurous places, such as Antarctica, you may have to take **zodiac boats** to go ashore. (A *zodiac* is a large rubber boat.) In other places, a ship may be too large or have too deep a draft to tie up to the dock. The ship will

FIGURE 4-6 Tipping guidelines
Source: *Costa Cruises*

Gratuities are customarily extended on the last evening of your cruise. Of course, tipping is a personal choice. The following are simply suggested amounts per person, per day: Waiter, $3.00; Assistant Waiter, $1.50: Stateroom Steward/Stewardess, $3.00; Head Waiter, $1.00. Envelopes for tips will be provided on the last night of your cruise. A 15% gratuity is added to all beverage checks for your convenience.

Your Name_____ Sailing Date: _____/_____/_____

Address_____ Table Number: _____

Dining Seating: _____

City_____ State_____ Zip Code_____

Stateroom Example:
Room
Number: A 110

Stateroom Number

A	0	1	1	0
■	■	0	0	■
B	1	■	■	1

- Use Pencil or Pen
- Darken Block Completely
- Make no Stray Marks
- Incorrect Marks
- ▨ ☑ ☒ Ⓦ
- Correct Marks
- ■ ■ ■ ■

Stateroom Number

A	0	0	0	0
B	1	1	1	1
	2	2	2	2
	3	3	3	3
	4	4	4	4
	5	5	5	5
	6	6	6	6
	7	7	7	7
	8	8	8	8
	9	9	9	9

ZIP CODE

0	0	0	0	0
1	1	1	1	1
2	2	2	2	2
3	3	3	3	3
4	4	4	4	4
5	5	5	5	5
6	6	6	6	6
7	7	7	7	7
8	8	8	8	8
9	9	9	9	9

ABOUT YOURSELF

Your Age:

18-24	☐
25-39	☐
40-54	☐
55-64	☐
65 & Over	☐

Number in your Party:

1-2	☐
3-4	☐
5-8	☐
Part of a Group	☐

THE SHIP	Excellent	Good	Fair	Poor
Overall appearance of the Ship	☐	☐	☐	☐
Cleanliness of outside Decks	☐	☐	☐	☐
Cleanliness in the Public Areas	☐	☐	☐	☐
YOUR STATEROOM				
Comfort	☐	☐	☐	☐
Cleanliness	☐	☐	☐	☐
Upkeep (Items in working order)	☐	☐	☐	☐
Supplies	☐	☐	☐	☐
QUALITY OF SERVICE PROVIDED				
Airport Meet & Greet Staff	☐	☐	☐	☐
Embarkation Staff	☐	☐	☐	☐
Reception Desk Staff	☐	☐	☐	☐
Bell Staff	☐	☐	☐	☐
Cruise Directors' Staff	☐	☐	☐	☐
Shore Excursion Staff	☐	☐	☐	☐
Casino Staff	☐	☐	☐	☐
Photography Staff	☐	☐	☐	☐
Beauty Salon Staff	☐	☐	☐	☐
Youth Counselors	☐	☐	☐	☐
Gift Shop Staff	☐	☐	☐	☐
Cabin Steward	☐	☐	☐	☐
Room Service Staff	☐	☐	☐	☐
Deck/Bar Staff	☐	☐	☐	☐
Lounge/Bar Staff	☐	☐	☐	☐
Buffet Staff	☐	☐	☐	☐
Waiter	☐	☐	☐	☐
Busboy	☐	☐	☐	☐

FIGURE 4-7 Passenger comment card
Source: *Courtesy of Premier Cruises*

Stern water platforms, a feature on some vessels, offer direct access to water activities.
Courtesy of Seabourn Cruise Line

instead anchor offshore. Small boats, called **tenders**, will ferry passengers between port and ship.

- On most cruises, you can dine far more than three times a day. In addition to breakfast, lunch, and dinner, there may be snacks or afternoon tea served between meals and a buffet at midnight.

- A spa or lean and light menu often refers to a low-calorie, low-fat dining alternative. Since so many passengers now watch what they eat, such healthy choices are becoming more common. The *CLIA Cruise Manual* contains a grid that summarizes each member line's special menu offerings. (See Figure 4-8.)

- "Themes" add an interesting spin to some cruises. A certain departure might focus on, say, basketball, with current and former basketball stars onboard. They mingle with guests, sign autographs, and teach volunteers how to improve their foul shooting. Other possible themes: jazz, filmmaking, finance, murder mysteries, and eclipse watching.

- Shore excursions are rarely included in the tour price. It's not necessary to book a shore excursion through the cruise line, either. You can buy one from a shore-side company, rent a car, stroll around, or do just about anything you please. But remember: If the cruise line-sponsored shore excursion is late getting back, the ship will almost surely wait. If you're on your own and you return late, though, you may have to wave good-bye to your fellow passengers as they sail off into the horizon.

CRUISE GUIDE FOR LEAN & LIGHT SHIPBOARD CUISINE	LOW CHOL/LOW FAT	LOW SODIUM	SPA PRESCRIBED	DIABETIC	VEGETARIAN	KOSHER	PROGRAM NAME
AMERICAN HAWAII CRUISES	●	SR	SR	SR	●	SR	Pu'uwai
BERGEN LINE, INC.	SR	SR		SR	SR		
CARNIVAL CRUISE LINES	●	●	●	SR	●		Nautica Spa Selections
CELEBRITY CRUISES, INC.	SR	SR		SR	●	SR	Lean & Light
COMMODORE CRUISE LINE	●	●	SR	●	SR	SR	Lite Cuisine
COSTA CRUISE LINES	SR	SR	SR	SR	●	SR	
CRYSTAL CRUISES	●	●	●	SR	●	SR	Lighter Fare
CUNARD LINE LTD.	●	●	●	●	●	SR	Spa Cuisine
DISNEY CRUISE LINE	SR	SR		SR	●	SR	TBD
FIRST EUROPEAN CRUISES	SR	SR	SR	SR	SR	SR	
HOLLAND AMERICA LINE	●	SR	●	●	●	SR	Light & Healthy Menu
MEDITERRANEAN SHIPPING CRUISES	SR	SR		SR	SR	SR	Regal Bodies
NORWEGIAN CRUISE LINE	●	●	●	●	●	SR	Lean Entree
ORIENT LINES, INC.	●	SR		SR	●	SR	The Lighter Choice
PREMIER CRUISES	SR	SR	SR	SR	SR	SR	SeaFit Cuisine*
PRINCESS CRUISES	●	●	SR	SR	●	SR	Healthy Choice
RADISSON SEVEN SEAS CRUISES	●	SR		SR	SR	SR	Our Light Selection
REGAL CRUISES	SR	SR	SR	SR	●	SR	Heart Line Selections
ROYAL CARIBBEAN, LTD.	●	SR		▲	●	SR*	ShipShape Menu
ROYAL OLYMPIC CRUISES	●	●	●	SR	SR	SR	Spa Cuisine
SEABOURN CRUISE LINE	●	●	SR	SR	SR	SR	Simplicity
SILVERSEA CRUISES	●	●	●	SR	SR	SR	Light & Healthy Cuisine
WINDSTAR CRUISES	●	●	●	SR	●	SR	Sail Light Cuisine/Vegetarian Cuisine

KEY   SR Special Request
   *   Must be requested four weeks prior to sailing.
       Kosher foods come in airtight frozen bags. No blessing on-board.
   ▲   On certain items only. (Not full menu)

FIGURE 4-8   Lean & light shipboard cuisine
Source: *Courtesy of CLIA*

Passenger questions

Yes, passengers really have asked the following:

- How will we know which photos are ours?

- Will trapshooting be held outside?

- Does the crew sleep onboard?

- Is there water all around the island?

- What do you do with the ice carvings after they melt?

- Why does the ship rock only when we are at sea?

- Does the ship generate its own electricity?

- Does the elevator go to the front of the ship?

- Will I get wet if I go snorkeling?

- What time is the midnight buffet?

▨ It's not unusual for a ship's officer to occasionally join passengers at their table. The most prestigious table to sit at, of course, is the captain's table (though this custom is becoming somewhat passé).

▨ In some cases, room service or dining at a special alternate venue requires a modest extra charge.

▨ Sometimes (especially on luxury ships) the tip is included in the cruise price—there's no need to tip again. Occasionally the policy is "no tip required," which means that the guest need not feel that tipping is obligatory. (Most tip anyway.) Some cruise lines offer an option to passengers to prepay their tips in advance of their sailing.

▨ Once all passengers have left the ship, staff rapidly prepare the vessel for the next cruise and its passengers. Amazingly, they often can "turn around" the ship within a matter of hours.

Questions for Discussion

1. Name at least six items that make up the cruise documents sent to a client before he or she leaves.

2. Outline briefly what happens on the first night of a cruise.

3. You're on a day at sea. What would *you* probably do? Name at least ten activities.

4. What goes on during the last evening of the cruise and the following day?

⚓ Activity

Obtain a cruise brochure. (It should be a different one from the brochure you used in Chapter 1.) After reading it carefully, describe below how the cruise and line you chose might offer cruise experiences that are different from the one given in this chapter. For example, does it have open-seating meals? Is there a casino? Look carefully for clues to what does—and doesn't—go on.

CHAPTER FIVE

WHO'S WHO IN CRUISING

After reading this chapter, you'll be able to

- Explain what sea-based cruise staff do

- Relate the responsibilities of land-based management and staff

- Describe how travel agents are a vital link to the cruise sales process

- Explain how and where professionals learn about the cruise vacation experience

E ver wonder what it would be like to be part of the cruise industry? In this chapter we're going to explore three occupational areas that you could consider: sea-based operations, land-based operations, and the segment that sells well over 90% of all cruises—the travel agency community.

Sea-Based Operations

You may be surprised to discover how many people work onboard a ship. Most vessels have *at least* one crew member for every three passengers. On some luxury ships, the ratio is closer to 1.5 to 1. The largest megaships may have more than 1,000 workers onboard.

Cruise lines divide operations onboard their ships into two broad categories: sailing operations and hotel operations. The captain is in charge of both operational sectors. He also attends many social functions onboard so that passengers can get to know him better.

A team of officers supervises those factors that directly relate to the ship's sailing operations:

- The *staff, deputy captain,* or *first officer* is in charge when the captain is busy or not onboard (e.g., at a port). On large ships, the staff captain supervises a team of senior and junior officers. Among his or her special duties is overseeing ship safety and security.

Bridge officers represent years of sailing experience.
Courtesy of Windstar Cruises

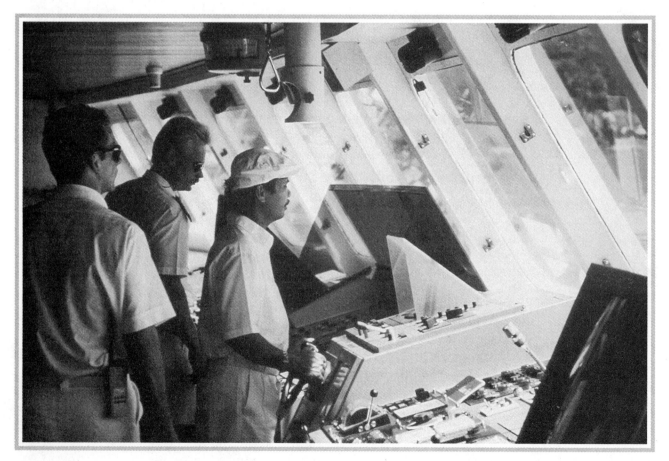

- The *chief engineer* oversees all mechanical operations, including the engines, electrical systems, lighting, plumbing, waste-management, onboard climate control, and the maintenance or repair of the ship itself. The larger the ship, the more specialist tradespeople work under the chief engineer.

- The *chief medical officer,* or *doctor,* tends to the health of passengers and crew. (All ships with 100 or more passengers onboard must have a doctor.) He or she may have a nurse and/or orderly to help out with medical concerns. (Medical services on a ship are not free of charge. Billings are handled as with any hospital or doctor's office.)

- In today's world, the responsibilities of *chief radio* or *communications officer* are complex. He or she oversees in-room satellite TV programming, ship-to-shore calls, and all other shipboard communication systems.

The team of people who comprise hotel operations is equally diversified:

- The *hotel manager,* or *hotel director* (also sometimes called the *chief purser*), conducts his or her business very much like the manager of a land-based hotel or resort, but with a specialized understanding of the cruise experience. Prime areas of responsibility include guest satisfaction and comfort, human resources, security, expenditures, and revenues.

- The *purser* is much like a hotel front-desk manager or assistant manager. Unlike the hotel manager—who tends to larger operational issues—the purser administers day-to-day affairs. Some examples include management of passenger accounts, mail, messages, printing, the storing of valuables, and immigration and customs requirements. On larger vessels, the purser has two assistants: the crew purser (who treats crew issues) and the hotel purser (who tends to passenger matters). The purser may have a large team of assistants who staff the purser's desk, coordinate publications, deliver messages, and handle other concerns.

- The *shore excursion manager* orchestrates the operation and booking of port-based packages. On certain lines, he or she is sometimes called the *concierge,* with broader responsibilities such as booking customized port experiences, changing flights, etc. On larger ships, a team of people tends to shore excursions, including an onboard travel agent who can book a passenger's future cruise needs. (If a sale occurs, the passenger's travel agent usually will still get the commission for that sale.)

- The *cruise director* coordinates all entertainment and informational activities that take place as part of the cruise experience. Part host, part entertainer, gregarious, and always gracious, the cruise director serves as a critical link between passengers and crew. He or she presides over many functions, including passenger orientation and disembarkation meetings. The cruise director also manages the musicians, entertainers, *social hosts* (who converse and dance with single women onboard), health club staff, photographers, and, in some cases, the shore excursion manager.

- The *executive chef* controls the preparation and serving of all food and beverages. He or she supervises the *assistant* or *sous chef,* the pastry chef, food preparers, and other kitchen staff.

- The *head housekeeper* or *chief steward* manages all stateroom, public space, and other shipboard cleaning. He or she supervises a squad of *cabin* or *room stewards* who tend to the passengers' stateroom needs. (Cabin stewards have a much more active, personal, and round-the-clock relationship with guests than do maids at hotels.)

- The *food and beverage manager* oversees the serving of meals and drinks. (On smaller ships this may be handled by the *executive chef.*) The food and beverage manager watches over the *dining room maitre d',* *table captains, waiters,* and *busboys.* The food and beverage manager also oversees the *bartenders, drink servers,* and *wine steward.*

To serve certain passenger needs, cruise lines contract with independent concessioners, contractors, or vendors. This is often true with shore excursion tour operators, onboard entertainer groups, and port operations staff. Casino and beauty salon workers, photographers, shop salespeople, and spa staff (e.g., aerobic instructors or masseuses) may also be independent contractors.

FIGURE 5-1 Concessioners

Responsibilities onboard a ship often overlap. The smaller the vessel, the more likely this is, especially when it comes to entertainment: The shore excursion director, the cruise director, and even the waiters may do double-duty as performers at the evening show. And on many ships, entertainers may serve in numerous other capacities. Note, however, that not all those working on a cruise ship are necessarily employees of the cruise line. (See Figure 5-1.)

Land-Based Operations

To summarize a cruise line's land-based operations is no easy task. Some cruise lines are relatively small, with fewer than 100 off-ship employees. Others are huge, with thousands of employees. What do they have in common?

Surprisingly, the layers of management are often similar. They parallel the standard usage employed in other North American corporations. (See Figure 5-2.)

Let's take a look first at the hierarchy of the typical large cruise line. At the top may be a *chairman* who presides over a *board of directors*. The chairman may be the principal or sole owner of the cruise line or may be responsible to the stockholders. He or she may also be referred to as the *CEO*, or *chief executive officer*. (Sometimes it's the president, not the chairman, who's referred to as the CEO.)

Reporting to the chairman and board is the line's *president*. He or she sets the company's direction in all areas: sales, marketing, operations, finance, and the like. Reporting to the president may be one or two *executive* or *senior vice presidents*.

In turn are a number of vice presidents, each with a set of responsibilities in a specific segment of the company's operations. A few possibilities:

- The *vice president of marketing* orchestrates the research, development, promotion, and follow-up of the cruise line's products.

- The *vice president of sales* oversees the actual selling of cruises, either through travel agencies or directly to the public. Below him or her are *district sales managers* or *sales representatives*, who are the spokespersons for the cruise line at trade shows and communicate with travel agents in their assigned geographic area. The vice president of sales is also in charge of the people who take calls from agents and clients, as well as those who supervise them.

- The *vice president of finance* administers and addresses all financial issues. If he or she is the company's CFO, or chief financial officer, he may well be a senior vice president.

- The *vice president of operations or passenger services* is responsible for all onboard and shore-side activities. This job is sometimes divided into two: a vice president of hotel operations (who manages shipboard hotel-like services) and a vice president of marine operations (who handles technical factors such as ship and port considerations).

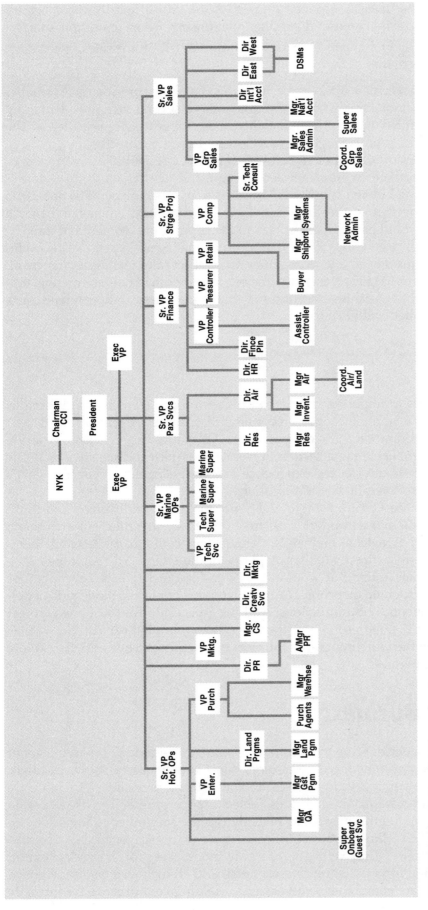

FIGURE 5-2 Organization chart

Source: Crystal Cruises

- The *vice president of national accounts* represents the cruise line to major agency chains, usually those in a preferred supplier relationship. (More about this soon.)
- The *vice president of groups and incentives* orchestrates all group sales, marketing, and operational activities.

Only the very largest cruise lines would have this many vice presidents. At smaller cruise lines, some positions might meld the functions of several vice presidents into one. Other lines might feel that the responsibility doesn't merit a vice presidency. The person in charge of, say, groups, might have a "lower" title (e.g., director).

What are the layers of management below that of vice president? As in the rest of the business world, they are, in order, *director, manager,* and *supervisor.*

A vice president might have one or two directors to oversee (or perhaps one assistant director who reports to a director). They in turn would have managers beneath them, the managers would have supervisors, and the supervisors would have staff.

One last point. At large cruise lines, district sales managers usually work exclusively for one cruise line. For smaller companies, the district sales managers may be independent, working for not only the cruise line but also for other, non-competing suppliers, such as tour companies and tourist bureaus. These independent sales representatives are called *multi-line reps.*

Travel Agencies

Why are travel agents so important to the cruise sales process? The reason is simple: Purchasing a cruise is a far more complicated matter than, say, buying an airline ticket.

A cruise isn't a commodity. It's an *experience.* All cruises *aren't* alike. To decide which cruise is the right one for a particular person is a complex and sensitive task, one that requires the analysis, advice, and experience of a professional travel agent. (That's why travel agents are often called *travel counselors.*)

People who purchase a cruise want to make sure that they'll fully enjoy and profit from it. They want one that will provide destinations, food, activities, entertainment, and an environment that matches their style. Perhaps they could do the research themselves and book the cruise directly (either by phone or the Internet) through the cruise line or some other sales entity. But wouldn't it be easier, quicker, safer, and perhaps cheaper to let an expert guide that choice? After all, cruises often cost thousands of dollars—they're investments, not transactions. And the cruise ship isn't just a way to get from Point A to Point B. It represents an experience, not a commodity.

Travel agents are therefore integral to the cruise sales process. Let's briefly explore how their industry operates.

The Travel Agency Business

About 40,000 travel agencies serve the North American market today, employing about 250,000 full-time and part-time travel counselors. Most of them are full-service outlets, providing air, rail, car, lodging, tours, cruises, and other travel products.

At one time, commissions on air tickets fueled agency profitability. However, in 1996 the airlines began a series of steps to severely cap the amount of commissions an agency could earn from selling air travel. Since then, many travel agencies have treated air sales as "loss leaders." They've begun charging modest fees for their services and have redirected their efforts to selling cruises, tours, and all-inclusive resorts. The reason: These products are comprehensive packages, yielding commissions on virtually

The dining room staff is essential to a successful cruise experience.
Courtesy of Commodore Cruise Line

everything that a client does while on vacation. Cruises generally require only one phone call or computer entry in order to book. A cruise produces extremely high satisfaction in clients, helping to ensure loyalty and repeat business. And most cruise lines treat travel agents as valued partners in the sales process. No wonder agents love selling cruises.

Kinds of Travel Agencies

There are three kinds of travel agencies:

- *Independent agencies.* These agencies are privately owned and unaffiliated with any larger institution. Often called *mom & pops,* they're the "corner store" of travel retailers, usually with small staffs and a keen sense of the communities they serve. However, independent agencies have limited economic leverage with suppliers and often find it a challenge to negotiate higher override commissions and preferred status.

  Yet some independent agencies have flourished in the current competitive business environment. Their strategy: focus on specialized travel products, establish a reputation for excellence, operate super-efficiently, and/or provide a high level of personal service. This is no easy task, however, so the number of mom & pop agencies—once the mainstay of the travel agency industry—has slowly diminished. Currently they represent a little less than 40% of all travel agencies.

■ *Agency chains.* As with most other retail industries, large groups of regionally or nationally branded agencies have developed in North America. Some embrace a dozen or more locations in a defined geographic area. Others count hundreds in their organization. Still others—usually called *mega-agency chains*—have a thousand or more.

Many of these chains have well-known names, creating public recognition and inspiring buyer confidence. Their size and reputation provide them with economic clout, too. It permits them to negotiate favored status with carefully selected "preferred" suppliers. In turn, these preferreds provide the chains with many advantages. (More about that soon.)

Within a chain may be two kinds of agencies: wholly owned and franchises. *Wholly owned* are what the name implies—the chain owns them. *Franchises* are semi-independent agencies who pay for the right to use a chain's name, preferred products, and services. They sign on, hoping that the fees they pay for franchise status will result in such benefits as brand recognition (which will attract more customers), training support, business guidance, higher commissions, and greater profitability.

■ *Consortium-affiliated agencies.* Consortia promise agencies greater independence than they would have if they were an agency franchise, with the leverage that a large national organization brings. (There's no brand name involved, however.) For a relatively modest fee (sometimes pegged to sales volume), an independent agency can affiliate itself with a consortium organization. In turn, the consortium forges preferred supplier relationships on behalf of its member agencies, and provides them with marketing aid, training support, financial advice, and possibly a 24-hour back-up reservation service. Some small or medium-sized chains also join consortia to further leverage their position in the industry.

Not all travel agencies are full-service. Some only sell tours. Some concentrate almost exclusively on business travel. And a good number sell only cruises.

Cruise-only agencies (sometimes called *cruise-oriented agencies*) are specialists. They pride themselves on their especially deep knowledge of ships, cruise lines, and ports. They may sell air and lodging, but only in conjunction with cruises. (They usually tap into the cruise line's air and hotel inventory.) Cruise-onlys can be independent, belong to a consortium, or be part of a chain. There are even cruise-only consortia and chains.

For other ways that people buy cruises, see Figure 5-3.

FIGURE 5-3 Other cruise distribution channels

Though travel agencies powerfully dominate cruise sales, other sellers of cruises exist. *On-line* companies sell cruises via the Internet. *Tour companies* sell cruises through their catalogs and other promotional avenues. They may even offer special group activities for their clients onboard, fold shore excursions into their package, and provide a tour director to tend to the group's shipboard needs. *Cruise consolidators* buy blocks of staterooms from the lines, often for resale at a discounted price and at the last minute (when a cruise line is trying to sell remaining inventory). Cruise consolidators generally sell through toll-free numbers or the Internet. The cruise lines often sell direct to the public, but most carefully avoid letting this erode their relationship with the travel agency community. A few don't permit the public to buy from them directly at all. Some omit their toll-free numbers from their brochures, directing the reader to "see your professional travel agent." Still others list their toll-free numbers and Web site addresses, but only as an information source for consumers or to reach those who would never use the services of a travel agent, no matter what.

In general, travel agencies sell a cruise for the same price as the cruise line does. Rarely is the price identical to what the brochure indicates, however. Early booking incentives, two-for-one offers, and other promotional discount strategies often lead to a lower price (which further underscores buying a cruise as a "deal"). If the cruise line is offering such a deal, the travel agency can offer the very same one, too.

Or better, they can offer "preferred" deals to their clients. Cruise lines routinely identify those agencies, consortia, or chains which sell —or whom they *wish* to sell—a large volume of their products. These productive agencies—through a negotiated process—become preferred sellers of the cruise line products. In turn, the agencies refer to the cruise line with whom they have a special relationship as a "preferred" vendor.

What are the advantages of being a preferred agency?

- The agency may be capable of offering its clients a *better cruise deal* than their competitors.

- The agency may be able to offer the client certain *value-added benefits,* such as an automatic two-class stateroom upgrade at no extra charge.

- The cruise line may provide *co-op funds* and promotional items to help the agency advertise its offerings.

- The cruise line may allow access to *inventory* that others cannot readily get. (In cruise lingo, inventory represents staterooms available.)

- Since agents have to *master only a few products* (typically, an agency will have only a few preferred cruise lines), they can better explain those products to their customers.

- *If a problem occurs, it's easier to resolve* the issue with someone you know—the preferred cruise line.

- The agency typically gets a *higher commission* for their sales performance.

This brings us to an important topic: How do travel agencies make money? When a travel agency sells a cruise, it receives a commission for its efforts. The traditional yield is 10% of the sale price. So if an agent sells a $2,000 cruise, the agency will receive $200 from the cruise line. Excluded are add-on costs such as port charges and taxes, which yield no commission.

If they enjoy a preferred arrangement, the cruise line will give the agency a commission over and above the 10%, known as an **override commission**. The greater the agency's productivity (or perhaps that of its consortium or chain), the greater the override might be. To find out why cruises are so important to agency profitability, see Figure 5-4.

FIGURE 5-4 How cruises can be an important profit center to an agency

In 1996 most airlines capped at $50 the commissions that a travel agency could receive from selling air tickets. Prior to 1996, for example, a $2,000 ticket would have yielded $200 to the agency. After the policy change, that same ticket generated only $50. The lifeblood of agency profitability had been cut severely.

Agencies immediately searched for new profit centers. Cruises were an obvious choice. To sell a cruise was to receive at least 10% commission on most of what a client bought on vacation: lodging, transportation, meals, entertainment, pre- and post-cruise packages and more. Air bought from the cruise lines (to get the client to and from the port) also yields 10% on the cost of the ticket. (Usually an override commission applies only to the cruise package itself, and not the air.) This is better than what the airlines offer. The most successful agencies, therefore, weaned themselves off their dependency on air tickets and shifted their attention toward selling the much more lucrative cruise experiences.

Travel agencies typically have two kinds of salespersons: *inside* and *outside* sales representatives. An inside salesperson works at the agency, fielding calls, responding to e-mail, and dealing with "walk-in" business. They may be paid straight salary or a percentage of their commissions. In many cases, agents receive a base salary *and* a percentage of commissions.

Outside salespersons—also called *home-based agents*—are allied to an agency and sell to friends, acquaintances, or customers referred by them. Paid a percentage of the commission, they usually work out of their home, though they may come into the agency to access its resources or to have an inside agent complete the transaction for them. In some cases, these outside salespeople are part of a chain-like enterprise composed entirely of home-based agents. Typically, the agent—like all agents—asks the client questions, then makes a recommendation based on that client's travel needs. He or she then turns over the client to a central phone booking center to handle the actual details of the trip.

How does a travel agent learn about cruise products and how to sell them most efficiently? Cruise lines may offer agents individualized print materials, videos, CD-ROMs, Internet training sites, visits to agencies by their sales representatives, seminars at key city locations, presentations at conferences, and inspections of their ships. (See Figure 5-5 for a ship inspection form.) Cruise lines also make it easy for travel agents to take cruises at a very reduced price, sometimes individually, sometimes with a group of other agents. These are called **familiarization cruises**, or **fams**, and they permit agents to have first-hand experience with the cruise product, the kind that helps them to better sell cruise vacations to their customers.

The Cruise Lines International Association (CLIA), which represents the vast majority of cruise companies, also makes available a highly diversified mix of training products and events. Indeed, CLIA's training program is regularly rated as the best in the travel business. Travel agents employed by CLIA-affiliated agencies may enroll in its Cruise Counsellor certification program. They can achieve two levels of certification: Accredited Cruise Counsellor (ACC) or Master Cruise Counsellor (MCC). Credits are earned via a combination of classroom, Internet, and/or video training; cruise experience; attendance at CLIA-endorsed conferences; ship inspections; analysis of case studies; and even by studying this book. After completion of each training component, the certification candidate must pass an exam. (For more details, you may contact CLIA at the address given in Appendix B.)

Here are some other North American organizations that offer education in cruise-related topics:

- *The Alliance of Canadian Travel Associations (ACTA)* is a non-profit trade association of travel agencies and suppliers who work together for the promotion, improvement, and advancement of the travel industry, while safeguarding the interests of the traveling public.

- *The American Society of Travel Agents (ASTA)* is a trade association that enhances the professionalism and profitability of member agents through effective representation in industry and government affairs, education, and training, and by identifying and meeting the needs of the traveling public.

- *The Association of Retail Travel Agents (ARTA)* is an organization that provides a forum for travel agents (especially at small- and medium-sized agencies) to emphasize to both the consumer and the supplier the important role they play in providing professional, unbiased travel information.

- *The Canadian Institute of Travel Counsellors (CITC)* encourages education and professionalism in the travel industry through support services, such as seminars, courses, agent education trips, newsletters, and special events.

Onboard entertainers add excitement to a ship's evening schedule.

Courtesy of Radisson Seven Seas Cruises

Name of Ship _____

Date of Inspection _____

Inspected by _____

In Port_____

At Sea_____

Checklist for Shipboard Inspections

Instructions: Identify each stateroom, restaurant or other facility inspected in the space provided and make appropriate comments. Review completed checklist with colleagues and insert into your travel agents' Cruise Manual.

1. Passengers' accommodations	Cabin____	Cabin____	Cabin____	Cabin____
Size of room _____				
Berth arrangement (upper/lower/sofa, etc.) ___				
Furniture comfort & arrangement_____				
Windows and portholes (sealed at sea)_____				
Floor covering _____				
Decor _____				
Self-controlled air temp. _____				
Television/radio _____				
Lighting _____				
Drawer space _____				
Wardrobe space _____				
Bathroom facilities _____				
Convenience Items				
Clothes hangers _____				
Clothes hooks _____				
Writing shelf _____				
Night light _____				
Reading light _____				
110 v electricity for hair blowers_____				
Refrigerator _____				
Potable water _____				
Bottle opener _____				
Clothes line _____				
2. Cabin service				
Promptness _____				
Courtesy _____				
Professionalism_____				
Efficiency _____				
Food and beverages _____				
Quality _____				
Quantity _____				
Eye appeal _____				
Hot/cold _____				

3. Entertainment	Professional	Movies	Semi-professional	Crew sponsored
Quality _____				
Frequency_____				
Variety _____				
Audience reaction_____				

FIGURE 5-5   CLIA's ship inspection form

Source: *Courtesy of CLIA*

4. **Restaurant**
   Seating arrangements
   Tables for two _____
               four_____
               six _____
               eight _____
               twelve_____
   Cleanliness _____
   Lighting_____
   Air conditioning _____
   Seating comfort _____
   Noise level_____
   Service
      Promptness _____
      Courtesy _____
      Professionalism _____
      Efficiency _____
   Food
      Quality _____
      Quantity _____
      Eye appeal _____
      Served hot (cold) _____
      Special diets available _____

5. **Lounges & other**
   public rooms
   Seating arrangements _____
   Seating comfort_____
   Cleanliness _____
   Lighting_____
   Air conditioning _____
   Acoustics _____
   Dance areas _____
   Bar accessibility _____
   View of sea _____

6. **Lido and deck area**
   Size _____
   Spaciousness _____
   Shaded areas _____
   Deck chairs _____
   Food & beverage service _____
   Deck surface _____
   Pool features _____
   Handrails _____

7. **Theater**
   Obstruction of view _____
   Air conditioning _____
   Acoustics _____
   Lighting_____

Seating comfort _____
Accessibility _____
_____
_____

8. **Passageways**
   Lighting_____
   Handrails _____
   Ashtrays_____
   Floor covering _____
   Width_____
   Height _____
   _____
   _____

9. **Service areas**
   Shops_____
   Drug store _____
   Beauty & barber shop _____
   Photo shop_____
   Tour office_____
   Purser's office _____
   _____
   _____

10. **Miscellaneous**
    Medical facilities _____
    Chapel facilities_____
    Casino
       Slots only _____
       Full casino _____
    Health club _____
    Sauna _____
    Indoor pool _____
    Children's playroom _____
    _____

11. **Pier facilities**
    Lighting_____
    Heating _____
    Ventilation_____
    Cleanliness _____
    Baggage handling
    areas _____
    Customs inspection
    facilities_____
    Parking facilities
    (indoor/outdoor) _____
    _____
    _____
    _____

FIGURE 5-5 *(Continued)*
Source: *Courtesy of CLIA*

- *The Institute of Certified Travel Agents (ICTA)* is a non-profit organization that has educated travel industry professionals for more than 30 years. Through quality training and certification programs, ICTA ensures that travel agents are skilled professionals who can expertly satisfy their clients' travel needs.

- *The International Airlines Travel Agent Network (IATAN)*, a wholly owned subsidiary of the International Air Transport Association (IATA), is a not-for-profit organization committed to upholding professional travel business standards. It endorses and appoints travel agencies, as well as travel service intermediary agencies (e.g., cruise-only agencies).

- *The National Association of Commissioned Travel Agents (NACTA)* is an association of travel industry cruise-oriented travel agencies, independent travel agencies, and other agencies that work with outside sales and independent contractors.

- *The National Association of Cruise-Oriented Agencies (NACOA)* is a non-profit trade association of travel agencies whose members have made significant professional commitment to the cruise vacation product. It is the only agency association dedicated to cruise specialists.

- *The National Tour Association (NTA)* is a professional trade association for the packaged travel industry, made up of tour operators, destination marketing organizations, and the suppliers (including cruise lines) that service them.

- *The Outside Sales Support Network (OSSN)* is an association established to represent independent travel contractor needs, providing education, fam training programs, and marketing directives to help sell and promote travel products for the outside travel agent.

- *The Society of Incentive and Travel Executives (SITE)* is a worldwide organization of business professionals dedicated to the recognition development of motivational and performance improvement strategies involving, among other things, cruises.

Questions for Discussion

1. Briefly describe the responsibilities of each of the following:

   - captain

   - chief purser

   - cruise director

   - executive chef

   - cabin steward

2. Briefly explain how the land-based operations are typically organized.

3. Why do most consumers buy cruises through a travel agent? Why do travel agents like selling cruises to them?

4. Describe four kinds of travel agencies.

⚓ *Activity*

Interview someone you know who has been on a cruise. (*Not* someone in the travel industry.) Ask the person the questions given below. Then summarize the responses in the spaces given.

Name of the person interviewed:

1. Did you buy your cruise through a travel agent? Why or why not?

2. In your opinion, who are the three most important cruise line staff members you came in contact with during your cruise? Why did you choose these three?

3. Did you ever entertain the thought of being a travel agent? Of working on a cruise ship? Why or why not?

CHAPTER SIX

THE PRE-, POST-, AND OFF-SHIP CRUISE EXPERIENCE

After reading this chapter, you'll be able to

■ Categorize various types of pre-cruise and post-cruise options

■ Describe how shore excursions enhance a cruise

■ Explain how a cruise experience is perceived differently according to client types

A s we've seen, what passengers can experience on a cruise ship is varied and impressive. Indeed, "cruises to nowhere," transoceanic voyages, and repositioning cruises manage to keep guests quite busy.

However, on most cruises, what takes place on *shore* is often crucial to the passenger's vacation. These port experiences can be divided into three categories: *pre-cruise, intermediary port stops,* and *post-cruise.*

Pre-Cruise Packages

Sometimes clients will travel to their cruise embarkation point and go directly to the ship. Often, though, they'll spend a day or more exploring the port. The simplest of pre-cruise experiences is the **air/sea package**. Usually through a travel agent, the passenger will purchase air, the airport-to-dock transfer, and perhaps lodging. The package can be obtained either from the cruise line itself, or it can be arranged independently, component by component (e.g., the travel agent will book the flight, transfers, and hotel separately).

What are the advantages—both to the client and the agent—of purchasing a pre- or post-cruise package through the cruise line?

- One phone call or computer transaction can set up the whole package.
- The agent will probably receive a higher commission on the air portion than if it were booked through the airline.
- The cruise line's *air deviation desk personnel* (flight specialists accessed by telephone) and meet-and-greet staff are there to help out if a problem occurs.
- Air and/or lodging rates may be lower via the cruise line, or the flight may even be included in the cruise package price. (This latter arrangement, once common, has become increasingly rare.)

There can be some advantages, as well, to arranging the pre-cruise experience directly with non-cruise line suppliers.

- The selection of airlines and flights may be better.
- The airfares may be lower than those offered by the cruise lines. (This is a case-by-case situation.)

One common misconception: If a passenger misses his or her cruise line-arranged connection to the ship (e.g., a flight is late or canceled), the cruise line will obtain, at no extra cost, a later flight that will connect to the ship's next port of call. This is only sometimes true. The cruise line's personnel will do all that they can with the airline to solve the problem. Ultimately, though, it's the airline's decision. More often than not, no matter how much the cruise line pleads, the airline *will* charge the passenger for the extra flight to the next port of call.

This is why it's so important for a cruise client to take travel insurance (and for a travel agent to offer it). For a reasonable fee, a cruiser can purchase insurance that will reimburse costs due to such things as:

- Trip cancellation, delay, or interruption
- Lost or stolen luggage
- Medical expenses for accident or sickness incurred onboard or overseas (including emergency transfer from the ship)

Both cruise lines and independent insurers offer travel insurance. Since problems may well go beyond an individual's or a cruise line's ability to resolve them without incurring cost, travel insurance is a very wise investment.

A modern cruise ship calls at centuries-old Venice.
Courtesy of Costa Cruises

Intermediary Port Stops and Shore Excursions

Most ships call on several ports as part of their sailing itineraries. When passengers arrive at each intermediate place visited, they have four options:

1. They may purchase a shore excursion through the cruise line.
2. They may buy a tour or activity (e.g., a dive package) from vendors who usually await them at or near the dock. They may be transported via a motorcoach, van,

FIGURE 6-1 Marrying aboard ship

An increasingly popular pre-cruise option is the wedding package. Thousands of marriages take place aboard ship each year. A common pattern: The ceremony and reception take place on the ship prior to departure—that way guests can attend. After they disembark, the ship departs, and the couple sails off on their honeymoon.

taxi, or even a private car. Two problems: There's almost no way to preassess the quality of the offering. Also, if the tour gets back to the ship late, the ship may have already left.

3. They may simply explore the port and its environs on their own. They can stroll a picturesque street, do some shopping, and engage in whatever else pleases them. For their reference, the cruise line or travel agent may provide a map of the port (the *CLIA Cruise Manual* contains port maps that can be photocopied). Passengers can even go back to the ship for lunch, then return to the port for the afternoon.

4. They may elect to stay onboard.
   (For a breakdown of what first-time cruisers do while in port, see Figure 6-2.)

In a few rare cases, some or all of the shore excursions are included in the cruise price. Most often, though, passengers buy them from the cruise line. Occasionally, this can be done in advance of sailing but is more commonly done onboard ship by:

■ Filling out a form that's in the stateroom upon check-in and then turning it in at the shore excursion desk (usually near the purser's office)

■ Buying it at the shore excursion desk during its open hours (there may be a waiting line, especially on the first day)

■ Doing it interactively via the stateroom video monitor (available on some newer ships)

Passengers find out about the content of each shore excursion through literature sent in advance of the sailing, in-cabin brochures, video presentations, port talks (usually held the day before arrival at each port), and/or the onboard cruise orientation meeting. Shore excursion personnel onboard the ship are also quite happy to counsel passengers individually on which port experiences might be best for them.

FIGURE 6-2 Participation in shore activities
Source: CLIA Cruising Dynamics Study

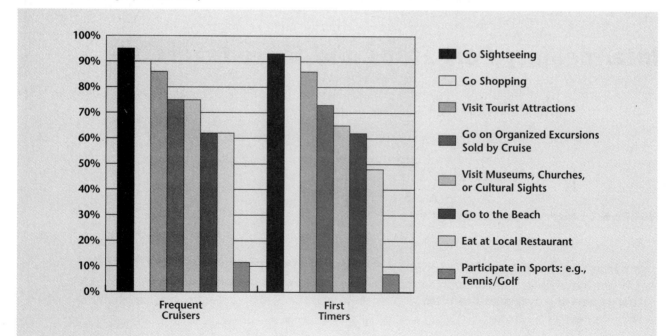

Categories of Shore Excursions

Shore excursions come in every size, shape, and theme. They can be divided into three broad categories:

Shore excursions are integral to the cruise experience.
Courtesy of Commodore Cruise Line

1. *Sightseeing excursions.* A group of people on a motorcoach—is this what sightseeing is all about? Not always. You could take a train from Skagway through the White Pass and Yukon Route. You might take an Atlantis Submarine ride down to view Bahamian coral reefs. Or perhaps a seaplane over New Zealand's fjords and icefields. Even a walking tour of New Orleans's Vieux Carre qualifies.
2. *Sports excursions.* Golf, tennis, sailing, snorkeling—you name the activity, and if it can be done at a particular port, there's probably a shore excursion that will make it possible.
3. *Miscellaneous excursions.* Shore excursions may take you to a faraway beach (e.g., Virgin Gorda's The Baths), to a legendary shopping area (e.g., Beverly Hills's Rodeo Drive), or to a world-class museum (e.g., St. Petersburg's Hermitage).

For more examples of shore excursion options, see Figures 6-3 and 6-4.

M/S FASCINATION TOUR ORDER FORM

NAME: _____   SIGNATURE: _____
CABIN #: _____   SAIL & SIGN FOLIO #: _____

Dear Guest, after reading the tour descriptions provided, please make your selections on the below listed order form. Please note that some of these tours will sell out early so make your selections for all tours as soon as possible to avoid any disappointments. Once completed, hand in the order form to the cruise staff member in the Palace Lounge located on Atlantic Deck Forward. The tickets will then be delivered to your cabin during the night, it's that easy.

NOTE: All tour tickets may be refunded prior to the tour departure but there will be a charge of 25% of the tour selling price applied to your Sail & Sign account.

All Tours Are Operated By Independant Contractors

♟♛ Tours with this symbol (♟♛) indicate that you must pick up your snorkeling equipment at the Snorkel Desk on Empress Deck BEFORE the Tour Departs!!

	BARBADOS TOURS	PRICE	# OF TICKETS	2ND CHOICE
506	BARBADOS ISLAND TOUR @ 9:15 am	$32		
508	BARBADOS ISLAND TOUR @ 1:15 pm	$32		
554	RUM FACTORY AT HERITAGE PARK @8:45am	$34		
556	RUM FACTORY AT HERITAGE PARK @1:30pm	$34		
514	BARBADOS CERTIFIED DIVE @ 8:15 am	$70		
515	ISLAND SAFARI TOUR @ 8:20am Adult	$57		
530	ISLAND SAFARI TOUR @ 8:20am Child	$48		
516	MOUNT GAY RUM TOUR @ 9:30 am	$23		
518	MOUNT GAY RUM TOUR @ 10:00 am	$23		
520	MOUNT GAY RUM TOUR @ 1:30 pm	$23		
522	MOUNT GAY RUM TOUR @ 2:00 pm	$23		
524	THE FLOWER FOREST TOUR @ 8:45 am	$32		
526	EXCELLENCE CHAMPAGNE CATAMARAN @8:45am	$49		
504	EXCELLENCE CHAMPAGNE CATAMARAN @12:00pm	$49		
528	A TOUCH OF JUNGLE TOUR @ 8:45 am	$32		
532	BEGINNING BARBADOS DIVE @ 9:15 am	$76		
534	BEGINNING BARBADOS DIVE @ 12:15 pm	$76	This Departure	Not Available
536	JOLLY ROGER PARTY @ 8:45am	$29	This Departure	Not Available
537	JOLLY ROGER PARTY W/ SNORKEL @ 8:45am ♟♛	$38	This Departure	Not Available
538	JOLLY ROGER PARTY @ 1:15 pm	$29		
539	JOLLY ROGER PARTY W/ SNORKEL @ 1:15 pm ♟♛	$38		
540	ATLANTIS SUBMARINE @ 9:45am adult	$79		
541	ATLANTIS SUBMARINE @ 9:45am Child	$38		
542	ATLANTIS SUBMARINE @ 10:45am adult	$79		
543	ATLANTIS SUBMARINE @ 10:45am Child	$38		
544	ATLANTIS SUBMARINE @ 1:45pm adult	$79		
545	ATLANTIS SUBMARINE @ 1:45pm child	$38		
550	HARBOR MASTER CRUISE @ 1:00 pm	$20		
552	HARBOR MASTER CRUISE W/SNORKEL@ 1:00 pm ♟♛	$29		
561	ATLANTIS SEATREC @ 9:45am	$39		
563	ATLANTIS SEATREC @ 9:45am Child	$19.50		
577	WEISERS BEACH PARTY Adult @1:30PM	$25.50		
578	WEISERS BEACH PARTY Child @1:30PM	$15.50		
579	MALIBU RUM DISTILLERY & BEACH TOUR @8:30am	$19		
580	MALIBU RUM DISTILLERY & BEACH TOUR @1:30pm	$19		
	SAN JUAN TOURS	PRICE	# OF TICKETS	2ND CHOICE
	ORDER DIRECTLY FROM TOUR SHEET			

FIGURE 6-3   Barbados shore excursions

Source: Courtesy of Carnival Cruise Lines

MED11—CITY TOUR (half-day)

Sightseeing tour of Barcelona, capital of Catalonia, and one of the most beautiful and interesting Spanish cities. Visit to the Cathedral and to the Gothic Quarter, dating back to medieval age. Short stop to admire the Sagrada Familia (outside), the unfinished Gaudi's Cathedral, and on to Casa Mija (outside) and Casa Batlo (outside). Visit to "Parque Guell" and short stop at Montjuich Hill, where, from the "Belvedere del Alcade," it is possible to enjoy a spectacular sight over the city. Return to the port to board the ship.

MED12—BARCELONA SHOPPING (half-day)

Sightseeing tour of Barcelona passing through the most interesting cultural places of this enchanting city of Catalonia. Short stop at Montjuich Hill to enjoy a spectacular sight over the city from the "Belvedere del Alcade." Stop at Cataluna Square and free time for shopping.

MED13—CITY TOUR (full-day with lunch)

Leaving from the port to drive to Montjuich Hill and enjoy a spectacular view of the city of Barcelona from the "Belvedere del Alcade." Visit to "Pueblo Espanol" (inside) and to the Miro Foundation (inside). Sightseeing tour of the capital of Catalonia passing through its main streets and squares, to admire Casa Mija (outside) and Casa Batlo (outside), built by Gaudi, and stop at Cataluna Square.

On to visit the Sagrada Familia (outside) before returning to the ship to have lunch onboard. In the afternoon the tour will continue with the visit to the Cathedral (inside), to the Gothic Quarter, to Picasso Museum (inside). Return to the port for embarkation.

FIGURE 6-4 Barcelona shore excursions
Source: Mediterranean Shipping Cruises

Veteran cruisers are especially savvy about shore excursions. Here are a few things they—and you—should know:

- Since ships often arrive at a port early in the morning and leave around dinner time, *it's often possible to take two shore excursions in one day.*

- *Shore excursions that include a meal often represent an especially good value.*

- Sometimes hundreds of people sign up for the same shore excursion, and a half-dozen buses will be waiting for them near the dock. *The earlier you disembark, the easier it will be to take the first coach to depart and return — leaving you more time later in the day.* Also, cruise ships don't always tie up at the dock. Because of the ship's draft and the harbor's depth, a ship may need to stay offshore and transfer passengers via small boat tenders. (This is call *tendering.*) Again, if you can take one of the first tenders out, you'll have more time later in the day.

- *The larger the ship, the more shore excursion choices are likely to be available.* Indeed, some see this as an advantage of a larger vessel.

- *Excursions sold by the cruise lines take into consideration ship meal and departure times.* If something goes wrong, the ship will almost always wait for the excursion to get back. (As mentioned, this is not necessarily so with independent excursions.)

- *Independent concessioners usually operate shore excursions.* Cruise lines do all they can to select quality excursion operators—after all, it reflects on their reputation. In some places (especially in Alaska) the cruise line may actually own the local tour operation, assuring even greater quality control.

Post-Cruise Packages

Post-cruise packages are exactly like pre-cruise ones. They're sold the same way. They represent the same possible components and experiences. Some passengers prefer to do a package before their cruise, others after, still others before *and* after. (Some, of course, don't schedule any at all. They just fly to the port on the day of departure and fly out the day the ship returns.)

We've just described only the simplest of packages. Some are complex, lasting for several days or even *exceeding* the length of the cruise. This sort of package is often called a *cruise tour*.

For an example of a 14-day cruise tour of Canada and Alaska, see Figure 6-5.

Port Experiences and Client Types

In Chapter 3 we briefly mentioned that the ship and port experience is very much perceived according to the passenger's likes and dislikes.

FIGURE 6-5   A Canada/Alaska cruise tour
Source: Holland America Westours

DAY 1. *Anchorage.* Arrive by air for a 2-night stay.

DAY 2. *Portage Glacier cruise.* Tour to Portage Lake and cruise to the face of the glacier aboard our mv Ptarmigan.

DAY 3. *Denali National Park.* Via the McKinley Explorer deluxe railcars.

DAY 4. *Denali Wildlife tour, Fairbanks.*

DAY 5. *Fairbanks river cruise, Tok.* Cruise the rivers by sternwheeler, then travel the Alaska Highway to Tok.

DAY 6. *Yukon River Cruise, Dawson City.* Motorcoach to Eagle to cruise aboard the Yukon Queen to Dawson City.

DAY 7. *Dawson City, Gaslight Follies.* Tour the town, relive Gold Rush Days. Tonight, enjoy the rousing Gaslight Follies show.

DAY 8. *Yukon Wildlife Preserve, Whitehorse.* Alaska-Yukon Explorer to Whitehorse. Stop en route to view the native wildlife.

DAY 9. *Skagway.* Travel by loungecoach and the narrow gauge White Pass & Yukon Railway to the Gold Rush town of Skagway. Overnight here with a sightseeing tour this afternoon.

DAY 10. *Sail from Skagway.* Sail this evening on your Inside Passage cruise to Vancouver.

DAY 11. *Cruising Glacier Bay.*

DAY 12. *Ketchikan port of call.*

DAY 13. *Cruising the Inside Passage.*

DAY 14. *Arrive Vancouver, tour ends.*

For example, families are strongly attracted to cruising because they're value conscious and time pressed. Cruises solve their needs nicely. Some lines feature special kids' menus. A few provide children with their own daily newspaper. Several have a "kids only" pool. Some cruise lines even go so far as to offer a full children's program, with a wide variety of special, age-appropriate activities supervised by counselors. (See Figure 6-6 for examples.) A few even have staff dressed as cartoon characters onboard. All these features leave time for mom and dad to relax together while still having loads of time to be with their children.

But what about port time? Parents usually select itineraries and ports that satisfy the goals they've set for themselves and their children. Want them to have fun? An itinerary out of Port Canaveral that features a pre- or post-cruise experience in Orlando is an obvious choice. How about children getting in touch with nature? Then Alaska's ports of call are ideal. Is the child about to study European history? A cruise among the islands of the Mediterranean would be a powerful, real-life motivator to academic success.

Indeed, port experiences can take altogether different shapes, depending on the client's profile. Let's say a ship visits Cancun. (It will actually dock at Playa del Carmen, about 40 miles away.) A culture-seeker may devote the entire day to visiting the magnificent Mayan ruins at Chichen Itza. A diver, on the other hand, may spend his time exploring the waters off Cozumel. A shopper will head straight for Cancun's hotel zone. A golfer will want to play Cancun's Poktapok course. And someone into fishing may want to deep-sea fish near Cancun or even at Isla Mujeres. Same port. Totally different experiences, depending on the client's interests.

One final but important topic: cruise travel for the physically challenged. As a result of the cruise lines' sensitivity to this issue and the nature of the cruise experience itself, many disabled travelers feel that cruising is *the* way to travel. Most modern

FIGURE 6-6   Examples of kids' activities

- "Kids-only" shore excursions

- Ping pong tournaments

- "Coke-tail" poolside parties

- Nintendo competitions

- "Parents-not-allowed" movies

- Special tours of the ship

- Camp nights, where kids sing around a "campfire," listen to stories and make s'mores (but don't get to sleep in tents!)

- Puppet workshops

- Beach parties

- Face-painting competitions

- Entertainment and performance programs

- Classes of all kinds: photography, computers, musical instruments, and more vessels are fully accessible to the handicapped, with specially equipped staterooms and maybe even a staff member or two onboard who specializes in the diverse needs of the physically challenged. Most cruise lines request that a physically challenged person be accompanied by an "able-bodied" companion.

A vessel departs Sydney Harbour.
Courtesy of Orient Lines

But what of the port experience? Some places, like Scandinavia, are especially sensitive to providing full accessibility for all people. Others (often underdeveloped countries) may provide a challenge to the disabled. Or if tendering between port and ship is required, it may be difficult for the physically challenged passenger to get to shore.

How, then, can the physically challenged maximize their enjoyment of a cruise? First, someone who is disabled should ask his or her travel agent to determine a ship's accessibility. (Both consumer and trade reference publications cover this thoroughly.) The agent will also find out if the line offers or can specially arrange a shore excursion customized to the client's needs, and if tendering situations will occur. Finally, many physically challenged travelers book with a cruise tour group made up entirely of physically challenged people, with tour directors who specialize in this market.

Another important point: Some travel agencies and tour operators are especially knowledgeable in arranging travel for the physically challenged. They may know the answers to these, and other questions, through their extensive experience.

Questions for Discussion

1. What are the advantages of booking a pre- or post-cruise package through the cruise line? What are the potential disadvantages?

2. What are the three options that a passenger has when disembarking at an intermediate port?

3. List five things a passenger should know about a shore excursion.

⚓ Activity

Study the two lists of shore excursions given on pages 78–79. If you could pick two from the Barbados list and one from the Barcelona list, which would they be and why? Give and explain your answers below.

Barbados

Shore excursion #1:

Reason:

Shore excursion #2:

Reason:

Barcelona

Shore excursion #1:

Reason:

⚓ Bonus Activity

In this chapter and others, we've emphasized (and we will again) how a cruise can satisfy a number of different client types. Which type would you be? What would you most want out of a cruise? Here's a quick quiz that will help you find out. The higher your score, the closer you are to that client profile.

For each item, circle the degree to which you agree with the following statements.

5 Strongly agree	4 Agree	3 Somewhat agree	2 Agree very little	1 Disagree

The Active Vacationer

On vacation, I like to choose from a wide range of activities, from shopping to sunning.	5	4	3	2	1
I like participating in sports, such as volleyball, racquetball, and basketball.	5	4	3	2	1
I'm a regular exerciser and like to keep up with it on vacation.	5	4	3	2	1
I'd be lost without my treadmill or stairclimber.	5	4	3	2	1
I'm interested in scuba diving or snorkeling.	5	4	3	2	1

Active Vactioner Total Score: _____

The Adventurous Vactioner

Visiting the world's capitals and seeing all the sites is something I've always wanted to do.	5	4	3	2	1
I like to visit places off-the-beaten-track and see unusual things.	5	4	3	2	1
I've often thought it would be exciting to walk on a glacier, climb a mountain, or explore a volcano.	5	4	3	2	1
Flight-seeing over exotic islands is my kind of fun.	5	4	3	2	1
I enjoy getting close to nature and wildlife.	5	4	3	2	1

Adventurous Vacationer Total Score: _____

The Romantic Vactioner

I like romantic dinners, dancing under the stars, and a show every night.	5	4	3	2	1
I like doing new things with a "special someone."	5	4	3	2	1
I like to make new friends on vacation.	5	4	3	2	1
A breathtaking view, a stroll under a full moon, and a quiet place to talk sound sublime.	5	4	3	2	1
I want our first vacation together to be something special.	5	4	3	2	1

Romantic Vacationer Total Score: _____

The Quick-Getaway Vactioner

I like to take several mini-vacations each year.	5	4	3	2	1
If I have a long weekend coming up, I want to make the most of it.	5	4	3	2	1
I try to sample as much as I can and visit a variety of destinations, even though my vacation time is limited.	5	4	3	2	1
When I take a short vacation, I want to be wined and dined, and I'd like to meet as many new people as possible.	5	4	3	2	1
It's hard for me to get away for long periods of time.	5	4	3	2	1

Quick-Getaway Vacationer Total Score: _____

The Family Vactioner

My spouse and I work and never seem to have enough time to spend with the children.	5	4	3	2	1
Even though we have different interests, our family enjoys vacationing together.	5	4	3	2	1
With a teenager, an eight-year-old, and a toddler, our family needs four vacations in one.	5	4	3	2	1
We need a restaurant that satisfies all our family's tastes—from burgers to continental.	5	4	3	2	1
We're planning a family reunion and are looking for a setting that will please Grandma as well as Johnnie.	5	4	3	2	1

Family Vacationer Total Score: _____

The Affinity/Special-Interest Vactioner

I like to have a focus to my vacation.	5	4	3	2	1
When I'm on vacation, I enjoy meeting people with interests that are similar to mine.	5	4	3	2	1
Learning something new can be as rejuvenating as relaxing by the pool.	5	4	3	2	1
I have a passion for _____ (fill in your special interest) and like to pursue it on vacation.	5	4	3	2	1
Rubbing elbows with a celebrity adds spice to my vacation.	5	4	3	2	1

Affinity Vacationer Total Score: _____

The Single Vactioner

When traveling alone, I enjoy being introduced to other singles.	5	4	3	2	1
I like meeting other singles in a relaxed and comfortable setting.	5	4	3	2	1

I prefer to share expenses with another single, so I need a vacation spot that will arrange this for me.	5	4	3	2	1
I'm a night owl and am looking for a lively crowd.	5	4	3	2	1
My dream vacation is one that offers ready-made bridge, golf, and dinner and dancing partners.	5	4	3	2	1

Single Vacationer Total Score: _____

The Sophisticated Vactioner

When I go on vacaion, I demand the very best.	5	4	3	2	1
I've traveled the world on business, and now I'm looking for a special way to revisit my favorite places.	5	4	3	2	1
I usually stay in a suite when I travel.	5	4	3	2	1
World-class cuisine and impeccable service are important to me.	5	4	3	2	1
The more exotic the destination, the more I like it.	5	4	3	2	1

Sophisticated Vacationer Total Score: _____

CHAPTER SEVEN

THE GEOGRAPHY OF CRUISING

After reading this chapter, you'll be able to

■ Describe the importance of geography to cruising

■ Define the world's major cruise regions and itinerary patterns

■ Match each region with the kind of traveler who favors it

■ Identify each region's seasonal patterns

G il Grosvenor, the president of the National Geographic Society, tells of the time when someone sitting next to him on a plane discovered who he was. "Oh, I just *love* geography," she enthused. "That's why I like to travel. One of these days I'll get around to taking a cruise. Probably to Las Vegas . . . ."

That would be quite an achievement, since Las Vegas is about 250 miles inland. The only bodies of water in Vegas are hotel swimming pools.

Las Vegas, though, is one of the few places on earth where cruises can't travel. Whether by sea or by river, cruise vessels can access thousands of ports. And those places not accessible by ship can be experienced through a pre- or post-cruise package.

Geography plays an essential role in cruising in many ways:

- Cruise clients often decide which voyage to take according to the itinerary, not the ship or the line. (This is especially true of first-time cruisers.)
- Certain places are *best* experienced by ship. To drive or fly from town to town in Alaska, for instance, is difficult, expensive, or, in some cases, impossible. Cruise ships, however, get around Alaska's coastal waters easily.
- Cruises are especially appropriate when you want to visit clusters of islands, such as those of Indonesia, the Greek islands, and the Caribbean.
- Air connections within these island groups are often awkward and, in the case of the smaller islands, non-existent.
- Travelers often prefer to visit underdeveloped countries via cruise. The ship is secure, the food familiar, the transportation dependable, and the lodging reliable.

Geography is relevant not only to passengers, but to those in the industry, too. The ship's staff must have an intimate knowledge of the ports they visit. Land-based personnel must understand how places impact the experience that they market and sell. Travel agents need to be fully familiar with geography, too. Their port knowledge establishes their credibility and professionalism, builds loyalty and trust, and maximizes the probability of client satisfaction.

So let's explore the world of cruising. To help you along, maps accompany each place described. Study them carefully as you read. Let's start with one of the most familiar places of all: North America.

Cruising North America

More cruises take place in the waters that surround and flow through North America than anywhere else in the world. To simplify things, we can identify five distinct cruise regions in North America: Alaska, the Northeast, the Mississippi River and its tributaries, Mexico's Pacific Coast, and the Caribbean. Let's examine each.

Alaska

Few places match the drama of Alaska. Pristine inlets, unpolluted skies, white-blue glaciers, jagged mountains, intimate towns—these are what have made Alaska one of the world's fastest growing cruise destinations. The cruise season here is limited to around May through early October, when daylight lasts longest and temperatures are most pleasant.

Two cruise itineraries predominate. The first, the Inside Passage route, usually begins in **Vancouver,** British Columbia, **Seattle,** Washington, and threads its way northward among narrow channels, past wooded islands to a turnaround point (usually at

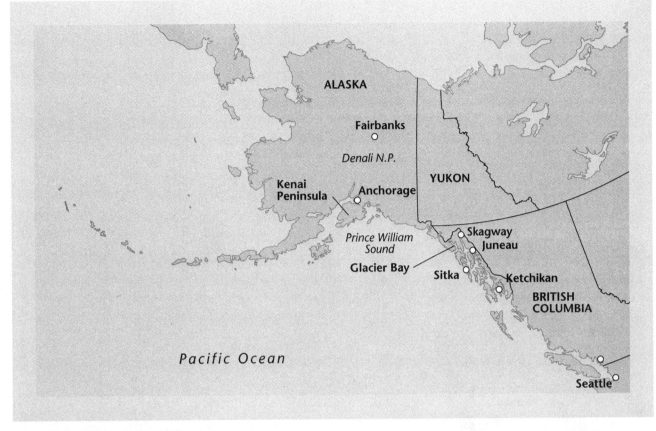

FIGURE 7-1 Map of Alaska

or near Skagway). The ship then returns southward to Vancouver. The vessel calls at three or four ports along the way. Among the most popular stops:

- **Sitka,** with its traces of Russian influence. (Sitka was once a Russian colonial outpost and capital of Russian America.)
- **Juneau,** Alaska's compact capital, picturesquely nestled at the base of a mountain.
- **Skagway,** a key town in Alaska's gold-rush era.
- **Glacier Bay,** where passengers see chunks of ice cracking off glaciers and thundering into the icy waters.
- **Ketchikan,** a center of Native American culture and the self-proclaimed Salmon Capital of the World.

The second common itinerary: a one-way cruise from Vancouver or Seattle to **Anchorage** (or vice versa). The ship stops at many of the same ports of an Inside Passage cruise, then continues northward to visit **Hubbard Glacier, College Fjord, Prince William Sound** and the **Kenai Peninsula.** From Anchorage, many cruisers extend their vacation experience by taking a 356-mile Anchorage-**Fairbanks** escorted railroad journey, with a layover stay at **Denali National Park.** (The park is the home of Mt. McKinley, North America's tallest peak.) Another land-excursion option: passengers disembark at Skagway for a trip to Canada's **Yukon** and on to Fairbanks (or the reverse).

What kind of people are drawn to an Alaska cruise? The ecology-minded, for sure, and those who appreciate scenery and a pure outdoors environment. Families with

A vessel passes the Isle of Capri.
Courtesy of Radisson Seven Seas Cruises

children are more likely to cruise during the summer months, while seniors predominate during the early and late Alaska cruise seasons.

A few smaller cruise lines explore the Pacific Northwest region south of Vancouver, including voyages up the **Columbia River.**

The Northeast

Passenger ships have plied the Atlantic waters off North America for well over a century. One of the most famous was the Fall River Line, made up of elegant steamers that served as transportation between New England and New York City. Another was the legendary *Bluenose*, a schooner that sailed between Maine and Nova Scotia. And, of course, the great ships of the early twentieth century followed a route from Europe to New York that curved along the Northeast's shores.

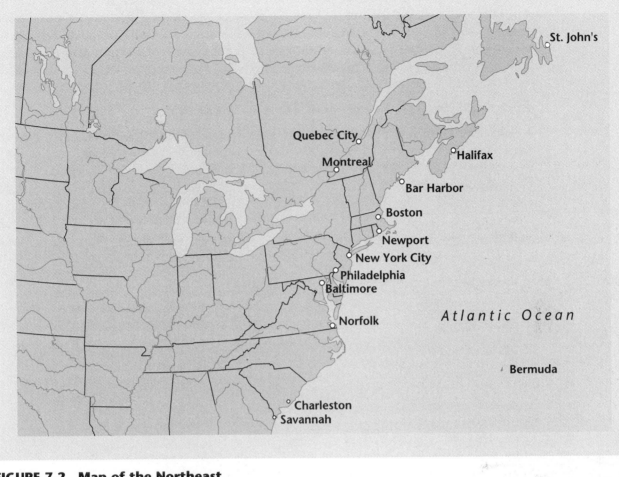

FIGURE 7-2 Map of the Northeast

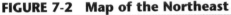

Today, coastal cruising in the Northeast is experiencing a renaissance, with ships sailing between two of North America's great cities, **New York City** and **Montreal.** The most common intermediary stops:

- **Newport,** Rhode Island, the site of some of America's greatest mansions.
- **Boston,** Massachusetts, the "cradle of liberty" of the United States.
- **Bar Harbor,** Maine, gateway to Acadia National Park.
- **Saint John's,** New Brunswick, and **Halifax,** Nova Scotia, two key cities of the Canadian Maritime Provinces.
- **Quebec City,** Quebec, a little bit of seventeenth-century France right here in North America.

The Northeast cruise season extends from late spring through fall. Fall foliage cruises in October are especially popular. The passengers who are found aboard a Northeast cruise are diverse. History and tradition are what attract them.

Ships occasionally venture into more southerly Atlantic waters, often as part of repositioning cruises from the Northeast to the Caribbean. Among the possible ports visited: **Philadelphia,** Pennsylvania, **Baltimore,** Maryland, **Norfolk,** Virginia, **Charleston,** South Carolina, and **Savannah,** Georgia.

A very popular cruise itinerary is the East Coast to **Bermuda** run. Operated from April through October (primarily from New York City), it provides an intriguing alternative to staying at a Bermuda hotel. (Bermuda limits new hotel construction, so land-based lodging is often at a premium.) Once there, cruise passengers can experience quaint towns and pink-sand beaches.

The Mississippi River and Its Tributaries

A quick quiz. Which of the following cities can you get to from the Mississippi or one of the rivers from which it flows? Pittsburgh. Minneapolis. Nashville. St. Louis. Little Rock. Memphis. New Orleans. Chattanooga. Charleston.

The answer: *All of them.* It's amazing how many fascinating places border the great rivers of America. Regular cruise ships rarely sail the Mississippi or its tributaries. The waters are too shallow. But two other kinds of vessels do—riverboats and large passenger barges.

FIGURE 7-3   Map of the Mississippi River and Its Tributaries

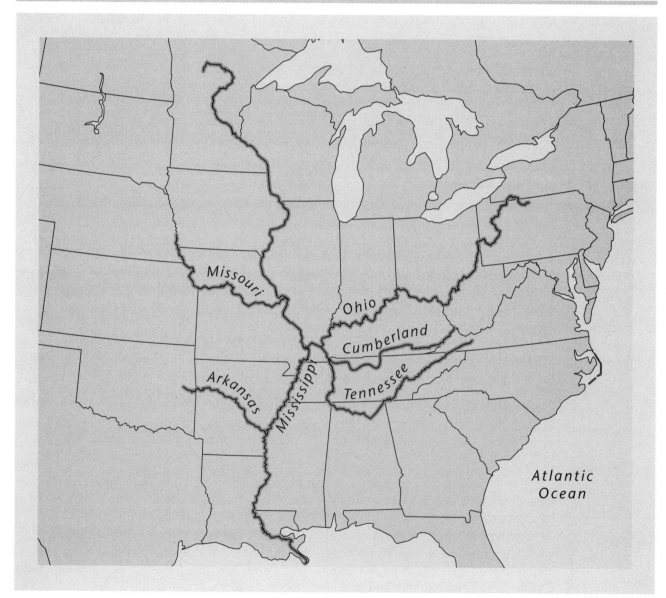

The great riverboats of the nineteenth century were legendary, the stuff of Mark Twain novels. In the early twentieth century, they virtually disappeared. Their comeback has been spectacular, with new paddlewheelers—every bit as ornate and majestic as the original ones—carrying passengers year-round to some of America's most interesting places. They're like time machines to America's past.

Who favors a North American river cruise adventure? Those passengers tend to be older and fairly upscale, with a deep interest in history. They're willing to forgo a resort-like onboard ship experience for the simple pleasures of visiting a restored plantation home, experiencing a Cajun music festival, exploring a vital city, or simply sitting in a rocking chair on the boat's "front porch," watching America's past and present glide gracefully by.

Mexico's Pacific Coast

Sun. Sand. Great shopping. Sensational food. A *fiesta* spirit. These and more attract tourists to Mexico. And these very same things appeal to those who wish to take a cruise along Mexico's Pacific coast.

Three itineraries are typical. The first is a three- or four-day round-trip out of **Los Angeles** or **San Diego** (often as an extended weekend getaway) to **Ensenada,** a festive town on the **Baja Peninsula.** Along the way, ships sometimes stop at **Catalina,** a charming island only 26 miles off California's coast. This itinerary operates year-round and often serves as a "sampler" for first-time cruisers. Typically, passengers are of all ages and interests.

The second itinerary is longer. It takes passengers one way between **Acapulco** and Los Angeles or San Diego (in either direction). This "Mexican Riviera" itinerary operates mostly in the winter and features the following ports:

FIGURE 7-4 Map of Mexico's Pacific coast

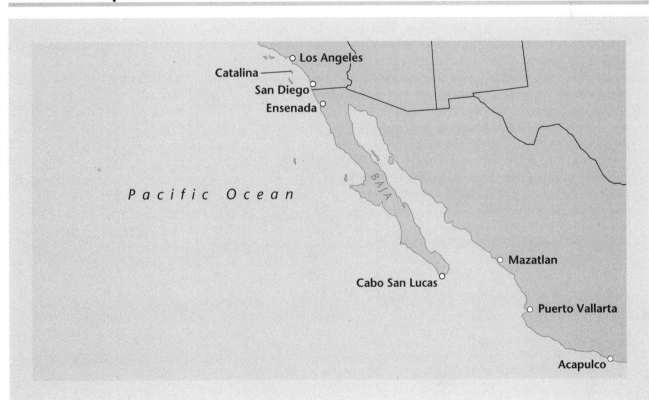

- **Cabo San Lucas,** at the southern tip of Baja. The big attractions here are beautiful coves, snorkeling, and superb deep-sea fishing.
- **Mazatlan,** another fishing paradise that offers jungle tours, shopping, folklore shows, and lively cantinas.
- **Puerto Vallarta,** with pristine beaches, an extensive market, and a dramatic golf course.
- **Acapulco,** Mexico's grand old resort. Numerous night spots, countless restaurants, and the famous cliff divers make Acapulco a dramatic beginning or end to a cruise.

The third itinerary is a variation of the previous two. The ship sails from Los Angeles, visits three ports, then returns to Los Angeles.

Often associated with the Mexican Riviera is a **Panama Canal** cruise. Beginning in Acapulco, this route takes passengers to the Canal, perhaps visiting a Central American port along the way. After passing through the Canal, the vessel may call on ports in **Colombia, Venezuela,** and the Caribbean itself. The itinerary, of course, can operate in reverse, from the Caribbean to Acapulco. Panama Canal cruises generally last 10 to 16 days.

The Caribbean

It's the number one cruise destination in the world. And it's one of the most misunderstood as well.

Here are three things the layman usually gets wrong. First, Bermuda is *not* in the Caribbean. It's nearly 1,000 miles north of the Caribbean, at about the same latitude as

FIGURE 7-5   Map of the Bahamas

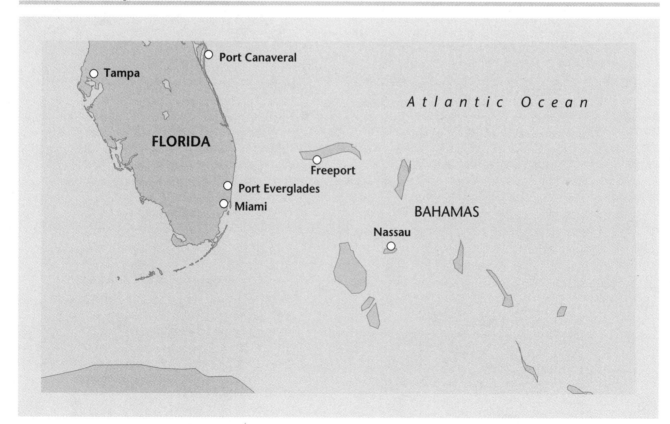

Charleston, South Carolina. (See Figure 7-2.) Second, the **Bahamas** aren't in the Caribbean, either. They, too, are in the Atlantic, just east of Florida and north of Cuba. (They are, however, often on Caribbean itineraries. More about that later.) And third, the Caribbean islands are *not* all alike. There are big ones, small ones, mountainous ones, and flat ones, with just about every culture and nationality represented.

Three basic Caribbean cruise itineraries exist: the Eastern Caribbean, Southern Caribbean, and Western Caribbean. For convenience, let's add the Bahamas as a fourth itinerary option. One proviso: What constitutes each region is open to debate. Some cruise lines, for example, call on Martinique as part of an Eastern Caribbean sailing. Others include it in their Southern Caribbean program. Still, we need to organize these islands in some fashion. What follows is the *general* pattern. Most of these cruises operate year-round, though fewer ships are positioned here in the summer than in the winter.

The Bahamas   A Bahamas cruise is to the East Coast what an Ensenada/Baja cruise is to the West Coast—a three- to four-day getaway that often provides travelers with their first taste of cruising. Most cruises to the Bahamas depart from **Miami** or **Port Everglades** (at Ft. Lauderdale). Others leave from **Port Canaveral** (just east of Orlando) or **Tampa**. As with an Ensenada cruise, the people onboard are highly diversified. The key Bahamian port is **Nassau,** with wonderful shopping, historical attractions, and great diving nearby. Four-day itineraries often include **Freeport.**

The Eastern Caribbean   This itinerary (seven days or more) usually begins and ends in Miami, Port Everglades, or **San Juan,** Puerto Rico, with its historic old city and

FIGURE 7-6   Map of the Eastern Caribbean

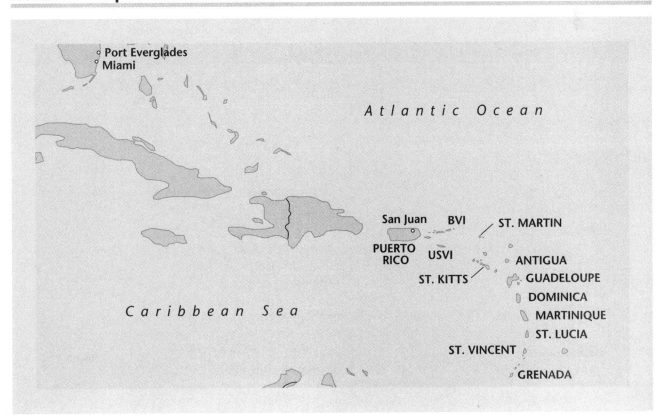

many lovely beaches. The ships then sail eastward, calling on a number of the following islands:

- **The U.S. Virgin Islands,** made up of **St. Thomas** (great scenery and shopping), **St. Croix,** and **St. John** (only the smallest ships anchor here).

- **The British Virgin Islands,** much less developed than their U.S. counterparts. On one of these islands (**Virgin Gorda**) is "The Baths," a unique beachside formation of boulders.

- **St. Martin/St. Maarten,** governed jointly by the French and the Dutch. Ships anchor on the Dutch side (St. Maarten), where most of the shopping can be found. The French portion (St. Martin) is famous for its fine restaurants.

- **Antigua,** a lush tropical island with a unique attraction, "Nelson's Dockyard," where the British Caribbean fleet was headquartered during the eighteenth century.

- **Guadeloupe** and **Martinique,** which share much in common: French culture, volcanoes, deep-green scenery, and plenty of shopping.

- Other islands that some cruise lines call on are **Dominica, St. Lucia, St. Vincent, Grenada,** and **St. Kitts.**

The Southern Caribbean   Less visited than the other Caribbean regions, the Southern Caribbean is a popular choice for those looking for a more exotic, port-inten-

FIGURE 7-7   Map of the Southern Caribbean

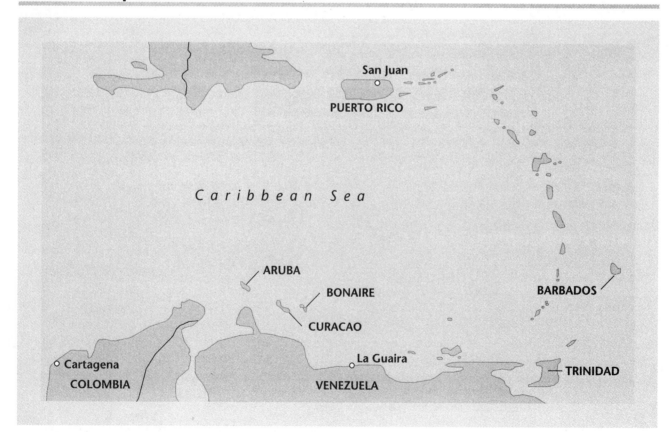

sive itinerary. Cruises generally leave and return from either San Juan or Aruba. Among the islands visited:

- The "ABC Islands" (for the letters that start each of their names): **Aruba** and **Curacao,** with their fine beaches, casinos, and picturesque Dutch buildings, and **Bonaire,** one of the Caribbean's greatest dive destinations.
- **Trinidad,** the home of steel drum bands, calypso music, and the limbo.
- **Barbados,** a busy island with old plantation homes and an underground wonder, "Harrison's Cave."

Southern Caribbean itineraries sometimes include ports on the South American mainland, such as **La Guaira** (the port for Caracas, Venezuela) and **Cartagena,** Colombia.

The Western Caribbean Conveniently accessed from the same Florida ports as Bahamas cruises, and occasionally from **Houston, Galveston,** or **New Orleans,** the Western Caribbean offers a broad spectrum of island and mainland experiences. Here are the most popular:

- **Cancun,** on the Yucatan Peninsula, one of Mexico's most popular resorts. Cancun has good shopping, great restaurants, and plenty of entertainment. Relatively nearby are several remarkable Mayan ruins. Off Cancun is **Cozumel Island,** where some ships dock, too. Diving and fishing have made Cozumel famous.

FIGURE 7-8 Map of the Western Caribbean

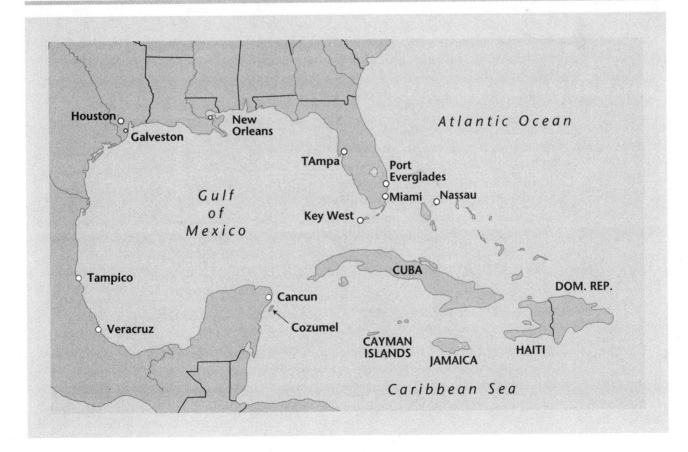

- **The Cayman Islands,** another legendary diving spot. Two famous attractions: a turtle farm and "Stingray City," where divers can swim with these ominous-looking yet gentle creatures.
- **Jamaica,** famous for its reggae music, varied landscape, and numerous attractions. The best-known: "Dunns River Falls," where a river cascades down a series of step-like stones that visitors can climb.
- **Haiti,** on the western side of the large island of Hispaniola. Its blend of French and African cultures is intriguing, and its folk art is widely collected.
- **The Dominican Republic,** occupying the eastern side of Hispaniola. It boasts historical sites, many golf courses, and shopping venues.

Sometimes included on a Western Caribbean itinerary are such Mexican mainland ports as **Tampico** and **Veracruz,** as well as **Key West,** Florida. If the political situation changes, **Cuba** will probably become a major cruise destination. Remember, too, that many Western Caribbean cruises stop at Nassau, Bahamas.

The huge variety of options in the Caribbean demonstrates why it's so popular. This diversity also reflects itself in the composition of cruise passengers. Caribbean and Bahamian cruises attract just about every kind and age group of passenger imaginable.

A cruise ship seems small as it passes through one of Norway's mammoth fjords.
Courtesy of Bergen Line

Cruising Europe

After North America, Europe is the world's most popular cruise destination. The combination of history, architecture, cuisine, and elegant living make Europe an especially seductive continent to cruise. Except for a few places (e.g., Switzerland), virtually every country in Europe is accessible to seagoing or rivergoing vessels.

Cruising offers many benefits that are especially well-suited to Europe:

- Cruises make visiting the Continent efficient. Transfers, border crossings, and the like are inconsequential if you're cruising.
- Language problems are minimized. There's no need to decipher road signs or figure out from which track your train will be departing.
- Cruises guarantee a consistent level of accommodations and dining, something that's somewhat unpredictable with land-based European lodging.
- Considering how expensive gas, tolls, and good European lodging can be, cruises offer a real value.

FIGURE 7-9 Map of the Western Mediterranean

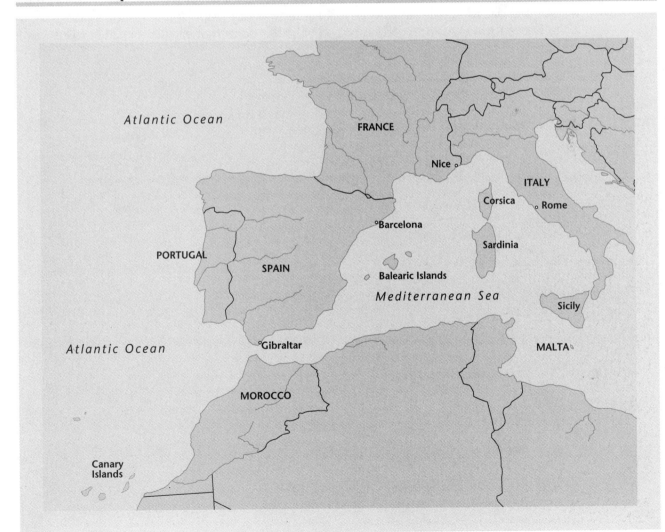

■ Cruises are especially interesting to veteran European visitors, since ships call on many ports off the beaten "land-based" path. Culture seekers and history buffs favor European cruises.

Six itineraries predominate: the Western Mediterranean; the Eastern Mediterranean; Atlantic ports; Ireland, Great Britain, and the North Sea; the Baltic Sea; and river cruises. Most are 7 to 14 days long and take place in late spring, summer, and early fall.

Let's review those six, keeping in mind that—as with the Caribbean—there can be plenty of variations.

The Western Mediterranean

Few regions offer as much culture as the Western Mediterranean. It's known for its sophisticated lifestyle: historic villages, chic boutiques, rich art galleries, fine wines, and refined cuisine. A Western Mediterranean cruise typically calls on ports on the mainlands of **Spain, France,** and **Italy.** The **Balearic Islands, Gibraltar,** and the islands of **Corsica, Sardinia, Sicily,** and **Malta** are popular, too. **Morocco,** a North African country south of Spain, often is included on Western Mediterranean cruises. And some ships venture out past the Straits of Gibraltar to the **Canary Islands,** in the Atlantic.

The three most popular ports of embarkation and debarkation in the Western Mediterranean are **Barcelona,** Spain, **Nice** (on the French Riviera), and **Rome,** Italy. Several dozen other ports are popular intermediary stops. (Note: Rome's port is actually the town of Civitavecchia. For a list of the ports that serve other major European and Middle Eastern cities, see Figure 7-10.)

FIGURE 7-10   European and Middle Eastern ports

Here are the ports that serve important towns and cities on European/Middle Eastern itineraries:

• *Alexandria*	Cairo, Egypt
• *Cadiz*	Seville, Spain
• *Civitavecchia*	Rome, Italy
• *Haifa*	Jerusalem, Israel
• *Kusadasi*	Ephesus, Turkey
• *Le Havre*	Paris, France
• *Leith*	Edinburgh, Scotland
• *Livorno*	Florence, Italy
• *Piraeus*	Athens, Greece
• *Southampton*	London, England
• *Zeebrugge*	Brussels, Belgium

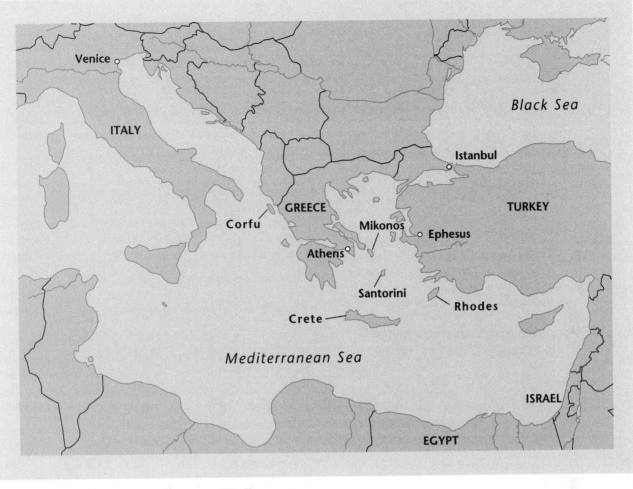

FIGURE 7-11 Map of the Eastern Mediterranean

The Eastern Mediterranean

For those who treasure ancient history, few places rival the Eastern Mediterranean. From the key ports of **Venice, Athens,** and **Istanbul,** ships sail forth to retrace the paths of Homer, Herodotus, and other greats from antiquity.

Which are the most popular places for ships to visit? **Greece,** of course, especially its islands of **Corfu, Mikonos, Crete, Santorini,** and **Rhodes.** The legendary ancient cities of **Turkey** (of these, **Ephesus** is the most famous). And, despite the fact that they're in the Middle East and Africa, not Europe, the ancient nations of **Israel** and **Egypt.**

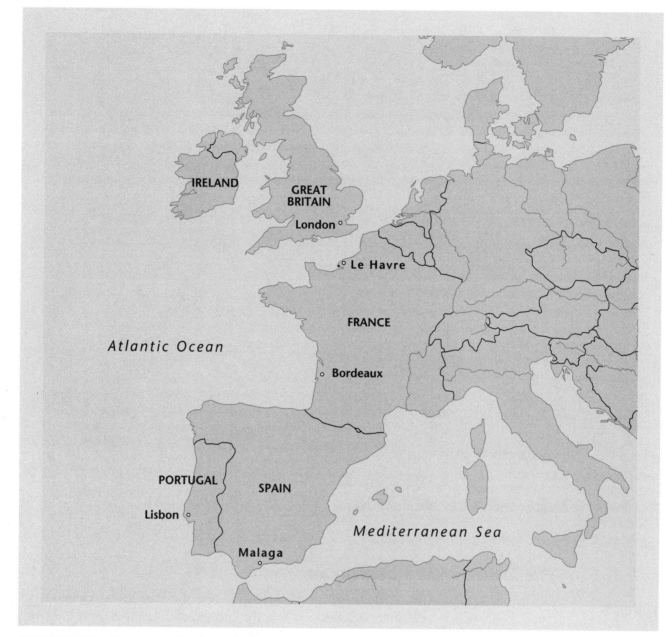

FIGURE 7-12 Map of Atlantic Europe

Atlantic Europe

Sometimes as part of a repositioning cruise (more about that later), other times an itinerary in itself, an Atlantic European cruise usually features **Portugal,** France, and, occasionally, Spain, **Ireland,** and **Great Britain.** If it were a long cruise, the itinerary might start at **Malaga,** on Spain's southern Costa del Sol, journey around to **Lisbon,** Portugal, continue northward to **Bordeaux,** France, and finish in **London,** England. Another variation might commence in Lisbon and finish at **Le Havre,** Paris's northern port.

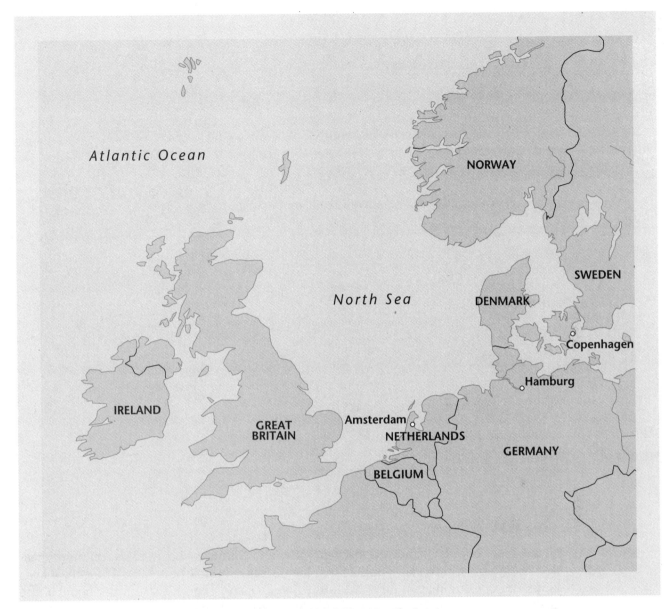

FIGURE 7-13   Map of Ireland, Great Britain, and the North Sea

Ireland, Great Britain, and the North Sea

Familiarity—that's what makes Europe's northwest regions especially attractive. The culture is familiar, the cities well known. But cruising enables even the veteran traveler to experience these places in an altogether different way.

The variations here are many. Some cruises circle Ireland, others go around Great Britain. A common itinerary starts in England and goes on to ports in **Belgium, the Netherlands** (especially **Amsterdam**), **Germany** (via **Hamburg**), **Norway** and its western fjord coast, and **Denmark** (the most important port here is **Copenhagen**).

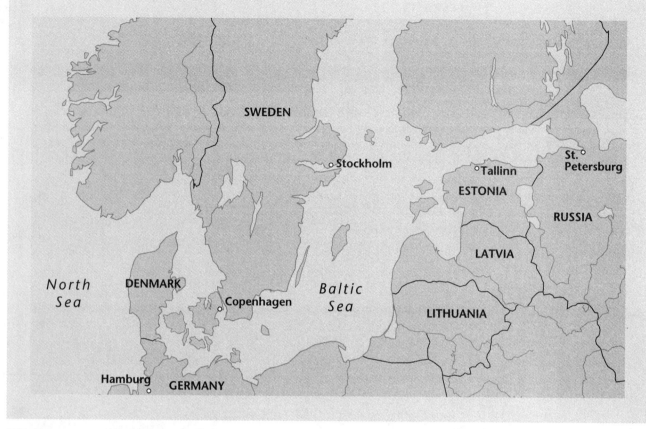

FIGURE 7-14   Map of the Baltic Sea

The Baltic Sea

Increasingly popular, a Baltic cruise takes in many countries that are less commonly visited than other European destinations. Here's one possible itinerary: The ship leaves Hamburg or Copenhagen for **Stockholm,** Sweden, and ends at that former home of the tsars, **St. Petersburg,** Russia. A more southerly route would take the ship along an uncommon path, past the three Baltic nations of **Lithuania, Latvia,** and **Estonia,** perhaps with a stop at **Tallinn,** Estonia.

River Cruises

Many tourists believe that those destinations in Europe's interior can't be part of a cruise. This is hardly true. Pre- or post-cruise tours, of course, offer limitless possibilities. But so do river cruises.

Among the most popular rivers for boat and barge cruises are France's **Rhone** (and the nation's many canals), Germany's **Rhine** and **Elbe,** and Russia's **Volga.** THE cruise river, though, is the **Danube.** Here are three cities that a Danube cruise might visit: **Vienna,** Austria, **Budapest,** Hungary, and Bratislava, Slovakia. A glittering trio of cities, don't you think?

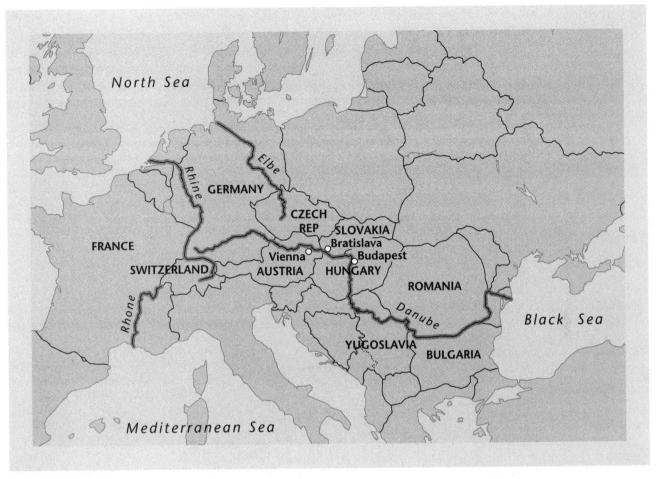

FIGURE 7-15 Map of European rivers

Cruising the Rest of the World

North America and Europe dominate today's cruise market. But there's every indication that more "exotic" places are becoming increasingly popular to today's more adventuresome traveler.

Cruising is well-suited to unusual destinations. Air, rail, and roads in Africa, Asia, and South America can be challenging. Border crossings are complex, monetary exchange rates confusing, lodging unpredictable, and safety a concern. A cruise cushions the traveler from much of this, providing a secure, reliable environment from which to explore adventurous destinations.

Four regions feature an especially favorable context for off-the-beaten-path cruising: Central and South America, the Pacific, Asia, and Africa. Let's look at each.

Central and South America

A land of diverse topography, cultures, and attractions, Central and South America offer a wealth of ports to explore. Central America—one of the world's prime ecological destinations—is sometimes visited as part of a trans-Panama Canal or Western

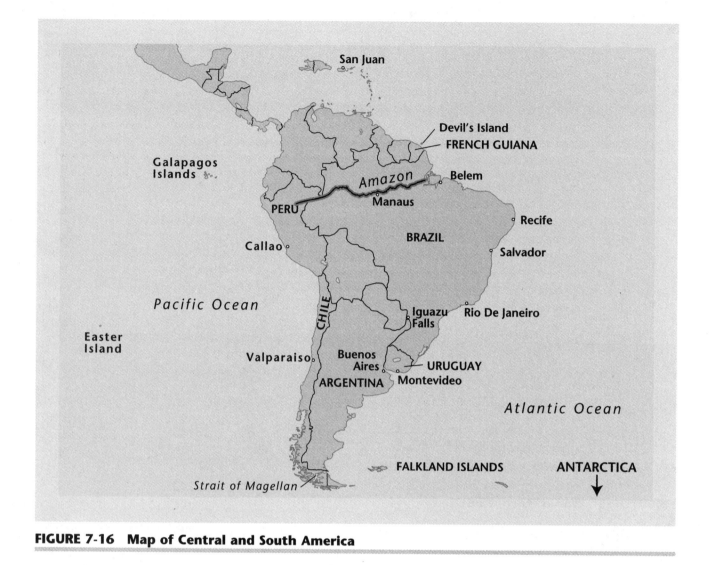

FIGURE 7-16 Map of Central and South America

Caribbean cruise. South America's Atlantic Coast is quite popular, too (especially from October to April), with departures typically out of San Juan, Puerto Rico, or **Rio de Janeiro,** Brazil. Intermediate stops might include **Devil's Island** (off French Guiana) and such Brazilian cities as **Belem, Recife,** and **Salvador.** Some ships journey up the **Amazon River,** all the way to **Manaus.**

Occasionally, cruise lines visit South America's Pacific coast or even offer a month-long itinerary around South America. The latter routing would go beyond Rio and visit **Montevideo,** Uruguay, **Buenos Aires,** Argentina, the **Falkland Islands,** through the **Strait of Magellan,** and on to South America's Pacific coast. Most likely Pacific ports of call: **Valparaiso,** Chile (**Santiago's** port), and **Callao,** Peru (**Lima's** port).

Before rounding South America's tip, however, the ship might "detour" to **Antarctica,** one of the most remote places possible. (Some cruises visit Antarctica from **New Zealand.**)

Many of South America's grandest attractions are inland, but can be visited as part of a shore excursion or a pre- or post-cruise package. Among the possibilities: mighty **Iguazu Falls,** accessed from Brazil, and Peru's **Machu Picchu** (reached from Lima via **Cuzco**). Two other remote destinations: **Easter Island** and the **Galapagos Islands,** both far off to the west of South America.

The interior of a cruise ship that reflects the destination it serves: Hawaii.
Courtesy of American Hawaii Cruises

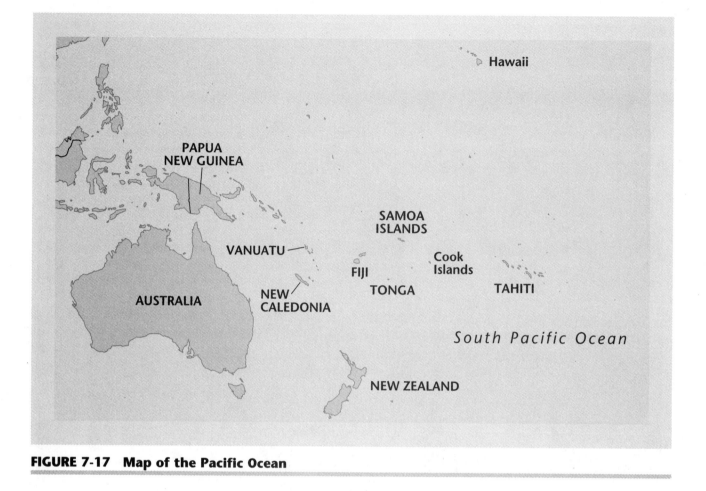

FIGURE 7-17 Map of the Pacific Ocean

The Pacific

The perfect tropical island—of such places dreams are made. That's why the Pacific is a fantasy destination for so many. There are *thousands* of picture-perfect tropical islands sprinkled about the Pacific's 64 million square miles of water.

And what more efficient way to sample them than on a cruise? In the South Pacific, ships primarily sail the islands of **Tahiti** and **Fiji**, but **Papua New Guinea, New Caledonia, Vanuatu, Samoa, Tonga,** and the **Cook Islands** are visited as well. Farther south, cruises around New Zealand and along the eastern coast of **Australia** are quite popular. Most South Pacific cruises operate November through April, when the Southern Hemisphere's climate is at its best.

In the North Pacific, **Hawaii** has been a popular cruise destination since the early twentieth century. (Prior to the jet age, ships were the primary way of getting there.) A cruise represents an efficient way of visiting several Hawaiian islands without having to pack and unpack. Some ships are permanently based there, while repositioning cruises in the spring and fall often stop in Hawaii along the way.

Asia

To summarize all the cruise itineraries that feature Asian ports is next to impossible. A few general patterns exist, though. Several highly popular sailings weave through the many islands of **Indonesia, Malaysia,** the **Philippines,** and **Singapore.** A second pattern: Southeast Asia, with **Thailand, Vietnam,** and Singapore as key countries. **India's**

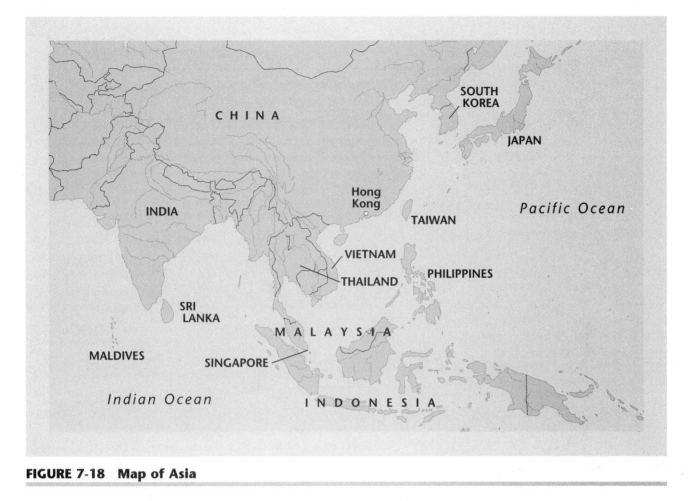

FIGURE 7-18   Map of Asia

ports are on a few itineraries, often in conjunction with **Sri Lanka** and the **Maldives.** **Hong Kong** and other major Chinese and Taiwanese ports constitute another typical itinerary. Finally, **Japan** and **South Korea** represent a natural geographic combination for cruising. Most cruises that visit Asia take place between October and May, though a few ships remain during the summer months.

Africa

Five major cruise itineraries for Africa predominate.

- The first includes the northwestern African nations of **Tunisia** and **Morocco,** sometimes in combination with the **Canary** and **Madeira** Islands. These generally take place from May through October.

- The second itinerary lies on and off Africa's east coast. The ports of **Mombasa,** Kenya, or **Dar Es Salaam,** Tanzania, are usually coupled with such Indian Ocean islands as **Zanzibar, Madagascar,** the **Seychelles,** the **Comoros, Reunion,** and **Mauritius.**

- The third pattern is a variation of the second. Instead of returning to either Mombasa or Dar Es Salaam, the ship sails on to **South Africa** (or vice versa).

- A fourth itinerary visits Africa's west coast. These last three itineraries typically take place in the Southern Hemisphere's summer, which is November through March.

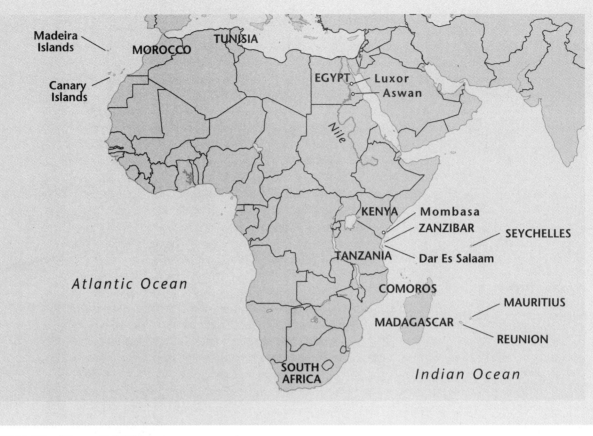

FIGURE 7-19 Map of Africa

■ Finally, there's one of the most legendary cruise itineraries of all, the **Nile River,** usually between Egypt's **Aswan** and **Luxor.** Nile cruises operate year round and employ boats specially designed for river cruises—unlike the Amazon, regular cruise ships cannot navigate the Nile.

For a summary of the destination information you've just read, see Figure 7-20.

Repositioning Cruises

Throughout this text we've referred to repositioning cruises. A *repositioning cruise* occurs at the end of one region's high season and the beginning of another's high season. It would be folly, for example, to leave two dozen cruise ships idle in Alaska's winter when they could be deployed elsewhere.

Here are the most common repositioning cruises in September, October, and November:

■ From Europe across the Atlantic to Bermuda, the Bahamas, the Caribbean, the Panama Canal, or even South America.

■ From the Mediterranean through the **Suez Canal** to Africa's east coast and its islands or into Asia.

Region	Starting/Ending Ports	Season
Alaska	Vancouver, Seattle, Anchorage	May–October
Northeast	New York City, Montreal	Late spring–fall
North America—Rivers	Mississippi River ports	Year-round
Mexico—round-trip	Los Angeles, San Diego	Year-round
Mexico—one-way	Los Angeles, San Diego, Acapulco	Winter
Bahamas	Miami, Port Everglades, Port Canaveral, Tampa	Year-round
Caribbean—Eastern	Miami, Port Everglades, San Juan	Year-round
Caribbean—Southern	San Juan, Aruba, Barbados	Year-round
Caribbean—Western	Miami, Port Everglades, Port Canaveral, Tampa, Houston, Galveston, New Orleans	Year-round
Mediterranean—Western	Barcelona, Nice, Civitavecchia	Late spring–early fall
Mediterranean—Eastern	Venice, Piraeus, Istanbul	Late spring–early fall
Europe—Atlantic	Malaga, London, Lisbon, Le Havre	Late spring–early fall
Europe—Ireland, Great Britain, North Sea	London, Copenhagen	Late spring–early fall
Europe—Baltic Sea	Hamburg, Copenhagen, St. Petersburg	Late spring–early fall
Europe—Rivers	Rhone, Rhine, Elbe, Volga, Danube ports	Late spring–early fall
Central and South America	San Juan, Rio de Janeiro, Callao	October–April
Pacific Islands	Various	November–April
Asia	Various	October–May
Africa—Northwest	Various	May–October
Africa—East coast	Mombasa, Dar Es Salaam	November–March
Africa—West coast	Various	November–March

FIGURE 7-20 Destination summary

■ From Alaska down the U.S. west coast to Mexico, the Panama Canal, and/or the Caribbean. (Sometimes the ship may "sidetrack" to Hawaii along the way.)

■ From Alaska across the Pacific to Hawaii and on to Asia or the South Pacific.

From March to May these repositioning cruises are reversed. For instance, a ship stationed in the Caribbean might cross the Atlantic to return to Europe.

Though repositioning cruises typically feature many days at sea (and are quite a value), every attempt is made to call on ports along the way. A ship sailing, say, from Northern Europe to the Caribbean might dock at the **Azores,** Bermuda, and Miami.

Some Miscellaneous Thoughts

- **Occasionally, cruise lines operate "cruises to nowhere."** Typically, the ship leaves a port, circles out for a few days, then returns—without making intermediate stops. Passengers are kept occupied by the activities that take place on the ship.

- **Allied to this is the concept of the ship *as* a destination.** The vessel is marketed as a floating resort, competing for the consumer's attention and dollars with land-based resorts in Las Vegas, Mexico, Hawaii, and Orlando. The goal is to make the passenger feel that the ship is every bit as interesting a place as the ports visited.

- **Sometimes a ship's "culture" is strongly affected by its crew's countries of origin.** The ambiance of a vessel with Greek crew members might be exuberant and hearty. Another with a crew from Britain might be more formal and refined.

- **On rare occasions, a port on the itinerary may be substituted or deleted.** Two possible reasons for such a change might be stormy weather conditions or political unrest at the port.

- **Some cruise lines call at their very own privately owned islands.** Most are in the Bahamas or the Caribbean and feature picnics, barbecues, nature trails, organized games, local craft vendors, all manner of watersports, and broad stretches of pristine sand.

- **Meals aboard ship are often themed with appropriate food and waiter "costumes."** One night might have a Caribbean theme, the next, Italian. Oddly, these might have no relationship to where the ship is traveling that night. A Polynesian night can occur in the Greek islands; a Greek night can occur in Polynesia. (The cruise lines do try to ensure, through entertainment or food, that the destination and shipboard ambiance, to some extent, match.)

- **Some cruise line chefs do believe, however, that food should reflect the region the ship is visiting.** But not in the way you might think. They argue that cold weather destinations make people want higher-calorie, more bland food, while warm tropical places make passengers want lighter yet spicier cuisine.

- **CLIA publishes a handy grid that cross-references major destination regions with its member lines.** This enables you to find out which cruise lines visit a certain area of the globe. For an example, see Figure 7-21.

CRUISE
GUIDE FOR
WORLDWIDE
DESTINATIONS

DESTINATION	AMERICAN HAWAII CRUISES	BERGEN LINE, INC.	CARNIVAL CRUISE LINES	CELEBRITY CRUISES, INC.	COMMODORE CRUISE LINE	COSTA CRUISE LINES	CRYSTAL CRUISES	CUNARD LINE LTD.	DISNEY CRUISE LINE	FIRST EUROPEAN CRUISES	HOLLAND AMERICA LINE	MEDITERRANEAN SHIPPING CRUISES	NORWEGIAN CRUISE LINE	ORIENT LINES, INC.	PREMIER CRUISES	PRINCESS CRUISES	RADISSON SEVEN SEAS CRUISES	REGAL CRUISES	ROYAL CARIBBEAN, LTD.	ROYAL OLYMPIC CRUISES	SEABOURN CRUISE LINE	SILVERSEA CRUISES	WINDSTAR CRUISES
WORLD CRUISES							•	•			•					•							
WEST COAST			•	•			•	•			•		•			•				•			
TRANS-PACIFIC							•	•			•					•	•					•	•
TRANS-ATLANTIC				•		•	•	•		•	•	•	•	•		•	•		•	•	•	•	•
SOUTHEAST ASIA							•	•			•			•		•	•					•	•
SOUTH PAC/TAHITI							•	•			•			•		•						•	
SOUTH AMERICA				•	•	•	•	•			•		•	•		•	•		•		•	•	•
SCANDINAVIA		•		•		•	•	•		•	•		•			•			•		•	•	
RUSSIA/EUROPE				•		•	•	•		•	•		•			•	•		•		•	•	
RIVER (EUROPE)																						•	
RIVER (CHINA)																						•	
RIVER (AMAZON)								•								•			•		•	•	•
RED SEA/SUEZ CANAL							•	•			•					•			•			•	•
PANAMA CANAL			•	•		•	•	•			•		•			•	•	•	•	•	•	•	•
NORTH CAPE		•				•	•	•			•					•	•		•		•	•	
NEW ENGL/CANADA			•	•			•	•			•		•			•		•	•		•	•	
MEXICO			•	•	•	•	•	•		•	•	•	•		•	•	•		•		•	•	•
MEDITERRANEAN			•		•	•	•	•		•	•	•	•		•	•	•		•	•	•	•	•
ISRAEL/EGYPT			•	•		•	•	•		•	•		•			•	•		•		•	•	
INDIA							•	•			•			•		•	•				•	•	
IBERIA				•		•	•	•			•		•			•	•		•		•	•	•
HAWAII	•		•				•	•			•		•			•	•		•		•		•
FAR EAST/ORIENT							•	•			•			•		•	•				•	•	
EUROPE (EXCL. MED)			•		•	•	•	•		•	•		•			•	•		•	•	•	•	•
CRUISES TO NOWHERE								•						•		•		•			•		
COSTA RICA				•		•	•				•	•	•		•	•	•		•		•	•	•
CARIBBEAN			•	•	•	•	•	•	•		•	•	•		•	•	•	•	•		•	•	•
CANARY ISLANDS/NORTH AFRICA				•		•	•	•		•	•	•	•			•	•		•	•	•	•	
BRIT ISLES/IRELAND						•	•	•			•		•			•	•		•		•	•	•
BLACK SEA				•		•	•	•		•	•	•	•		•	•	•		•	•	•	•	
BERMUDA			•				•	•			•		•			•	•	•	•		•		
BALTIC			•		•	•	•	•		•	•		•			•	•		•	•	•	•	
BAHAMAS			•	•		•	•	•	•		•	•	•		•						•		
AUSTRALIA/NEW ZEAL						•	•	•			•			•		•	•					•	
ALASKA			•	•			•				•		•			•			•		•		
AFRICA				•		•	•	•		•	•		•	•		•					•	•	

FIGURE 7-21 Cruise guide for worldwide destinations
Source: Courtesy of CLIA

Questions for Discussion and Activity

This chapter's Questions for Discussion and Activity are combined. They're also different from the ones you've done before. Below is a list of cruise ports. Your assignment: to identify the country or U.S. state for each port. Use any resource at your disposal. (An atlas might be a good start.) A clue: Some—but not all—are mentioned in this chapter.

Port	Country/State	Port	Country/State
Auckland		Mazatlan	
Bali		Mombasa	
Bar Harbor		Montego Bay	
Barcelona		Montevideo	
Barranquilla		Nassau	
Bergen		New Orleans	
Bombay (Mumbai)		Nice	
Budapest		Ocho Rios	
Buenos Aires		Odessa	
Cairns		Papeete	
Callao		Philipsburg	
Cape Town		Piraeus	
Casablanca		Port Everglades	
Catalina		Port Kelang	
Charlotte Amalie		Port of Spain	
Civitavecchia		Portofino	
Cozumel		Pusan	
Dakar		Recife	
Ensenada		Santorini	
Fort-de-France		Seward	
Haifa		Shanghai	
Halifax		Singapore	
Hamilton		Sitka	
Istanbul		Southampton	
Juneau		Stockholm	
Key West		Tallinn	
Kusadasi		Tunis	
Lahaina		Valletta	
Leith		Valparaiso	
Mahe		Vancouver	
Manaus		Yokohama	
Manila		Zanzibar	
Marigot		Zeebrugge	

CHAPTER EIGHT

PROFILING THE LINES

After reading this chapter, you'll be able to

- Identify the major sources of insight into a cruise product's personality

- Access the most important industry and consumer research resources

- Recognize general patterns among cruise products

- Profile each cruise line specifically

T hink of your best friend. What words come to mind? What is it about him or her that makes you two get along? Almost surely you've thought of some very specific adjectives. Now think of a cruise line that you've heard about or experienced. What words do you think of? What is it about that cruise line that appeals to people? As with your best friend, some very precise adjectives will come to mind.

Like people, cruise lines and even individual ships have specific "personalities." They're even sometimes part of "families" of cruise lines, with several different lines under one corporate umbrella. Later in this chapter you'll read how the cruise lines describe themselves. But first, here are some general guidelines so you can discover more about each cruise line.

The Cruise Lines Themselves

One of the best sources of information about any cruise line is directly from the cruise line. Here's how you can find out more about each:

- *Cruise line promotional pieces,* such as brochures, ads, commercials, videos, and Internet Web sites, are rich sources of information and insight. Some of the most important information, however, requires a little "digging."

  Look at the people portrayed in a cruise line's promotional pieces. Are they mostly families? Older people? Younger couples? In each case the photo reveals a clue to the cruise line's specialty. Suppose all these kinds of consumers and more are represented? Then this company is communicating mass-market appeal. It's one that attracts every kind of passenger.

  What the people in these photos are doing is also important. If they're mostly observing wildlife, then this cruise line probably takes an eco-approach to its product and targets a more narrow type of client than does a more mass-market cruise product. Even what the people wear is an important clue to their income and lifestyle.

  Images aren't the only way to understand whom cruise lines target to buy their product. Words, slogans, colors, and even brochure paper texture are all indicators to a cruise line's personality. What might a brochure for a company that targets very upscale consumers, for example, look like? The paper would be thick, connoting high quality. Photos would show people who are mature, well-dressed, and wearing expensive jewelry. The prose would be very literate—the more educated people are, the more money they usually make. The food depicted would be beautifully presented and of gourmet quality: Studies show that fine food is the most important cruise factor to upscale consumers.

- *Seminars* are another source of critical information. Cruise lines regularly offer seminars where travel agents can learn more about the cruise line's product. A few cruise companies actually give workshops that, in an unbiased manner, analyze each cruise product, including those of their competitors. In essence, the cruise line is saying: We're so confident in our product that we can tell you what's good about our competitors, too.

- *Ship inspections* (while a ship is in port) and *familiarization cruises* (offered at greatly reduced prices) are powerfully effective ways to experience first-hand the personality of a ship and its parent company.

- *District sales representatives* are an important link between the cruise lines and travel agencies. They also represent their companies at consumer trade shows. Deeply informed about the demographics and psychographics of their company, they're often quite happy to provide insights on their cruise products. They may even be willing to share passenger research reports with preferred travel agencies who consistently sell their product.

Trade Publications

Four resource publications regularly offer in-depth information on cruise lines and ships. Travel agents are their primary customers:

- Throughout this book we've cited the *CLIA Cruise Manual,* which is CLIA's yearly compendium of important data. This publication doesn't really analyze product—it is, after all, a resource vehicle created by the cruise lines. Nonetheless, it provides such valuable content as ship data, sample menus, key telephone numbers, sales policies, itineraries, port maps, sample forms, and grids detailing offerings to client-types such as honeymooners, wheelchair travelers, children, and singles.

- *The Official Cruise Guide* offers interpretive information on virtually every cruise line in the world. Among its features: ship profiles (including what kinds of clients are likely to be aboard) and information on theme cruises, specialized programs, ports of call, and sailing schedules. Its full-color format is easy to use, its content global.

- *The Official Steamship Guide International* contains sailing itineraries, port maps, ship facts, and specialty cruise products (including freighters, ferries, and barges).

- Most travel agents forget that *The Star Service,* a massive compendium of hotel reviews, also profiles cruise ships. Thoroughly opinionated, *The Star Service*'s analyses are solid and often entertaining. Each ship is rated according to a 1-to-5 star system.

About a half-dozen cruise-specific trade magazines and newsletters regularly analyze lines, ships, destinations, and itineraries. So, too, do the industry's more generic publications. For a list of these periodicals, see Appendix C.

Trade Shows

Many travel industry trade shows feature at least a few seminars on cruising. Several magazines and organizations also sponsor conferences devoted entirely to cruising. Among the best known:

- *Cruisealong* and *CRUISE-A-THON,* both sponsored by *Travel Trade* magazine
- *CruiseFest* and *ASTA School At Sea,* offered by ASTA
- *Ship-to-shore,* staged by Tourism British Columbia

Consumer Publications

The public's growing enthusiasm for the cruise vacation experience has led to a plethora of consumer publications. Here are the most popular books:

- Berlitz *Complete Guide to Cruising*
- Blum's *The Total Traveler Guide to Worldwide Cruising*
- *Bon Voyage: The Cruise Traveler's Handbook*

- *Fielding's Worldwide Cruises*
- *Fodor's Worldwide Cruises & Ports of Call*
- *Frommer's Cruises*
- *Garth's Profile of Ships*
- *Stern's Guide to the Cruise Vacation*
- *The Unofficial Guide to Cruises*

These consumer magazines regularly offer cruise-related articles: *Travel and Leisure, Conde Nast Traveler, Arthur Frommer's Budget Travel,* and *Travel Holiday. Cruise Travel Magazine* and *Porthole* devote most of their content to cruising.

These and other travel-related consumer publications are also listed in Appendix C.

A cruise line's profile is shaped by both its ships and the places they visit.
Courtesy of Princess Cruises

Video and the Internet

Virtually every cruise line offers at least one video that showcases its product. Some have many more. A one-stop source of cruise line videos is *Vacations On Video.* Their address is 7741 E. Gray Road, Suite 2, Scottsdale, AZ 85260.

As for the Internet, there seem to be as many Web sites devoted to cruise analyses as there are passengers. The problem: How can you be sure the person giving an opinion is truly knowledgeable and reliable? One of the few professional sites is *Cruise Center,* a service of America Online. Most cruise lines now also have Web sites. Each site is usually divided into two sections: one for consumers, the other for travel agents. For a complete list of CLIA member Web site addresses, see Appendix A.

CLIA has its own extremely useful Web site at www.cruising.org. It enables consumers to find CLIA-affiliated agencies and Certified Cruise Counsellors in their geographic area. It also offers answers to typical questions on cruising, information on specific lifestyle needs, data on over 100 worldwide cruise destinations, and current news and features on cruising. Its agent-specific center lists valuable marketing and training resources that are available.

Another impressive resource is *National Geographic*'s Cruise Finder, at www.nationalgeographic.com.traveler. This Web site, among other things, allows consumers to input key information on their preferences, then provides specific cruise line recommendations. But it can be valuable to travel professionals, too. It's a solid research tool and simulates the kind of client counseling a truly proficient travel agent should do.

CLIA's Education and Certification Programs

Through CLIA's Cruise Counsellor Certification Program, travel professionals receive comprehensive training in how to maximize cruise sales. Though the program doesn't profile individual cruise lines, the extensive experiential learning it requires inevitably leads to a deeper understanding of products, along with greater client recognition, confidence, and sales success.

This highly rated certification program offers two achievement levels: Accredited Cruise Counsellor (ACC) and Master Cruise Counsellor (MCC). Enrollees profit from a rich mixture of learning components: live seminars, videos, Internet-based courses, ship inspections, cruises, and, yes, this book. Nearly 10,000 cruise professionals have achieved certification, and thousands more are completing their requirements.

For more information on the program, contact CLIA at 212-921-0066.

General Patterns

Each cruise line has its own personality. But distinct patterns also mark certain *categories* of cruise products. For example, low-cost cruise lines tend to

- Visit mass-market destinations
- Encourage a casual onboard style
- Offer plentiful food
- Attract younger passengers, families, and seniors on a budget
- Make use of older (but well-maintained) ships
- Provide a vacation experience that's still usually more impressive and represents a better value than what a budget or even mid-priced hotel offers

It's important to realize that these are *generalizations*. Exceptions do exist. Some upscale cruise lines offer very casual experiences, for example. Some budget lines call on exotic ports. And young passengers and families are sometimes found on more expensive cruises.

General patterns also mark mid-level, mass-market cruise lines. They're more likely to have

- A very diversified mix of passengers
- Large to very large ships, offering many activities and options
- Major entertainment shows
- Dining with two seatings

Deluxe cruise lines refine the experience even more. Their ships feature larger staterooms, near-gourmet food, a somewhat more formal atmosphere, and extra touches—like artwork throughout the ship. The *most* expensive cruise lines tend to

- Feature many unusual ports and itineraries
- Have open seating in their dining room, with gourmet cuisine
- Attract older, more experienced travelers (and wealthier, of course)
- Deploy more intimate-sized ships
- Have large staterooms (most or all are outside staterooms)
- Emphasize learning and culture
- Offer less-structured activities and low-key entertainment
- Provide an astonishing level of service, sometimes with no tipping required

There can be variations of product level even aboard an individual ship. Nothing like the old "class" system—where first-class passengers never interacted with those in third class—exists today. But guests in suites and on a "concierge" level deck often get a higher level of amenities and services than do those in standard staterooms. There may be a bathrobe for their use while onboard, premium soap and shampoos, free laundry services, and even a separate dining room.

Generalized Versus Niche Cruise Lines

Most of us think of cruising as a product so broad that it can satisfy almost every type of traveler. In most cases, this is true. For example, the majority of cruise lines offer special packages for honeymooners. Families with children also find plenty to do on most cruises, as do very active adults. (The *CLIA Cruise Manual* contains grids that display what each member line offers to such specialized clients. For an example, see Figure 8-1.)

On the other hand, some lines target narrow segments of consumers who have something in common. In marketing, these categories of customer types are called **niches.** A niche is defined as a group of people who have a very specialized set of needs and wants. A niche company provides products and services that suit the ways their niche clients buy.

For example, some cruise lines don't simply provide options for the active adult—as generalized cruise lines do—but *stress* them. Adventure is what they're all about. Comfort, pampering, and elegant cuisine may be low on their clients' priority list. (There are, however, some niche cruise lines that provide *both* adventure and pampering.)

Another specialized market: education. For some lines, learning is at the *core* of the cruise experience. These companies may offer only limited entertainment and no casino. The people who take their cruises care very little about anything but learning. Still other companies appeal to clients who are highly independent and want as unstructured a cruise experience as possible. A plethora of activities onboard ship is precisely what they *don't* want.

The CLIA Member Cruise Lines

No one understands its product better than the cruise line itself. What follows is a description of each CLIA-member cruise line in "its own words." It should help you understand what makes each cruise company special in its appeal to consumers and why those cruise lines that are members of CLIA are especially favored by travel agents.

CRUISE GUIDE FOR ACTIVE ADULTS

Cruise guide table (Figure 8-1). Rows list cruise lines; columns are grouped under **ON-BOARD** and **ASHORE** activities.

CRUISE LINE	ON-BOARD																				ASHORE*									
	AEROBICS	BASKETBALL	LOW CAL MENU	GOLF DRIVING	GYM	JOGGING	MASSEUSE	PADDLE TENNIS	SAIL BOATING	SAUNA	SCUBA DIVING	SKEET/TRAP SHOOTING	SNORKELING	SNORKELING LESSONS	SPA POOL	SWIMMING	TOTAL FITNESS PROGRAM	VOLLEYBALL	WATER/JET SKIING	WINDSURFING	BICYCLING	CHARTER FISHING	GOLF	HIKING	HORSEBACK RIDING	SCUBA DIVING	SNORKELING	TENNIS	WATER SKIING	WINDSURFING
AMERICAN HAWAII CRUISES	A		A		A	A	A		A/I		A/I		A/I	A/I		A			A/I	A/I	A/I	A/I	A/I	A/I	A/I	A/I	A/I	A/I	A/I	A/I
BERGEN LINE, INC.		S			S					S																		S		
CARNIVAL CRUISE LINES	A		A	A	A	A	A	A		A	A/I	A	A/I		A	A	A	A			I	I	A/I	A/I	S/I	A	A	I	I	I
CELEBRITY CRUISES, INC.	A		A	A	A	A	A	A		A		S	I	I	A	A	A	A	I	I	I	I	I	I		I	A/I	I	I	I
COMMODORE CRUISE LINE	S	S	S	S	S	S	S	S		S	S/I	S	S	S	S	A	A	S	I	I	I	S	S	S	S	S	S	S	I	I
COSTA CRUISE LINES	A		A	A	A	A	A	A		A	S	A	S	S	S	A	A		I	I								S		I
CRYSTAL CRUISES	A	S	A	S	A	A	A	A		A		A			A	A	A													
CUNARD LINE LTD.	A	A	A	S	A	A	A	A	S	S	S	S	S	S	S	A	S	S	S/SP		S	S	S	S	S	S	S	S	S	S
DISNEY CRUISE LINE	A	A	A	A	A	A	A	A		A	S/SP	A				A	S	A	S/SP											
FIRST EUROPEAN CRUISES	A		A		A	A	A	A		A					A	A	A					A	A	S	S	A	A	A	A	A
HOLLAND AMERICA LINE	A		A		A	A	A	A		A					A	A	S								S	A		A	A	A
MEDITERRANEAN SHIPPING CRUISES	A		A	S	A	A	A	S			A				S	A		S												
NORWEGIAN CRUISE LINE	A		A		A	A	A	A		A	A	A	A/I	A	S/I	A	A	S	I	I					S		A	A		
ORIENT LINES, INC.	A		A		A	A	A	A	S/I	S			A		S	A	A		S/I	S/I	S/I	S/I	S/I	S/I	S/I	S/I	S/I	S/I	S/I	S/I
PREMIER CRUISES	A	S/I	A	S/I	S	S	A	A	S/I	S	S/I	S	S/I	S/I	S/I	A	S	A	S/I	S/I	S	S	S/I	S	S	S/I	S	S/I	S/I	S/I
PRINCESS CRUISES	A	S	A	S	A	S	A	S	I	S	S	S	S	S	S	A	A		I	I	S	S	S	S	S	S	S	S	S	S
RADISSON SEVEN SEAS CRUISES	A	A	A	A	A	A	A	A	A/I	A	A	A	A/I	A	I	A	A/I	A	A	A	A	A	A	A	A	A	A	A	A	A
REGAL CRUISES	A		A		A	A	A	A	A	A	I	A	A/SP		S	A/SP	A		A	A	S/I	A	A	A	S	A	A/SP	I	A	A/SP
ROYAL CARIBBEAN, LTD.	S	S	A		A	S	A	A	S/I	A	A	A	S/I	A	S	A	A	S		A	S/I	S/I	S/I	S/I	S/I	S/I	A/SP	S/I	S/I	S/I
ROYAL OLYMPIC CRUISES	S		A		S	A	A	A	A/I	S	A		S/I	S/I	S	A/SP	A/I		S	A	S/I	S	S/I	S	S	A/I	A/I	I	S/I	S/I
SEABOURN CRUISE LINE	A		A	A	A	A	A	A	A	A	A	A	A/SP	A	A	A/SP	A		A	A	A	A	A	A	A	A	A/SP	A	A	A
SILVERSEA CRUISES	A		A		A	A	A	A		A	I		I		A	A	A		A		A	A	A	A	A	A	A/SP	A	A	I
WINDSTAR CRUISES	S		A		A	A	A	A	A/SP	A	A/SP		A/SP		A	A	S	A/SP	A/SP	A/SP	A/SP	A/SP	A/SP	A/SP	A/SP	A/SP	A/SP	A/SP	A/SP	A/SP

KEY
A—All ships
S—Some ships
I—Information on local facilities provided by shipboard staff
SP—Ship(s) equipped with aft water sports platform

NOTE*

(1) There is an additional charge for most shore-side activities. Some shipboard activities such as skeet-shooting, are also extra.

(2) Some water and shore-side sports aren't available in every port or destination (i.e., snorkeling in Alaska).

(3) Unless marked "I", available shore-side activities are provided through shore excursions and sports programs OR arranged at a passenger's request

FIGURE 8-1 Cruise guide for active adults
Source: Courtesy of CLIA

American Hawaii Cruises

American Hawaii Cruises' classic U.S. flag ocean liner, the *S.S. Independence,* is the only ship cruising exclusively among the Hawaiian Islands year round. The convenient seven-day, five-port, four-island cruise departs each Saturday from Honolulu, Oahu, and visits Nawiliwili, Kauai; Kahului, Maui; Hilo and Kona on the Big Island of Hawaii. Optional hotel extensions and special golf and wedding/honeymoon packages are available.

American Hawaii's shore excursions, named "Best of the Best" by *Travel Holiday* magazine, offer 50 ways to experience the beauty and individuality of the Hawaiian islands. On board, passengers enjoy authentic Hawaiian entertainment and culture through the cruise line's "Hawaiiana" program, winner of Hawaii's top tourism award, "Best of Show" in the 1997 "Keep It Hawaii" competition, sponsored by the Hawaii Visitors and Convention Bureau.

The *Independence,* created by renowned designer Henry Dreyfuss, is considered among the finest passenger vessels ever built. Launched in 1951, it has been refurbished several times, most recently in 1997. The ship carries 1,021 passengers and features spacious cabins and public areas as well as 23,000 square feet of deck space.

American Hawaii cruises announced plans to double its fleet and more than quadruple its passenger capacity in the next eight years. The company will build two new, $400 million cruise ships in U.S. shipyards.

Carnival Cruise Lines

Carnival Cruise Lines is the world's largest and most popular cruise brand. The emphasis aboard Carnival's sleek and modern SuperLiners is on fun and relaxation. Interesting and entertaining activities or a spot for reading and relaxation along a stretch of open deck space—there's something for everyone aboard Carnival.

Carnival was the first cruise line to introduce lavish Vegas-style shows in elaborate multi-deck theaters. And the first to introduce expansive health and fitness facilities: 12,000-square-foot Nautica Spas with aerobics rooms, state-of-the-art equipment, and luxurious European spa treatments.

Carnival led the way with innovations in casual alternative dining. In addition to meals served in the main dining rooms, the "Fun Ships" feature 24-hour pizzerias and casual restaurants serving breakfast, lunch, and dinner—no extra cost and no reservations required.

Carnival is the industry leader in children's programming with its year-round "Camp Carnival" program run by trained child-care professionals. And Carnival boasts cruising's most popular wedding program, offering a variety of shipboard or port-of-call ceremonies.

Carnival is so confident in its product, it is the only cruise line offering a Vacation Guarantee: Guests may disembark a Carnival ship in the first foreign port of call for any reason and receive a pro-rated refund, as long as they notify the purser's office prior to arrival at that port.

Carnival's "Fun Ships"—including the world's first totally smoke-free cruise ship, the *MS Paradise*—offer cruises of 3-16 days to The Bahamas, Caribbean, Mexico, Alaska, Hawaii, the Panama Canal, and the Canadian Maritime Provinces.

Celebrity Cruises

What is Celebrity style? It's museum-quality works of art and bouquets of fresh-cut flowers. Hand-polished brass railings and crystal-clear glass. It is an air of understated elegance and a festive, carefree ambiance on one of the youngest and most modern fleets in the industry.

Celebrity offers award-winning cuisine created by master chef Michel Roux. All food is prepared from scratch, using only the freshest produce, herbs, aged beef, and fish, providing Celebrity guests with a multitude of choices: exquisite five-course dinners, vegetarian and children's menus, as you like it omelet and pasta bars, elegant tea, gourmet bites, and midnight buffets with multiple buffet lines for no wait service.

With the highest staff ratio in the large-ship category, every Celebrity guest experiences refined, courteous, attentive, but never intrusive, service. Suite guests enjoy butler service and added amenities. And the exclusive AquaSpa^{SM} facilities and custom-designed programs offer the comprehensive beauty, health, and fitness amenities of a world-class spa.

Standard staterooms start at 172 square feet, with suites ranging up to 1,219, all with a full list of amenities, including multi-channel televisions and music systems, the interactive Celebrity network, satellite telephones, in-room safes—even hairdryers. Celebrity also offers a high percentage of ocean-view rooms with over-sized verandahs.

Celebrity offers Michael's Club, the first cigar lounge at sea, Martini Bars, Champagne and Caviar Bars, the Cova Cafe, luxurious public spaces, original artwork, and state-of-the-art theaters with unobstructed views. Daily activities include culinary demonstrations, wine tastings, lectures, and active shore excursions.

Commodore Cruise Line

Commodore Cruise Line, founded in 1966, was one of the first lines to offer year-round, seven-night cruises out of Miami, the first cruise line to establish regular service to Cap Haitien in northern Haiti, and the first to call at Puerto Plata, Dominican Republic.

The company's pioneering spirit is also evident in being the first to popularize "theme" cruises, as well as seven-night cruises from the Port of New Orleans. Both of these traditions are carried on today as the cruise line sails two vessels, the *Enchanted Isle* and the *Enchanted Capri*, from New Orleans.

Selected by *Travel Holiday* magazine as "the best cruise for the money," Commodore is proud of the value it offers its many first-time and repeat passengers. Because of the medium size of Commodore's vessels, the line focuses the majority of its marketing efforts on building relationships with its passengers and repeat business. It's a system that not only builds business but enhances the cruise experience for the passenger and Commodore's onboard staff. Passengers are greeted by name and remembered from their previous cruise. The ships' accommodating size also allows for high levels of passenger interaction between the cruise staff and the dining room staff, a luxury not always available on a larger vessel. To assure that this level of satisfaction is maintained, passenger comment card reviews at the end of each and every voyage are a high priority. Many of the current activities are a direct result of passenger recommendations.

Costa Cruises

Costa, Europe's #1 cruise line, offers 189 sailings throughout the breathtakingly beautiful ice-fringed fjords, the stone monuments and onion-shaped towers of the Baltic and Russia; the romantic flavors of Italy, France, and Spain; the ancient wonders of Egypt and Israel; the whitewashed beauty of the Greek Isles; and everything between. With 40 different itineraries ranging in length from 5 to 16 nights, Costa brings the best of the Eastern and Western Mediterranean, North Cape/Fjords, Baltic and Russia, and the transatlantic, with a sailing sure to fit any client's time frame. Passengers experience the youngest fleet and most experienced cruise line in Europe aboard six Italian-inspired ships, the *CostaAllegra, CostaClassica, CostaMarina, CostaRiviera, CostaRomantica,* and *CostaVictoria.*

The *CostaVictoria* and *CostaRomantica* are stunning five-star ships that combine the elegance of European style with the sophistication of American comforts. Only Costa offers *Cruising Italian Style* with plenty of Caribbean sun and fun, and Italian activities. From the first Buon Viaggio Celebration to the last Bacchanal Parade, Costa sets the stage for a week of unforgettable enjoyment. Passengers stow their inhibitions behind Venetian masks or wrap themselves in togas and party like the Romans. They enjoy the carnival atmosphere of Fest Italiana, while taking in Italy's favorite pastimes like Bocce Ball, Tarantella dancing, Italian karaoke, pizza (dough) tossing, and more. They indulge in all of the magic that cruising *Italian Style* has to offer, and experience the best time of their lives on Costa.

Crystal Cruises

Crystal Cruises, voted "World's Best Cruise Line" by readers of *Travel & Leisure*, restores the grandeur of the past while adapting to the modern age of cruising. Aboard the *Crystal Harmony* and *Crystal Symphony*, guests experience six-star service, elegantly appointed staterooms (most with private verandahs), an unprecedented array of dining options (including Italian and Asian alternative restaurants), and critically acclaimed entertainment. Plus, there's the lavish Crystal Spa and Salon, extensive exercise facilities, golf instruction and a golf driving cage, and Caesars Palace at Sea Casino. Not to mention a spectacular assortment of worldwide destinations.

Crystal's philosophy: Each instant of a cruise must be memorable, every detail sublime. It is true not just in the grand design of our ships, but in the smallest details: the right vintage, a turned-down bed, a simple smile—each is in its own way a vital part of the whole. Crystal's ultimate goal is to create, for each guest on every cruise, a perfect experience. People are the cornerstone of Crystal's commitment to quality. Norwegian captains and their staff of officers are among the finest at sea. Officers and crew are hand-picked for their professionalism, pride, and dedication to service.

Cunard Line

Cunard Line, with its flagship *Queen Elizabeth 2*, is one of the world's most recognized brand names, providing the ultimate in deluxe ocean travel experiences for the past 158 years. Cunard has been in the forefront of passenger shipping since Samuel Cunard began the first regularly scheduled transatlantic steamship service in 1840. During its history, Cunard has operated more than 190 ships, including such legends as the *Queen Elizabeth, Queen Mary, Mauretania,* and *Caronia.*

Today, all Cunard ships are rated as five star by leading industry guidebook *Berlitz Complete Guide to Cruising and Cruise Ships,* 1998, and four Cunard ships are rated as number one in the world in their size category. A Cunard cruise is noted for luxurious accommodations, exquisite personal service, gourmet cuisine, attention to detail, and exciting and exotic destination opportunities.

In May of 1998, Carnival Corporation and a group of Norwegian investors purchased Cunard, simultaneously merging it with Seabourn Cruise Line to form Cunard Line Limited. The resulting eight-ship fleet represents nearly 50 percent of the world's luxury cruise market and includes: *Queen Elizabeth 2, Seabourn Sun* (formerly the *Royal Viking Sun*), *Caronia* (formerly the *Vistafjord*), *Seabourn Goddess I* and *II,* and Seabourn's original three ships: *Seabourn Pride, Seabourn Spirit,* and *Seabourn Legend.*

Disney Cruise Line

Disney Cruise Line is the first and only cruise line built and operated by the dreammakers of Disney. This land and sea vacation combines the magic of the Walt Disney World® Resort and the romance of the Golden Age of cruising. Onboard, guests of all ages enjoy unforgettable dining experiences, Disney-style entertainment, and areas and activities created specifically for adults, families, and children.

While most cruise lines offer the same dining room for the entire cruise, Disney Cruise Line guests find a unique restaurant every night at sea. Disney Cruise Line offers more entertainment than any other ship afloat, including original Disney-created Broadway-style productions, a nighttime entertainment district, and a full-screen cinema offering a variety of films every day. Onboard is one of the most comprehensive and entertaining children and teen's programs afloat, with almost an entire deck dedicated to them. Every cruise visits the Port of Nassau and Castaway Cay, Disney's private 1,000-acre Bahamian island, offering white sand beaches and crystal blue water. On Castaway Cay, guests indulge in water sports, casual dining, and open-air massage cabanas. Special honeymoon packages are available.

With the charm and classic lines of the magnificent ocean liners of the past, the Disney Cruise Line fleet features some of the most modern vessels afloat. Guests are enveloped by the ships' casual elegance, accented with distinctly Disney detailing throughout. The 875 staterooms per ship are among the most spacious in the cruise industry: 25% larger than average. Its ships sail round-trip from Port Canaveral, Florida.

First European Cruises

1998 marked the debut of First Europeans Cruises in the U.S. travel market. First European Cruises is an offshoot of one of Europe's top cruise lines, the Festival Group, which is the first company to have designed cruises for the pan-European market. The line has carried over 150,000 passengers from all over the continent on destination-rich voyages aboard its three classic cruise liners—*Bolero, Flamenco,* and the *Azur,* sailing exclusively in and around the Mediterranean and Northern Europe. The *Mistral* ventures into the Caribbean.

First European Cruises' itineraries are planned to be fresh and exciting for both its European and American passengers. During the winter, the vessels sail in the Red Sea and Canary Islands. Spring and fall destinations are Egypt, Israel, Turkey, the Black Sea, Italy, Spain, and the Western Mediterranean, including Morocco, Tunisia, and West Africa. Summer voyages explore the Greek Islands and Turkey, Scandinavian Fjords, and the Baltic Sea to St. Petersburg. Cruises range from 4 to 17 days in length, and, for American travelers, are packaged with air and pre- and post-cruise land options.

The onboard atmosphere is casually elegant and unpretentious. First European Cruises' ships are immaculate, onboard service is warm and professional, and the dining experience is similar to a fine European restaurant, with fresh and delicious selections from a menu designed to satisfy demanding international palettes.

Holland America Line

In 1998, Holland America Line celebrated its 125th anniversary as the purveyor of premium cruises the world over. Eschewing the vogue for mega-liners, Holland America focuses instead on the comfort of guests aboard a fleet of eight mid-size, five-star–rated vessels that emphasize pampering service, understated elegant decor, and exotic itineraries. Multimillion–dollar art and antique collections grace public rooms designed to enhance a historic maritime tradition.

Holland America has introduced a new ship each year since 1993 and has committed one billion dollars for three additional deliveries through the millennium. This modern, technologically advanced fleet offers cruises in Alaska, the Caribbean, Europe, Panama Canal, South America, Mexico, Canada and New England, the Orient, Australia and New Zealand, and the South Pacific. The industry leader in World Voyages, Holland America embarks its flagship on an annual global circumnavigation. Signature Explorer Cruises and Grand Voyages—featuring a Flagship Forum lecture series, local cuisine, folkloric entertainment, and the ballroom services of Gentleman Hosts—remain a hallmark. Innovative Late Nite activities, Club HAL youth programs, Passport to Fitness activities, sports lounges, theme cruises, and the University at Sea add contemporary flair.

Holland America, including sister companies Westours, Gray Line of Alaska, and Westmark Hotels, is a leader in Alaska travel. Fourteen Westmark hotels, more than 250 motorcoaches, 16 luxury domed McKinley Explorer railcars, dayboats at Portage Glacier and on the Yukon River, plus 2,500 Alaska employees support an array of seamlessly integrated cruise and land tour options in Alaska, the Yukon, and the Canadian Rockies.

Mediterranean Shipping Cruises

Mediterranean Shipping Cruises began service a decade ago as a one-ship fleet with a limited schedule. Today, the company has grown to a fleet of four ships operating over 140 departures on a worldwide basis. Based in Naples, Italy, and a subsidiary of Mediterranean Shipping, MSC is now the second largest cruise line operating in the Mediterranean. In addition, its ships offer cruises to South Africa, South America, the Caribbean, and transatlantic.

MSC strives to provide unique and diversified itineraries, enhanced with the flavor of Italian hospitality. In addition to its commitment to its passengers, MSC is equally committed to enhancing its relationship with its partners in the travel agency community.

The clientele on board MSC vessels is of a far greater international makeup than most other cruise lines. This mix of passengers creates a challenge when developing onboard product components, food, entertainment, etc. Yet over 90% of MSC passengers rated their cruise as very favorable. The majority of the crew is Italian and represents a significant resource in maintaining the line's cruise experience.

Mediterranean Shipping Cruises is poised, with the financial backing of its parent company and ten years experience in international cruising, to become a major factor in the growing worldwide cruise market in the next millennium.

Norwegian Coastal Voyages Inc/Bergen Line Services

The foremost provider of cruises and passenger ship services in Scandinavia, Bergen Line is the North American sales and marketing arm for the Norwegian Coastal Voyage. This century-old scenic journey navigates the stunning west coast of Norway 365 days a year, carrying cruise and local passengers as well as cargo. The ships call on 34 picture-perfect ports as they sail from Bergen in the south to Kirkenes, far above the Arctic Circle. The Norwegian Coastal Voyage offers six-, seven-, and twelve-day itineraries.

The 11 ships in the fleet are divided into three categories: new, mid-generation, and traditional. Built since 1993, the six new ships accommodate 490 cruise passengers and feature spacious, art-filled public areas, a glass-enclosed panorama lounge, elevators, and cabins with two lower berths, including several cabins that are wheelchair accessible. The three mid-generation ships were built in the 1980s and refurbished in 1995. Each holds approximately 320 cruise passengers. Reminiscent of classic steamer vessels, the two traditional ships are the most intimate, accommodating approximately 200 cruise passengers.

Bergen Line also handles reservations for five other Scandinavian cruise companies, offering services on more than 30 ships throughout Scandinavia and Northern Europe.

Norwegian Cruise Line

Founded in 1966 as Norwegian Caribbean Lines, Norwegian Cruise Line revolution-ized the cruise industry with the introduction of the concept of one-class cruising to the Caribbean in an atmosphere of informal luxury. Renowned for its entertainment, din-ing, theme cruises, and sports programs, NCL today operates a modern fleet of nine ships on itineraries throughout the Caribbean, Europe, the Mediterranean, South Amer-ica, Bermuda, Alaska, Canada/New England, Hawaii, the Bahamas, and Mexico. Cruises range from 3-day getaways to 12-day or longer vacations.

NCL's highly acclaimed fleet includes the 2,032-passenger *Norway*; the 1,504-pas-senger *Norwegian Sea*; the 950-passenger *Leeward*; the 1,052-passenger *Norwegian Crown*; the 800-passenger *Norwegian Star*; the 800-passenger *Norwegian Dynasty*; the 1,056-passenger *Norwegian Majesty*; the 1,726-passenger *Norwegian Wind*, and the 1,726-passenger *Norwegian Dream*.

Orient Lines

A specialist in destinational cruising, Orient Lines has been named the top cruise line in the world for "Destinations/Itineraries" in a *Conde Nast Traveler* readers' survey and "Best Cruise Value" by the World Ocean & Cruise Liner Society for three years in a row. The line's 800-passenger *Marco Polo* offers moderately priced 5- to 26-day cruises to the Greek Isles and Mediterranean from May through October, while offering exotic destinations such as Australia, New Zealand, Africa, India, Egypt, Asia, and Antarctica in the balance of the year.

Itineraries, presented as complete "cruise-tour" vacations, include hotel stays and sightseeing in embarkation and disembarkation cities, detailed port lectures, and local cultural performances wherever possible. On all except Europe cruises, top name guest lecturers are aboard to enhance the destination experience, and gentlemen social hosts serve as dance partners for single female passengers.

The classic and elegant *Marco Polo* offers every four-star luxury amenity, superb Continental cuisine, and gracious service by Scandinavian officers and a warm and friendly Filipino crew. Facilities include cabins equipped with televisions, personal safes and hair dryers, an elegant main dining room, special bistro, several lounges, health club, library, card room, outdoor swimming pool and Jacuzzis, duty-free boutiques, and casino. To appeal to younger and first-time cruisers, Greek Isles and Mediterranean itineraries are marketed as casual cruises with no formal dress required.

Premier Cruises

In September of 1997, Cruise Holdings Ltd. merged three cruise lines—Dolphin, Sea-Wind, and Premier—under one banner: Premier Cruises.

Based in Miami, Premier Cruises is the world's fifth-largest cruise operator. It provides guests an intimate, charming yet affordable cruise experience, offering personalized service and unique itineraries to exotic destinations on its fleet of smaller ships: the *Big Red Boat*, *IslandBreeze*, *Rembrandt*, *SeaBreeze*, *OceanBreeze*, and *SeaWind Crown*. Premier Cruises' ships sail from Miami, Fort Lauderdale, Port Canaveral, New York, Montego Bay, Santa Domingo, Aruba, and Barcelona.

Out-of-the-way itineraries, cuisine ranking among the best at sea, accommodating service, and outstanding entertainment offer everyone—from the first-time cruiser to families to seasoned travelers—the best cruising has to offer.

Princess Cruises

Founded in 1965, Princess Cruises was a pioneer of the modern-day cruise industry and the star of the *Love Boat* television series, which catapulted cruising to the forefront of consumer consciousness. Beginning with one ship cruising to Mexico, the now-famous fleet of Love Boats has expanded to nine, and the line is one of the three largest in the industry.

Purchased in 1974 by the British company P&O, one of the oldest and largest shipping firms in the world, Princess began a course of expansion. Sitmar Cruises was acquired in 1988, adding three additional ships, and three brand-new ships followed, one each in 1989, 1990, and 1991.

Today the fleet includes the *Crown Princess, Island Princess, Pacific Princess, Regal Princess, Royal Princess, Sky Princess, Sun Princess,* and *Dawn Princess,* which debuted in May 1997. The line introduced the largest and most expensive cruise ship ever built, the 109,000-ton *Grand Princess* in 1998 and the 77,000-ton *Sea Princess,* sister to the *Sun* and *Dawn Princess,* in 1998, followed by the *Ocean Princess* in 1999.

Providing one of the widest varieties of destinations and itinerary choices in the industry, Princess Cruises offers cruises to the Caribbean, Alaska, Panama Canal, Mexico, South Pacific, Hawaii/Tahiti, Europe, Asia/Orient, India, Africa, Holy Land, South America/Amazon, and Canada/New England. The line's richly appointed ships are known for large staterooms, offering more balconies at sea than any fleet afloat, as well as overall spaciousness and the onboard experience of fine dining, entertainment, and service.

Radisson Seven Seas Cruises

Radisson Seven Seas Cruises—with a capacity of 1,524 berths—is the fourth largest luxury line, operating the six-star, 350-guest *Radisson Diamond,* and the six-star, 180-guest *Song of Flower.* The 320-guest, 18,800-ton *Paul Gauguin* is the most deluxe cruise ship ever to be based year-round in Polynesia. A 30,000-ton, all-suite cruise ship offering worldwide itineraries is under construction. The fleet reaches over 500 ports of call worldwide on every continent, including the two polar regions.

The 20,000-ton *Radisson Diamond,* launched in 1992, combines small-ship intimacy with large-ship amenities. Her inimitable profile owes to her twin-hull design, which cuts down on pitch and roll movements. Of her 177 spacious staterooms overlooking the sea, 123 feature private balconies. From December through April, she operates a distinctive Trans-Panama Canal program featuring Costa Rica and the Caribbean, with summers devoted to Mediterranean and Baltic Republics cruises from major European cities.

The 8,282-ton *Song of Flower,* renowned for her yacht-like ambiance, Scandinavian refinement, and destination-intensive explorations of exotic ports, sails seasonally in India, the Red Sea, Arabia, and the Far East, including China, Burma, Vietnam, and Indonesia, with summers spent exploring classic Mediterranean, Scandinavian, Baltic Republics, and Northern European destinations.

The 9,000-ton, 184-guest *Hanseatic* is one of the most luxurious adventure cruise ships in the world and boasts the highest possible ice-class rating for a passenger vessel. She all but circumnavigates the globe with exploration cruises in the Arctic and Antarctic, and operations in lesser-visited regions such as the Spitsbergen Archipelago, Iceland, and Greenland.

Regal Cruises

The *Regal Empress's* classic elegance, born of an era of transatlantic crossings when ships were legends of spaciousness, style, and stability, recently completed a $6 million renovation.

From October to May, the ship sails out of Port Manatee, Florida to such ports of call as Playa del Carmen and Cozumel, Mexico; Key West; Grand Cayman; Montego Bay, Jamaica; and partial transit of the Panama Canal on four-, five-, six-, seven-, and ten-night cruises.

For the spring and summer seasons, the ship cruises out of New York to Provincetown, Massachusetts; Bar Harbor, Maine; the Bahamas; Martha's Vineyard, Massachusetts; St. Andrews, Canada; Newport, R.I.; and Hamilton, Bermuda on five- and six-night cruises. The line added a very popular overnighter to Bermuda. There are also one-, two-, and three-night cruises to nowhere.

In September, Regal offers a 12-night "Fall Foliage" cruise to New England, Nova Scotia, and Canada. In addition, Regal has introduced two 12-night voyages to the Canadian Fjords, visiting Nova Scotia, Newfoundland, and Labrador. Regal also offers a 56-night "Cruise of the Americas" that sails from New York, featuring 25 ports of call throughout Latin America. Travelers can choose from any one of seven legs of this spectacular trip.

Royal Caribbean International

The 12 ships of Royal Caribbean serve the volume contemporary and premium segment of the cruise vacation market. With a capacity of 23,000 at double occupancy, the line offers over 60 different itineraries, ranging from 3 nights to 15 nights and calling on more than 125 destinations on five continents.

The line attracts a broad array of vacationers in the contemporary segment of the volume market by providing a wide variety of itineraries, varying cruise lengths, and multiple options for dining and entertainment. The consistent quality of its product throughout its fleet represents excellent value, especially for couples and families traveling with children.

While Royal Caribbean is positioned at the upper end of the contemporary segment, the line believes that its quality enables it to attract consumers from the premium segment as well, thereby achieving very broad market coverage.

What are Royal Caribbean's passenger demographics? The average passenger age fleetwide is mid-40s (mostly ranging from 25-54 years old). On average, they are married or are traveling as a couple, with a household income of $30,000 to $50,000. They are typically professional, white collar, and college educated. Though this is the center focus of Royal Caribbean's demographics, a wide range of passengers on both sides of the demographic center enjoy Royal Caribbean cruise vacations.

Royal Olympic Cruises

Specializing in unusual and innovative itineraries, Royal Olympic Cruises caters to seasoned North American travelers with premium, culturally oriented destinations customarily associated with much more expensive cruise lines. The seven-ship fleet, ranging from small to mid-sized, evokes the charming, gracious, and personable ambiance of a European villa.

The line's signature service and European staff reflect a special family-style warmth. Its outstanding cuisine—considered among the best afloat—is prepared from scratch daily by master chefs and features a variety of continental entrees with Greek specialties.

Entertainment, ranging from classical music concerts and Theatre Guild performances to an extensive onboard enrichment program with expert guest lecturers, is highlighted by a special "Greek Night"—celebrating the folkloric songs, dances, and traditions of the line's homeland.

Royal Olympic's unique combination of intriguing itineraries, intimate shipboard atmosphere, and warm service has special appeal to seasoned travelers looking for a more personal, culturally enriching vacation piqued by a spirit of discovery.

In the summer, Royal Olympic is the largest cruise line in the Mediterranean, with the only three-day to three-week sailings round-trip from Athens to the Greek Isles, Holy Land, Turkey, and Black Sea. Cruises to the Baltic and Scandinavia from Copenhagen further complement the line's European portfolio.

In the winter, soft-adventure cruises in South America explore the mighty Amazon River in Brazil and the jungle wilderness of Venezuela's Orinoco River. Caribbean and Panama Canal cruises, plus special interest themes ranging from the Solar Eclipse to the Maya Equinox, complete the line's spectrum of provocative itineraries.

Seabourn Cruise Line

Widely regarded as one of the finest vacation experiences available, Seabourn is among the world's most celebrated cruise lines, having consistently won awards and top ratings in authoritative travel and cruise guidebooks and other publications.

The line's all-suite sister ships, the *Seabourn Pride, Seabourn Spirit*, and *Seabourn Legend* are full-sized cruise vessels, carrying just 200 pampered guests in magnificently appointed suites that feature five-foot picture windows, walk-in closets, marble-clad bathrooms and fully-stocked bars. Wines and spirits are complimentary throughout the cruise. The vessels' registry and officers are Norwegian, and its 155 staff are mostly European. Service is warm and friendly, yet impeccable.

Seabourn's cuisine compares with the finest restaurants ashore, served either in the elegant Restaurant or in alternative, casual venues. Along with spa and beauty facilities and a fitness center, each ship has a swimming pool, whirlpools, and a fold-out watersports Marina at the stern of the ship.

Seabourn operates a variety of itineraries worldwide, taking advantage of the size and capacity of its ships to provide exclusive and unique travel experiences for its guests. Optional or included land extensions maintain the same high standards of quality.

Seabourn is now a division of Cunard Line Limited, owned by Carnival Corporation and a consortium of Norwegian investors. Cunard Line Limited operates both Seabourn and Cunard, with a total of eight ships comprising the largest fleet in the luxury segment of the cruise industry.

Silversea Cruises

Silversea Cruises is distinguished within the ultra-luxury market by its elegant, all-suite ships, all-inclusive pricing, and genuine hospitality. In only its second year of eligibility, Silversea was named the "World's Best Cruise Line" in the *Annual Conde Nast Traveler Readers' Choice Awards* for the second year in a row.

Silversea's yacht-like sister ships, *Silver Cloud* and *Silver Wind,* carry just 296 guests in true splendor. At 16,800 GRT, the ships' unique size enables them to navigate some of the world's more intimate waterways. Spacious suites—75% featuring private verandahs—offer spectacular views of the world's most treasured destinations.

The line's exclusive partnership with *Le Cordon Bleu* allows guests to learn "l'art culinaire" from Master Chefs. Its *National Geographic Traveler Series* allows guests to explore the world with photographers and journalists who have traveled on assignment for *National Geographic.* Another guest enrichment program, the *Silversea Golf Series,* features the world's most prestigious golf courses.

Silversea's imaginative itineraries include voyages to the Mediterranean, Northern Europe and the Baltic, Africa and the exotic spice islands, India and the Red Sea, the Far East, South America and Canada, and New England.

The line's all-inclusive fares are among the most comprehensive in the industry and feature round-trip economy air transportation; pre-cruise deluxe hotel accommodations; all beverages including select wines, spirits, and champagnes; all gratuities; all port charges; all transfers and porterage; and on selected sailings, the Silversea Experience®, a special shoreside tour designed to give guests a greater understanding of the places they visit.

Windstar Cruises

When guests step onboard a Windstar vessel, they experience the most unforgettable destination of all. Teak-lined decks and towering sails are a first inkling of a truly unique cruise adventure. The intimate atmosphere, unpretentious pampering, and out-of-the-way ports confirm this notion.

A guest might rise with the sun and explore ruins, rain forests, Rome, or Rhodes, or watch palm-fringed beaches come into view from the 24-hour open-air bridge. Guests can enjoy a full-service day spa, casino, and an array of water sports, from snorkeling to sailboarding, kayaking and water-skiing. Or they can retreat to a luxurious state-room for the magnificent view and amenities, including plush, queen-sized beds, spacious bathrooms, fully stocked mini-bar, CD stereo, and VCR.

Freedom is the greatest luxury on a Windstar cruise, and service is elevated to an art. The international staff treats guests to spontaneous, gracious service that fulfills their every desire. Drinks are refilled in a twinkling, fluffy beach towels appear magically, and room service is always available.

Windstar's cuisine is one of the most creative at sea. The Restaurant offers exquisite signature dishes or delicious Sail Light selections. Guests can leave their ties and formal gowns at home and dine with whom and when they please.

Along the way, guests enjoy smooth sailing, thanks to each ship's computerized ballast system that automatically adjusts to changes in wind and current.

Windstar's exquisite cuisine, enhanced amenities, and sheer unadulterated pampering onboard are only equaled by the striking beauty and charm of the ports visited along the way.

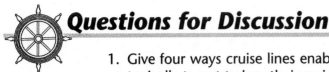

Questions for Discussion

1. Give four ways cruise lines enable you to understand their profile and whom they typically target to buy their cruises.

2. Cite four publications of in-depth information on cruise lines and their product.

3. What product patterns generally characterize a budget cruise product? A mass-market one? A deluxe one? The most expensive cruise products?

4. Is it possible for a person to have a "deluxe" experience on a budget or mass-market cruise ship? Explain why.

⚓ Activity

Select one cruise brochure. Explain how each of the elements listed below is used and what this may say about the clients that the cruise line targets:

Name of cruise line:

Name of brochure:

Colors used on the cover:

Colors used inside the brochure:

Quality of paper:

Quality of the prose inside:

Photo selection:

Overall design:

CHAPTER NINE

SELLING CRUISES

After reading this chapter, you'll be able to

■ Analyze six types of experienced cruisers

■ Apply the cruise sales process to the travel counseling process

■ Interpret cruise brochures

■ Propose an effective cruise solution to most clients' needs

■ Overcome barriers to the cruise sale

■ Carry out a cruise reservation

W ho sells cruises? The most obvious response: travel agents. But there's a more subtle answer to that question. *People who've been on cruises sell cruises.* The number one reason people buy the cruise vacation experience is word-of-mouth—someone told them how great it is. (Other motivators, in order of importance, are a travel agent's recommendation, an ad, a brochure, and an article.)

Who Buys Cruises

Let's take a look at the other side of the equation. Who *buys* cruises? As we indicated in Chapter 2, only about 11% of the North American market has thus far been on a cruise. To help travel agents and its member lines understand people who have already cruised (and probably will again), CLIA decided that it might be useful to identify their demographic and psychographic profiles. They identified six categories of cruise consumers. Here they are, with some facts about how they think and buy:

- *Restless Baby Boomers* constitute the largest segment of cruisers (33%). They're in their 40s and early 50s, are thrifty, family-oriented, and a little wary of new things. Because they're still supporting children, they respond positively to the cost-saving value of a cruise. Their lives are complex, so they like the simplifying, all-inclusive nature of cruising. They also perceive cruising as a fun family vacation.

- *Enthusiastic Baby Boomers* are the second largest category of current cruisers (20%). They're a little younger than our previous category (they're in their early 40s). Like older Baby Boomers, they're fun-loving and family oriented. They're a little more adventurous and gregarious than Restless Baby Boomers. They see cruising as an entertaining way to do many things and meet many people. The romance of cruising very much appeals to them.

- *Consummate Shoppers* represent 16% of today's cruisers. They're age 55 and over, well-traveled, and like the pampering and fine dining available onboard cruise ships. Because they're thrifty, however, they very much want to feel that they're getting the best deal for their dollar. More than most, the ship is as important to them as the destination.

- Even more than Consummate Shoppers, *Luxury Cruisers* (14% of current cruisers) value ships that provide fine dining and ever-present pampering. Unlike Consummate Shoppers, though, cost isn't a major issue for them. As long as they perceive value, they're quite willing to pay for the best. In young middle age (they average 52 years old), they're cultured, well-educated, experienced, and active.

- *Explorers* are a small (11%) but influential segment of the cruise market. They see a cruise as a vehicle for discovering the world. Destinations are far more important to them than the ship itself. They're well-educated and use their sightseeing to learn even more. They're older (average age: 64) yet still very active. They plan their cruises far ahead of departure, not so much to get a better deal (they're quite well-off) as to get the vacation that they want.

- *Ship Buffs* are the study's smallest segment (6%) and the oldest, too (68 years old). The most cruise-savvy of all, they possess an unusual knowledge of ships and itineraries. They love being taken care of, to be comfortable and pampered. They like longer cruises and are very flexible in their cruise choices.

The Cruise Sales Process

Understanding who buys cruises is an important step toward effective sales. So, too, is knowledge of the product. But that's not enough. It's essential for travel agents (and cruise line reservationists) to be familiar with effective sales techniques.

Unfortunately, travel agents sometimes see themselves as service people or order-takers, rather than salespeople. They think that their job is to respond to client requests, rather than to lead their buying behavior. Why? Because, like many people, they have a very negative image of a salesperson: aggressive, exploitative, greedy, and self-serving. Imagine the stereotype of a car salesman. That just about says it all. Agents don't want to be stereotyped as such.

But the sales process need not be manipulative. In fact, today's consumers recognize and reject old-fashioned "hard" sales techniques. They prefer sellers who are sensitive to their needs, who wish to establish ongoing business relationships with them, who, as a result, don't do things *to* people, but *for* and *with* them.

This paradigm suits the selling of travel well. A cruise vacation evokes pleasant emotions. Relaxation, pampering, joy—that's what a cruise is about. The sales process should parallel those feelings. The cruise vacation experience doesn't start when a passenger gets on the ship. It begins *in the client's mind*, when he or she hears a friend's positive comments about a cruise, when a brochure is skimmed, an ad is seen, an article is read. And it can really take hold right there in the travel agency, when a wish is about to become reality.

So let's examine the entire sales process through the eyes of a travel agent. Let's examine what the best travel counselors do.

Opening the Sale

Most people decide if they like someone in *six seconds*.

So concludes a Stanford University study. A salesperson has only a fleeting moment to achieve two things: create a favorable impression and put a client at ease.

Let's assume that the prospect has visited his local travel agency. (That's more probable for a cruise purchase, which is a more complicated purchase than, say, an airline ticket.) What should you do if you're the travel agent?

- Stand up and greet the client. Your action communicates your eagerness to *take action* for the client.
- Establish eye contact with the client.
- Smile, conveying your pleasure with the opportunity to help.
- Give your name, then obtain the client's name. (The exchange of names helps personalize the sale.)
- Shake hands. (A genuinely warm and open gesture.)
- Invite the client to sit down with you. If your office layout permits it, have the client sit to the side of your desk. It's a much more friendly gesture than having a customer sit across from you.

Opening a phone sale is a greater challenge. You and the client can't see each other. Your voice must convey everything. Here's how:

- *Use the four-part greeting:* "Good morning. *[Your agency's name].* This is *[your name].* How may I help you?" Experts have determined that this four-part greeting is by

The dining experience—and, here, a wide selection of desserts—are prominent features in cruise brochures.
Courtesy of Holland America Line

far the most effective. A few cruise specialist agents even customize its end, dropping the "How may I help you?" in favor of something like the disarmingly friendly: "How can I help you with your cruise vacation?" Note also that both of these endings elicit an open-ended response, leading to conversation and clarification.

- ▧ *Smile.* Yes, smile. Phone callers can somehow perceive a smile over the phone.
- ▧ *Communicate energy and enthusiasm.* The client is excited about the possibility of cruising. You should mirror that fervor with your own.

Qualifying the Client

A standard term in sales jargon, "qualifying" means asking questions to uncover a client's needs. The types of questions you'll ask, though, will depend on why the customer came to you.

Travel agents deal with three general scenarios:

Scenario #1. *Clients have only the vaguest idea about what kind of vacation they want.* Maybe they only know they want to go someplace "warm" or experience something "different." For such clients, you must ask *many questions* to discover what's right for them. An early question should be: "Have you ever cruised before?" If the answer is yes, you should try to probe the reasons that motivated them to select a cruise. Their answers should enable you to classify your client in one of the CLIA survey categories. Is your customer an Explorer? A Luxury Cruiser? Perhaps a Restless Baby Boomer? Your conclusion will help you steer the sales process in a direction appropriate to the client's needs.

What if this customer has never cruised? Does such a client fit the same categories as a cruise "veteran"?

Somewhat. CLIA commissioned a study of those 89% of the population who've never cruised. Certain categories emerged that were very similar to those in the other study. But new categories appeared, too. That's understandable—certain personality traits may have inhibited them from buying cruises before.

The survey discovered that some people probably will never cruise. But it also concluded that *74 million people* have an interest in trying out a cruise. (See Figure 9-1.)

FIGURE 9-1 Future potential next 5 years
Source: CLIA study

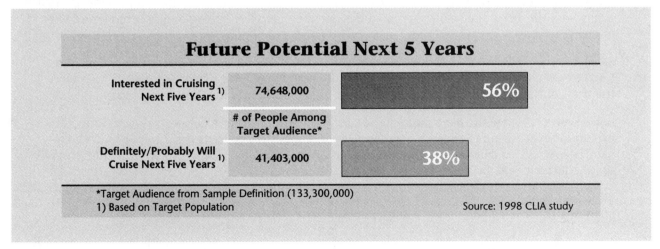

Figure 9-2 lists the five psychographic types the study identified and what could appeal to them about a cruise vacation.

Scenario #2. *Clients have a rough idea of what they want.* They may be interested in a cruise, but they don't know which itinerary and ship is right for them. Or they may have already selected their destination (let's say the Far East), but don't realize that a cruise might be a great vehicle for experiencing Asia. As with Scenario #1, probe with questions that will profile the client's traveling style. Try to classify them in the appropriate category. The insights you achieve will assist you when it's time to recommend.

FIGURE 9-2 Prospective cruise clients

Here are the five kinds of prospects who haven't yet cruised but would potentially find a cruise vacation appealing:

- *Family Folk* (31%) are younger, practical, and down-to-earth. They're cautious with their money and have traditional values. They think that cruises are too expensive and/or offer little in the way of family activities.

  Sales Strategies: Explain that many cruise lines offer a wide spectrum of family options. Stress cruising as a form of escape from routine. Do a cost comparison, showing how a cruise can be more affordable than a land-based family vacation.

- *Comfortable Spenders* (25%) are older, wealthier, active, and seek the finer things in life. They're ambitious and worked hard for what they have. They may not realize that many cruise products can match and even exceed their high expectations.

  Sales Strategies: Underscore the luxury and comprehensiveness of cruising. Recommend lines that offer fine dining.

- *Want It Alls* (17%) are younger versions of the Comfortable Spenders. Ambitious and hard working, they like to indulge themselves with quality products, services, and experiences. They tend to be impulsive and often live beyond their means. They believe that cruises are too structured or not upscale enough for them.

  Sales Strategies: Explain how luxurious, pampering, and stress-free a cruise can be—that it's a unique experience. Contact them regarding last-minute promotions. Remind them that cruises are trendy. Mention to them that they've worked hard—they deserve a cruise.

- *Cautious Travelers* (15%) favor familiar travel experiences. They're somewhat timid and wary. Safety is a concern with them. They're never cruised because they perceive cruising as a little too out-of-the-ordinary.

  Sales Strategies: Emphasize that ships are safe and secure. Suggest familiar, mass-market itineraries. Explain how a cruise cushions them from "overly foreign" experiences. Point out how a cruise takes the stress out of a vacation: no looking for places to eat, no driving long distances, etc.

- *Adventurers* (12%) are the direct opposite of Cautious Travelers. They like to experiment, learn, and explore. They're willing to spend a good amount of money on a product that promises such benefits. They've resisted cruising because they think it's too regimented and confining, with little emphasis on education and too much on entertainment.

  Sales Strategies: Explain how flexible a cruise vacation is. Recommend itineraries with unusual ports. Suggest a cruise line that offers learning opportunities and/or adventure.

Scenario #3. *Clients know exactly what they want.* They've come to you to save time, get a good price, or verify their own research. And they have a specific cruise in mind. These customers are using your services because they are too busy. Even though they seem to know what they want, you should still ask a few questions. Perhaps there's a cruise product the client knows little or nothing about that would fit their needs *better.* Or even a "hidden" need that the customer doesn't realize. Precise questioning will also underscore your commitment to getting to know this client.

What if the client has telephoned with a specific cruise in mind and wants only a price? Telephone shoppers can be trying. You know your chance of getting the sale is low. They'll just keep calling agencies until they get the best price. Just give them a quote. No need to ask questions. Right?

Wrong. Asking questions before quoting a price will set you apart from other agents. In effect, you're not just trying to sell a cruise. You're selling your *agency,* what's unique about it, what benefit there is to doing business with you, showing that you care enough about them and their trip, and that you're willing to take the time to explore their needs. You might also offer to try to match the best price quoted once the prospect has finished shopping. If you made a solid, favorable impression, this shopper might just call you back to buy.

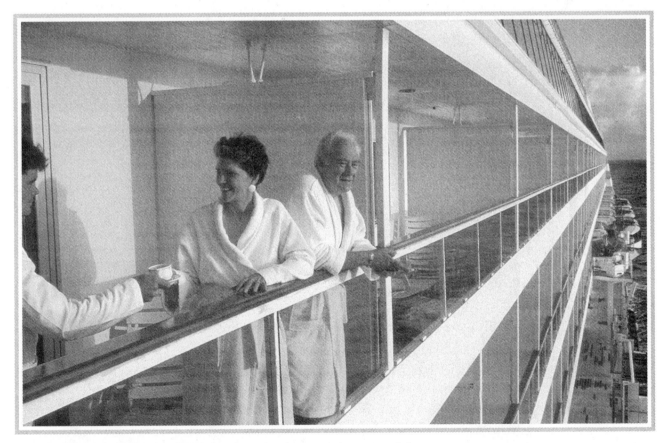

Some clients are willing to pay more for a stateroom with a verandah.
Courtesy of Crystal Cruises

Another tactic: Give a reason for the shopper to actually come to your agency. One effective strategy is to offer to loan them a video on the cruise line they're considering. If they borrow one, they'll have to return it. That means *two* visits to your agency. And research shows that a sale is much more likely in person than over the phone.

Here's the flip-side to Scenario #3. The client knows what he or she wants, but it's not a cruise. Should you therefore dismiss a cruise as a recommendation option? No! Maybe this client is someone who'll never cruise. Perhaps, though, he or she is indeed a cruise prospect, but just doesn't know it. Be alert. If your questions reveal that the client fits one of the five prospect profiles and if their mental barriers to buying a cruise prove false, then a cruise may be precisely what satisfies their needs.

Qualifying Questions

Two kinds of questions help you determine a client's needs: Closed-ended and open-ended.

Closed-ended questions require simple, factual responses. They're essential to ask in all three scenarios we describe above. Here are the classic ones:

- *Who* is going on the trip? (It's essential to get the client's name, phone number, etc., for potential future follow-up.)
- *What* do you have in mind for your trip?
- *When* do you want to go and for how long?
- *Where* do you want to go?
- *How much* do you want to pay? (A better phrasing: "Tell me your price range.")

The answers are generally entered onto a reservation sheet (see Figure 9-3). In addition to filling out this form, you should take notes of everything the client says. It helps keep you alert and conveys how important you consider the client's responses to be.

Taking notes is especially important when asking open-ended questions, the kind that elicit complex and telling responses. Good open-ended questions provide you with important clues to a client's needs. They're especially important to counseling customers with vague ideas of what they want. Even customers who have a rough idea or know exactly what they want should be asked a few open-ended questions. Here are seven classic open-ended questions:

- How do you picture this cruise in your mind?
- Describe your typical vacation.
- What's the best travel experience you've ever had and why? What's the worst?
- Have you been on an escorted tour? At an all-inclusive resort? Did you enjoy it? (An affirmative answer means they may like a cruise, too.)
- What do you like to do while on vacation?
- What did you do on your last vacation? Where did you stay? Do you want this vacation to be similar or completely different?
- Have you been on a cruise? What did you most like about it and why? What did you least like and why?

You can also pose "lifestyle" questions. Some of these seem to be closed-ended, but they yield open-ended results:

- Where do you live? (An important clue to a person's lifestyle.)
- What do you do for a living?
- What kind of car do you drive?
- What's your favorite place to eat and why?

Clubs _____

Organizations _____

CRUISE DATA AND RESERVATION SHEET

Bold face type indicates information essential **before** making a call to the reservation department of a cruise company.

1. **Name of Client** _____ Date: _____

2. Address _____ Zip Code _____

3. Telephone: Home (____) _____ Business (____) _____

4. **Total Number of Party**_____ Comprised of: _____Adults _____Children (Age) _____

_____ A or C

_____ A or C

_____ A or C

6. New_____ Repeat_____ Last Traveled_____ Source _____

7. Departure Date_____ Alternate Departure Date:_____ Total Vacation Days: _____

8. Prior Vacations _____Successful/Unsuccessful

_____Successful/Unsuccessful

_____Successful/Unsuccessful

_____Successful/Unsuccessful

9. Special Interests/Destinations: _____

· · · · · · · · ·

10. Line: _____ **Ship:** _____ **Sailing Date:**_____

11. Alt. Line _____ Alt. Ship:_____ Alt Sailing Date:_____

12. Accommodations: Requested   Offered

   A. **Type, Category, Cabin No.,**

      or Description (Bed Type)   _____   _____

   B. **Price (Cruise only)**   _____   _____

      AIR ALLOWANCE . . . .   _____   _____

      Air/Sea . . . .   _____   _____

      Air/Sea City . . . .   _____   _____

   D. **Option Date** . . . .   _____   _____

   E. Deposit Amount . . . .   _____

      When Due at Line . . . .   _____

   F. Cancellation Insurance: ❑ Offered ❑ Declined . . . .   _____

   G. Port & Departure Taxes . . . .   _____

   H. Extras (Pre/post cruise package) . . . .   _____

   I. Amount Final Payment from Client . . . .   _____

      When Due at Line . . . .   _____

   J. Form of Payment . . . .   _____

   K. Commission . . . .   _____

   L. Net Due to Line . . . .   _____

13. Citizenship_____ Special Diet/Occasion _____

14. **Dining Room Sitting: 1st**_____ **2nd**_____   **Smoking: Yes**_____ **No**_____

15. **Table For:** _____   **Seated with:** _____
       (number)   _____

· · · · · · · · ·

16. **Reservations Made By:** _____ **Date:** _____ 17. Air/Sea Only:

    Booking #:_____   Flight Nos. _____/ _____

    Offered by: _____   Departure Times: _____/ _____

    Accepted by:_____   Arrival Times: _____/ _____

    Gift Order Sent: _____   Seat Assignment: _____/ _____

18. Documents Received: _____ Delivered: _____

FIGURE 9-3 Cruise reservation sheet

Source: Courtesy of CLIA

- What kinds of hotels do you prefer? (Since a cruise ship is like a floating resort, the answer to this question will give you important clues as to which ship and line to recommend.)
- Do you like to drive while on vacation? (A yes answer may indicate that the customer likes independence on a trip or perhaps is a budget traveler.)

So as not to seem prying, pose your lifestyle questions very carefully. And be alert to what may lie behind each response. For example, a young woman who says she lives in a toney part of town, practices law, drives a BMW, likes to eat gourmet cuisine, stays in Ritz-Carltons, and hates driving while on vacation is probably a "Want It All" and a strong prospect for a luxury cruise. Don't assume, though, that an attorney who lives a modest, conservative lifestyle wants a budget trip. This very well may be an Adventurer or a Comfortable Spender.

Recommending a Vacation

You've asked plenty of questions. You've collected many clues. You've placed your client in a clear-cut category. And you're pretty sure that a cruise will be the right recommendation. In fact you have several possibilities in mind.

Before you make your suggestion, however, take a minute to review what your client has told you. This will serve as a reality check for both of you. *Then make a single, best recommendation.* (You can have one or two alternates in mind.) Show how it solves each need and want that the client expressed. Describe your recommended cruise vacation's features, then its benefits. (See Figure 9-4 for an explanation of the difference between the two.) Paint a picture in the client's mind as to what the cruise will be like, *and put the client in that picture.* This will make the client mentally rehearse the trip. Buying a cruise will become far more likely. Sell the *value* of a cruise vacation—don't fall into the trap of selling by price. And make your client *feel good* about a cruise—that's precisely what is wanted in the vacation.

FIGURE 9-4 Features vs. benefits

Most salespeople fall into the trap of mentioning a product's features, but not its benefits. Benefits inject energy and reality into a sale. Here are the differences between each:

Features	Benefits
• Answer the question "What?"	• Answer the question "So what?"
• Represent facts	• Represent the payoff
• Sometimes have the word "you" in them, sometimes not	• Almost always have the word "you" in them
• Are usually impersonal	• Are personal

For example, a ship may be "fast" (a feature), but the real advantages of the ship's speed is that it can stay longer in one port before moving on to the next. Or it will reduce an itinerary's at-sea days. (Both are benefits.) If a stateroom has a verandah, that's a feature. The benefit: Your own private and intimate experience of the itinerary's destinations.

What if your recommendation doesn't "click" with the client? Find out why, clarify any misconceptions, then, if necessary, go on to your backup recommendation.

The Cruise Brochure

Cruise brochures aren't simply sources of information. They're powerful sales tools as well. They fall into five categories:

- *The All-In-One Brochure.* This kind of brochure encompasses every itinerary and ship that the cruise line has. It may be subdivided according to geographic region or individual vessel. As you can imagine, it's usually a thick document.

- *The Specific Ship Brochure.* This brochure lists only those itineraries that a single ship follows. The vessel is generally unique in the line's fleet.

- *The Specific Region Brochure.* Increasingly common, each brochure explains what the line offers in a distinct geographic region: the Caribbean, Alaska, Mexico, Europe, Asia, etc. Usually only the larger cruise lines publish these kinds of brochures.

- *The Seasonal Brochure.* Most often employed to ignite sales at a certain time of the year, this brochure might highlight, say, all the winter cruises that the line offers.

- *The Targeted Brochure.* This brochure is highly specialized. It touts a special promotional sailing, such as a reduced-price trip, an around-the-world cruise, a cruise targeted to members of an organization, etc. It may simply be a slightly customized version of a regular brochure.

Though variations do appear, brochures have a rather standardized, predictable three-part format.

1. *A sales presentation* sets the mood and tone of the promotion piece, while presenting the broad benefits that this company's cruises offer. This section includes the cover (usually with the brochure's effective dates), a table of contents, photos, promotional text, and perhaps an overview map.

2. *The cruise itineraries section* shows the reader where the cruise line travels. (Some cruise lines call this "The Invitation To Choice.") Here's where you'll usually find each ship's sailing schedule, individual itinerary maps, promotional and informational text, photos, deck plans, and fares. (Sometimes fares and deck plans appear in the third section.) If the cruise line offers pre- and post-cruise land options, these will be listed here, too.

3. *The back-of-brochure information section* contains descriptions of airfares, transfers, amenities packages (e.g., for a honeymoon), insurance, payment and refund policies, helpful hints, frequently asked questions, and other general information. A common industry saying: "Clients read brochures from the front to the back, but travel agents read them from the back to the front." In other words, a client is initially interested in what a cruise is all about. Travel counselors already know this. They're initially more concerned about information and policies.

The cruise line's chief vehicle for information and promotion, the brochure can also serve as a cogent sales tool in the hands of a travel agent. Here's what you should do—and not do—with brochures if you're a travel counselor:

- Once you've arrived at your primary cruise recommendation, *bring out a sales "file" copy of the brochure.* Use its photos to illustrate the benefits of your recommendation. An alternative: Share a new brochure with your client, "personalizing" it with Post-its, highlighting, and underlining. Make the experience depicted as "theirs."

- Just as you shouldn't give more than one initial recommendation, *you should share, at first, only one brochure with your client.* If your first choice doesn't work, go to your back-up one—and a second brochure.

- Above all, *don't give your client a stack of brochures to take home,* telling him or her to peruse them "to figure out which one you like." A brochure is a device to help you recommend and close the sale. Once you close the sale, *then* give them the brochure for reference. If you can't possibly close the sale, then perhaps it's all right to offer the take-home literature. But remember: If the client is out of sight, you may be out of a sale.

- For the same reason, *brochures shouldn't be displayed on racks accessible to a client.* A customer may read them while waiting and be led to the wrong product. Or the customer may leave with them if the agency's service is sluggish, never to return.

Overcoming Barriers

Some clients find it difficult to make decisions. Their minds swirl with concerns. Isn't this too expensive? Won't I feel confined? Or seasick? Or bored?

It's time to overcome their resistance. In Chapter 2 we discussed 14 objections to cruising. Figure 9-5 reviews them, with possible responses. Become thoroughly familiar with them. At one time or another, no matter what segment of the cruise industry you're in, you're sure to encounter these barriers to a sale and will need to know how to respond.

No matter what objection a client gives, you should always reinforce your "counter" by reminding the client of the extremely high satisfaction rate that cruises achieve among consumers.

Adding Value

The pattern is the same in virtually every retail industry: The highest satisfaction is almost always with the most expensive product. The top-of-the-line auto. The dishwasher with all the bells and whistles. The most expensive suit in the store. These are what please customers best.

It's the same with travel products. That's why you should always offer the clients the best product within their budget range. (In fact, you should offer them something that costs a little more than their top amount, since clients usually give very conservative figures about what they're willing to spend.) This is called upselling. Some examples:

- An ocean-view stateroom instead of an inside one
- A stateroom on a higher deck
- A stateroom with a verandah instead of one without
- A suite instead of a standard cabin

You can also offer the client something *in addition* to the cruise itself, but related to it. This is called cross-selling. Like selling up, it's used all the time in other industries. "How about fries with your hamburger?" "Would you like our extended service warranty?" "Do you want your car waxed after it's washed?"

Objection	Counter
1. Expense	• Cite cost as per-diem
	• Compare to a similar land-based vacation
	• Stress inclusiveness and value
	• Recommend a cruise line that mirrors their budget
	• Suggest a repositioning cruise
2. Boredom	• Show a daily activity log
	• Cite their favorite activities
	• Cite testimonials from other clients
	• Recommend an active cruise
	• Mention the people-meeting nature of cruising
3. Old people	• Recommend a cruise with a younger passenger profile
	• Point out brochure photos of younger people
	• Explain this was once true, but no longer
	• Cite a testimonial from another client of about the same age as your client
4. Formality	• Recommend an informal cruise product
	• Explain alternate "casual" dining options
	• Look up dress requirements as stated in the brochure's information section
5. Regimentation	• Recommend a flexible cruise product (e.g., upscale cruises, sailing ships, and adventure/education cruises)
	• Cite the "do it all or nothing at all" nature of cruising
	• List flexible features (e.g., multiple dining options)
	• Suggest independent pre- and post-cruise packages
6. Limited port time	• Select itineraries that offer maximum port time
	• Suggest shore excursions as an efficient way to experience a port
	• Offer pre- and post-cruise packages

(continues)

FIGURE 9-5 Overcoming barriers

7. Confinement	• Recommend a ship with a high space ratio
	• Recommend an ocean-view stateroom or one with a verandah
	• Sell up to a larger stateroom or suite
	• Reinforce that ships are really large, floating resorts
8. Forced socializing	• Underscore the do-it-all/nothing-at-all nature of cruising
	• Recommend a product with alternate, open-seating and/or Lido deck dining
	• Sell up to a product with all open-seating dining
	• Suggest a stateroom with a verandah
9. Navy experience	• Stress the features inconceivable on a military ship (e.g., entertainment, pampering)
	• Emphasize that this isn't a seagoing military base, but a sea-going *resort*
10. Ship safety	• Explain how safe today's cruise ships are and how the few problems that have occurred have been rapidly contained
	• Underscore the fact that security is emphasized on today's vessels
11. Too much food	• Cite healthy, "spa" dining options
	• Point out exercise opportunities
12. Too far	• Underscore that it's worth it
	• Choose a closer port or one that requires fewer plane changes
	• Remind them that, once there, a cruise maximizes their vacation time
13. Motion discomfort	• Explain ship stabilizers
	• Inform them of Sea Bands®
	• Recommend that they discuss this with their physician; pills or Transderm Scop patches may be prescribed
	• Recommend a river cruise
	• Book during a time when the climate is at its best
14. Level of knowledge	• Give more information
	• Help them visualize themselves on the cruise
	• Describe how they'll feel on a cruise
	• Loan them a video about cruising

FIGURE 9-5 *(continued)*

Some cross-sell opportunities in cruise sales:

- Travel insurance (this should be an automatic offer, since it protects both the client and the agency from potential hassles and losses)
- An amenities package (e.g., wine in the stateroom upon arrival)
- Pre- and post-cruise packages (tours, lodging, etc.)
- Air to and from the cruise (either purchased from the cruise line or independently)
- Meet-and-greet services, if the air wasn't purchased through the cruise line

A reminder: Upselling and cross-selling not only enhance the profitability of a sale, they almost always improve the client's cruise vacation experience, too.

Getting the Business

What's the most important thing a seller of travel should do? Close the sale. The obvious reason: A salesperson is employed to make a profit for the company. The more subtle reason is to make a customer happy. Few travel products make people happier than a cruise. Remember that 95% satisfaction rate.

Unfortunately, some clients are indecisive. They're afraid to make a commitment to cruise. Even worse, some *salespeople* are afraid to ask for the business. They fear they'll be rejected. Their efforts, they think, may lead to failure.

There's nothing sadder than a salesperson who does everything right, then falters. He or she greets warmly, qualifies thoroughly, recommends with intelligence, and overcomes resistance with skill. But then, when it's time to close . . . .

Perhaps the momentum of the sale will cause *the client to close the sale*. Out comes the credit card, in goes the booking. No need to ask. Other times customers give you subtle signals that they're ready to buy. They might do the following:

- Lean toward you
- Ask you a question that shows that they're already imagining themselves on the ship (e.g., What kind of clothes should I wear? What will the weather be like?)
- Become especially excited as they speak
- Nod their head in a small "yes" motion
- Push away some object that sits on your desk and that formed a symbolic barrier between buyer and seller

At such times—or even when the client seems "neutral"—you should deploy at least one of these closing techniques:

- Explain that it would be better to put down a deposit now, since the availability of what the client wants may disappear. (One line's research shows that 95% of people who make the commitment of a deposit actually buy. Without a deposit, that rate drops precipitously to 35%.)
- Just before you ask for the sale, review how your recommendation exactly fulfills your client's vacation needs.
- Point out that an advance deadline is approaching, after which the cruise promotional offer may or will disappear.
- Ask the client why he or she is hesitating. If the concern seems misconceived, explain why.

- Give the client a series of choices as you reach the end of the recommendation stage: "Do you think you'd prefer an ocean-view stateroom or an inside one?" "Do you think the 4-day or the 7-day cruise best fits your needs?" The more choices the client makes along the way, the easier it'll be to make the final choice to cruise.

- Sometimes a simple "So shall I reserve it?" or "So let's do it!" is all that you'll need to say. Because you carried out the sales process so well, the client will be ready to buy.

Are closing techniques manipulative? No more than helping someone across the street. Unless, of course, crossing the street isn't where they want to or should go. If your client is one of those few for whom cruising is *really* wrong, you'll know long before you get to the close. You'll already have gone off in another sales direction.

The Nuts and Bolts of a Reservation

How does a cruise booking actually unfold? It's quite simple, though at first it can seem challenging to both a travel agent and a cruise line reservationist.

First, though, you should know a few things about how staterooms sell:

- The first products that sell out are suites, followed by large staterooms (often with verandahs).

- The next are the least expensive ones, especially inside cabins.

- Mid-ship cabins sell first. (Less walking and less motion perceived.)

- Each cabin on a ship is "sold" several times. Someone books a cabin, then has to cancel. Others book a cabin, but ask for and get a better one when it becomes available. And cabins are held on an "option" but are eventually "released." (More about options soon.)

Before making the reservation, a travel agent should first complete a cruise reservation form. (See Figure 9-3 for a sample.) This maximizes booking efficiency. He or she should also carefully review the back-of-brochure information section.

The travel agent has three main avenues for booking a cruise: the *telephone*, the *computer reservation system (CRS, also sometimes called the GDS, or global distribution system)*, or the *Internet*. Internet bookings are still in the development stage. They may, however, someday dominate the cruise reservation process. The airline CRSs in agencies have become a very viable way to book cruises, too. Since each CRS system has a different set of procedures, we won't go into detail here on how a cruise computer reservation is done. A little agency training, plus following the formats and prompts that appear on the screen, make this a relatively easy thing to learn.

For now, phone transactions remain the most popular way to make a reservation. Brochure and reservation sheet in hand, the agent gives the reservationist all the information requested. (He or she should inform the reservationist—at the beginning of the call—if the client is present.) The cruise line reservationist, in turn, confirms all requests if available, recommends alternatives if necessary (the agent should have these in mind as well) and discusses the booking choices available. Three are commonly offered (see Figure 9-6 for a fourth possibility):

1. *A confirmed category, stateroom number, and price.* Many first-time cruisers are surprised that this is possible. Hotels don't offer room pre-selection at all. It's best not to provide exact cabin selection from the brochure to the client, though, until the reservationist or computer gives the inventory available.

2. *A guarantee, run-of-the-ship reservation or TBA (to be assigned).* The cruise line confirms the date and price but doesn't give the precise stateroom number. It guarantees a

On some lines, passengers traveling alone may have a fourth booking choice: the **guaranteed share.** On most modern cruise ships, a stateroom is designed to hold two or more passengers and prices are basis two. If a cruise line sold such a stateroom to a single passsenger at the double occupancy rate, it would potentially lose money—it might have been able to sell that stateroom to two passengers. Therefore, most cruise lines add a **single supplement** to the fare (anywhere from 15 to 100 percent of the per-person rate). To avoid this supplement, a single passenger may be allowed to book a guaranteed share. The cruise line will try to find another passenger (of the same sex) also traveling alone to share the same stateroom; each passenger would pay the double occupancy rate. Even if the cruise line can't find anyone to share the stateroom, the passenger won't have to pay the supplement.

FIGURE 9-6   Guaranteed shares

cabin at the category desired or possibly *higher*. Guarantees are offered when the category requested isn't available (but other, higher ones are) and cancellations in the category requested are anticipated. If the cancellations don't materialize, the client gets the higher category stateroom for the same price. Guarantees aren't a good idea for certain clients who may desire or need a specific location and type of cabin. Examples: the physically challenged, seniors, honeymooners, and people who desire a specific cabin location or bed arrangement.

3. *A guaranteed upgrade.* The specific stateroom isn't assigned, but the client is promised a cabin at a category higher than what he or she paid for.

Once the booking choice is determined and availability is confirmed, the agent has two options:

■ *Get a deposit.* Whether refundable or not (it generally is), a deposit solidifies the customer's commitment. As we explained, if you don't get a deposit, the probability that the sale will occur drops dramatically.

■ *Offer an option.* This means that the cruise line will hold the reservation without a deposit (usually for about five days). Options are advisable only for the customer who seems to absolutely need time to think about it or talk it over with a travel partner. The travel agent should give the client a deadline that's ahead of the cruise line option date. That way if the client is a day or two late in getting back to the agent, the sale won't be lost. Agents who haven't heard from a client usually follow up with a reminder phone call. If the option won't be exercised (the client decides not to go), the travel agent, out of courtesy, should call the cruise line to cancel. If it will be exercised, then the travel agent should contact the cruise line, in case the deposit arrives after the option date. (The cruise line will extend the option date, just in case.)

But let's assume the client immediately says yes to a wonderful cruise vacation. Here's what happens:

1. The client pays the deposit by credit card, cash, or a check to the agency. If it's by cash or check, the agency deposits the funds, then sends an agency check to the cruise line. (Cruise companies usually don't accept the client's personal check.) Credit card policies differ among cruise lines. The *CLIA Cruise Manual* and the cruise line brochure usually outline credit card practices.

2. The agent informs the client when final payment will be due. (That's explained by the reservationist and in the brochure.) It's best to express it as an *exact* day of the week and due date (e.g., Monday, June 6), not "six weeks prior to departure."

3. The cruise line sends a confirmation of booking and/or invoice to the travel agency.

4. The client makes final payment to the agency, which in turn moves the funds on to the cruise company.

5. The cruise line sends the documents to the agency. (See Chapter 4 for what they include.) As protection against loss, the agent photocopies the essential elements of the documents, then presents the documents to the client, either in person or by mail (preferably registered). If it's a last-minute booking, the documents will be held for the client at the departure pier.

6. The client cruises!

Following Up

Is the sale "closed" when it's over? Not if you're a good salesperson. You know that you're creating a loyal client, not just a sale. According to the White House Office of Consumer Affairs, it costs six times more to attract a new customer than to keep a current one.

One of the proven ways of keeping that customer is through follow-up. There are four kinds of follow-up situations:

1. *Follow up on an unclosed sale.* If clients only want an option, or even less than that, remind them before they leave the agency how great their cruise could be. Perhaps loan them a cruise video. Call them within 24 to 48 hours to get their decision. If they say yes, great. If not, gently ask them why. You may be able to clarify things. If they still say no, thank them for the opportunity to have counseled them. You never know. They may someday return, this time with the will to buy from someone who cared.

2. *Follow up a closed sale.* Send a thank you note. Leave a bon voyage phone message. If the commission warrants it, arrange for an onboard amenities package for them. Show them that you appreciate their business.

3. *Follow up when they return.* Send a welcome back card, perhaps with a satisfaction survey enclosed. Call them to see how they enjoyed their cruise. Have a welcome back gift delivered to their door.

4. *Follow up at the same booking time next year.* You know when these clients will think about their next vacation. Why not contact them at the same time the following year? Offer to discuss their next vacation plan. It just might well be a cruise.

Though this chapter is lengthy, its subject—cruise sales—could easily fill a book. And it does. Several. Here are publications that focus, entirely or in part, on travel agency cruise sales:

- *Cruises: Selecting, Selling and Booking,* Jules Zvoncheck
- *Sea Travel: The Book,* Douglas Shachnow
- *Selling Cruises: Don't Miss the Boat,* Tom and Joanie Ogg
- *Selling The Sea,* Bob Dickinson and Andy Vladimir
- *Selling Cruises,* Claudine Dervaes

Questions for Discussion

1. Give at least three traits for the following buyers of cruises:
   (a). Restless Baby Boomers:

   (b). Enthusiastic Baby Boomers:

   (c). Consummate Shoppers:

   (d). Luxury Cruisers:

   (e). Explorers:

   (f). Ship Buffs:

2. List five things you can do to make a good impression on a client in person and three things if the sale is over the phone.

3. What's the difference between a closed-ended and open-ended question? Give at least three examples of each.

4. Explain at least three ways a feature differs from a benefit.

5. Name and describe the five kinds of cruise brochures. What three sections does each kind probably have?

6. Give at least one counter to each of the following objections:
   (a). "Cruises are too expensive."

   (b). "Cruises are too formal."

   (c). "Cruises are too regimented."

   (d). "I'll feel confined."

   (e). "I'm afraid of seasickness."

7. Give four ways that you could upsell a cruise client and four cross-sells that you could offer.

8. What are the four kinds of possible bookings?

9. Outline the major steps in a phone cruise booking.

10. Cruise professionals often say that a ship sells from "the top down and the bottom up" and "from the middle to the ends." What does this mean?

⚓ *Activity 1*

In this chapter, we examined the five kinds of people who are likely prospects to take a cruise. Review the profile of each type, then try to think about someone you know who fits each category. If you can't think of someone you know who fits any of these categories, substitute a famous person or even a well-known character from a book, play, or film.

List the person in the middle column. In the right, explain your selection.

Category	Person	Why?
1. Family Folk		
2. Comfortable Spenders		
3. Want It Alls		
4. Cautious Travelers		
5. Adventurers		

⚓ *Activity 2*

Read the agent-client scenario below. Try to identify the things the agent does right—and the many things she does wrong. Write your analysis in the space provided.

AGENT: "Travel, this is Mary."

CLIENT: "Yes, someone gave me your name. I'm interested in taking a vacation . . . ."

A: "OK—where do you need to go?"

C: "I don't know. I was actually looking for some advice. I've got, like, a week and a half off in May, in the spring, and, I don't know, like maybe Florida."

A: "Well, personally, I'd probably consider a seven-day cruise—a cruise package to the Caribbean. You only have to pack and unpack once. And it includes all your meals and all your entertainment."

C: "Don't you get seasick on a cruise?"

A: "There are a lot of things you can do to combat it. Nowadays, they have these little patches you can put behind your ears, and that cures any kind of motion sickness. I have a friend that used one, and it was great. There are all kinds of things."

C: "Now, aren't cruises expensive? How much are the cruises?"

A: "Generally, for, like a 7-night cruise, with meals and everything included—it starts at about one thousand dollars, or twelve hundred dollars per person."

C: "Well . . . I guess I can afford something like that. What's the advantages of that over, say, going to Florida or something?"

A: "Well, it's the type of thing you can really sit back and relax, and all your meals are included—you can literally eat all day long. They've got lots of activities aboard the ship—and you can get sun at the same time. Uhh, you stop and see different ports—so you do more traveling."

C: "Well, where do the ships go for the most part? Which one would you do?"

A: "I like the Eastern Caribbean, but they have all different destinations. They leave out of Miami, they go down to St. Thomas, St. Martin—different islands in the Caribbean—different itineraries. Uh, there are some very interesting ones. Uh, there are different islands—you may be there for a couple of hours, you may be there all day long, depending on the itinerary. But at least you get out, and get to explore, and get some fresh air. If you want, you can swim in the pool. You know, you have a lot of things to do, and it's all included in one price."

C: "OK, maybe a cruise would be a good idea."

A: "Well, if that's what you want to do, I mean, you know, if that's what you want to do—maybe you want to see EPCOT, you want to see Disney World, Universal Studios, I guess a cruise is different from all that—it's a different type of thing. Yeah, definitely, it's probably gonna run you about the same, by the time you get your hotel, your car, your transfers, uh, admissions, your meals, your entertainment—uh, adding all that up, it's pretty costly."

C: "Well, what do you get, like, free on a cruise?"

A: "OK. What would be included in the price would be all your meals—you can eat non-stop all day long—you've got all kinds of entertainment onboard—lounges, discos—or quiet areas—library and movies. Then at night, you know, they've got different shows—Las Vegas reviews, with singers and dancers, all kinds of different entertainment. Ummm, different contests every night. The only thing that would not be included would be any special services, such as a massage, or if you want to get your nails done or your hair done. And your liquor, your drinks. But generally the prices of the drinks aren't that expensive. The prices are comparable to what you get on land. They don't really jack up the prices for the drinks."

C: "Well, that sounds good."

A: "Like I said, there's all kinds of entertainment. You can do as much as you want, or as little as you want. You want the sun—you want to explore different points in the Caribbean, umm, it's kind of an all-inclusive type of package."

C: "Well, again, it sounds like a pretty good thing. Let me talk to my wife about it."

A: "OK."

1. What has the agent done right?

2. What has the agent done wrong?

CHAPTER TEN

CRUISE MARKETING, GROUPS, AND INCENTIVES

After reading this chapter, you'll be able to

- Analyze and apply a cruise marketing campaign

- Create a marketing plan

- Operate a cruise group departure

- Explain how incentives operate

Y our alarm clock rings. Out of bed, off to the kitchen for some Rice Krispies that you bought yesterday at the grocery store. You watch TV, surfing through the channels until you pause at the Food Channel. There's Chef Emeril Lagasse, showing how to make a great crepe and inviting his viewers to actually join him on a culinary cruise of the French Riviera—a toll-free number is given on the screen. You write it down. You've always wanted to learn how to really cook, to go beyond cereal. And to do it with a famous chef in a legendary region? Sounds good to you.

Before leaving for work, you browse through yesterday's mail. Here's a credit card solicitation. There's an invitation to join a book-of-the-month club. Maybe . . . You put it aside. Oh, and a flyer from your travel agent about a special cruise departure. Sounds interesting.

So what has just happened? A distribution system has provided your breakfast, your psychographic profile has led you to a niche promotion hosted by a pied piper, several of your hot buttons have been hit, and you're clearly a prospect in several databases. Oh, yes, you've considered purchasing both tangibles and intangibles from companies whose mission statements probably address your needs and whose promotional mix has successfully targeted you.

All this in the first hour of your day.

Yes, marketing—and its language—can be intimidating. But why is it so critical to understand it at all? One reason: Marketing permeates your life. Every day, hundreds of companies direct thousands of marketing efforts and millions of dollars in your direction. Whether you like it or not, marketers are constantly analyzing your behaviors, affecting your ideas, and steering your purchases.

And if you intend to go into the cruise business, you must understand how the cruise industry markets itself. Whether as a travel agent or a cruise line employee, you're part of a formidable marketing engine.

Definition

What is marketing? Many people think it's the same as selling. But it's much more than that. One description: *Marketing* is the defining of a need and the development of products and services to meet those needs. That short sentence encompasses a world of implications.

A solid and effective marketing campaign includes the following elements:
1. Consumer and product research
2. Product/service design
3. Pricing
4. Promotion
5. Distribution
6. Follow-up

When executed properly, marketing yields predictably excellent results. And few industries over recent decades have generated results as spectacular as those of the cruise business.

The Elements of Marketing

Cruising is a near-textbook example of how to achieve marketing success. Let's look at the six steps we gave to you above and how the cruise industry has put each into practice. It'll give you an insight into what good marketing is all about.

The look of ship's interior spaces reinforce the cruise experience that each cruise line sells.
Courtesy of Carnival Cruise Lines

1. Research

In marketing two types of **research** are common: **consumer research** and **product research**. Consumer, or market, research tries to discover who the public is, how they think and what they like to buy. The many studies we've cited in this book are examples of consumer research: What do people want in a vacation? What barriers exist to buying a cruise? How do consumers compare cruises to other vacation options? The responses to this research serve to guide cruise lines as they develop and refine their offerings.

Product research is somewhat different. It focuses on the elements of what is to be sold. Let's say you want to develop a new cruise line. You would want to research the history of cruising, isolating what succeeded and what didn't. You'd certainly find out what other cruise lines have done and perhaps what they haven't—especially if your research indicated that certain consumer needs weren't currently being met.

A company need not carry out its own research. It can plug into the research of others. CLIA studies, for example, are useful not only to its member lines, but also to agencies, tour operators, and many other segments of the travel business.

2. Design

Once you've examined the results of your research, you then design a product or service that addresses what you've learned. For example, you might decide that the opportunities in mass-market cruising are few—too many companies are already doing it right. But how about a cruise line that emphasizes learning? Your studies showed that a huge number of Baby Boomers are in their peak earning years and will be increasing their travel as they approach retirement. A significant number of them like to learn things while vacationing. Maybe a cruise line that's a sort of "floating extension school" might work well. You've discovered that several companies are already doing this, and doing well. But it seems that there's room for another such product—the demand, you think, exceeds current and future supply. And perhaps you can give a different "spin" to your cruise line product.

In the cruise business, product design isn't limited to cruise lines. You could, for instance, design a chain of travel agencies that specializes in educational travel products,

FIGURE 10-1 Unusual cruise statistics

Source: Ambassador Magazine

- Number of photographs shot by photo department per year on Carnival ships: 12.5 million

- Pounds of caviar consumed on a 7-day Celebrity cruise: 40

- Weddings performed on a typical 7-day Costa Caribbean cruise: 17

- Pieces of tableware (other than glasses) used on one Cunard *Queen Elizabeth 2* sailing: 64,531

- Highest toll ever paid by a Princess ship: $141,344.97, to go through the Panama Canal

- Number of ice sculptures carved on a 7-day *Radisson Diamond* sailing: 15

- Bottles of champagne consumed, per passenger, on a 14-day Seabourn cruise: 1

- Most popular bread-sculpture form on a Windstar cruise: a bear including tours as well as cruises. Your research could lead you to those communities where learning is highly valued: for example, near major universities or even upscale retirement communities.

3. Pricing

But for how much should you sell your educational cruises? First, you need to budget out what it will cost to operate and sell your product. This is no easy task. (That's what cost accountants are for.) You'll need to include everything: building or buying the ships, salaries, promotion, overhead, and all the rest. Then you'd have to project how many cruises you'll expect to sell and in what time period.

Eventually—and it's a long, tricky process—you'll know what it will cost to operate each departure. So how much should your profit be? That depends almost entirely on what consumers will pay for your cruises and how many of them there will be. Research has told you that people who take educational vacations make quite a bit of money. The people you surveyed also told you what they might be willing to spend on a learning cruise. It was more than you expected. So perhaps a relatively high cost and profit margin is possible.

Let's be honest, though. This marketing step requires plenty of interpretation, assumptions, and guesswork. The superstars of marketing are those who excel at making educated, well-based "guesses."

4. Promotion

No matter how well-researched, designed, and priced your cruise product is, it won't sell unless people know about it. Promotion solves that. It gets the word out.

There are two kinds of promotion: publicity and advertising. **Publicity** is promotion that is nearly or completely cost-free. Some examples: articles in magazines, TV coverage, a free education-oriented Web site, a regular column you write for a newsletter. **Advertising**, on the other hand, is promotion that costs: a listing in the Yellow Pages, a magazine ad, a radio commercial, a poster, a brochure. (See Figure 10-2 for the strengths and weaknesses of various types of advertising.)

FIGURE 10-2   Media comparison
Source: Holland America Line / Windstar

It's often difficult to decide which direction to go with limited marketing funds. The following is a comparison of strengths and weaknesses that may assist you in making your decision.

MEDIUM	STRENGTHS	WEAKNESSES
Newspapers	Local market penetration	Usually black & white
	Some targeting available	Size = level of impact
	Current message	Affected by ad clutter
	Flexible	Short lifespan

(continues)

Newspapers Inserts	Low cost	Can't specifically target
	Good for local market	Cheap image
	Coupons possible	Short lifespan
	Measurable results	Read quickly
Magazines	Target opportunities	Ad buy made far in advance
	Distinctive	Limited formats
	Good repro. quality	Placement is critical
	Involves reader	Targeting is questionable (except for niche magazine)
	Adds prestige	Expensive
	Direct response capability	
	Long message lifespan	
	Trade/consumer option	
Radio	Target potential	30-60 seconds is short
	Cost-effective for repeat spots	Short lifespan
	Widespread medium	Not good for visual folks
	Supports other advertising	Segmented audience
	Can be local and promotionally oriented	Very competitive
Television	Powerful reach/awareness	Cost to produce and air
	Prestige	"Clutter" concerns
	Creates credibility	Placement
	Mass market	30-60 seconds is short
	Appeals to many senses	
Cable TV	Powerful reach/awareness	Limited range
	Lower cost	Lower ratings
	Target market	Spotty coverage
		Cost to produce ad
Billboards	Ability to move consistent ad to multiple billboards	High cost
	"Silent" salesperson	Time frame limited
	Dramatic presentation	Clutter/image consideration
	Geographic targeting	Message limitations
		Mass market, not targeted

FIGURE 10-2 *(continued)*

Direct Mail	Most easily targeted	High cost/thousand
	Measurable	Image considerations
	Creates awareness	Possible confusion with junk mail
	Economical compared to other media	Design and testing costs
	Personalized medium	Inaccurate mailing lists
	Offers variety of methods	
	Testable	
	Most bang for your buck	
Telemarketing	Human contact	List purchase expenses
	Quick implementation	Excellent communication skills needed
	Instantaneous feedback	Low results-rate (except for existing clients)
	Good for existing customers	Bad image among consumers
	Lead generator	
Brochures	Convey enough info for customer to buy	Can be expensive to produce
	Visual imagery	Needs to be read
	Creates visibility	
Yellow Pages	Puts you with competition	Possible limited usage
	Huge audience	Not targeted
	List and display opportunities	Not current message
	People are ready to buy	Ad blends in with others
	Convenient	Not especially attractive
	Long lifespan	
Window Displays	Exciting	Requires creativity
	Visual	Location important
	Draws potential clients into agency	Need strong message
	Economic	Limited reach
	Long lifespan	

FIGURE 10-2 *(continued)*

The cruise lines, of course, have entire departments that fashion their promotional campaigns, often using multiple advertising channels. But what of travel agencies? Do they have the resources to do the same?

Certainly it's a challenge for travel agencies to create solid promotional campaigns. But they don't have to start from scratch. Both the cruise lines and CLIA provide ready-made materials, like generic PR releases, brochures, radio/TV copy and collateral material such as postcards, posters, and mail stuffers (often assembled in a "marketing kit"), that agencies can tailor to their own situation. CLIA also provides "how-to" materials that advise agencies about the best ways to promote their cruise products.

It's not enough, though, to have quality promotional materials. For real success, your promotion should target the kinds of people most likely to buy your product. You probably would get more responses for your educational cruise by placing an ad in *Smithsonian*, rather than in *Time*. It would cost less, too. (Conversely, a mass-market cruise line would be better off advertising in *Time*.)

To target effectively, you must also keenly understand what appeals to your prospects—and what doesn't. For example, your **prospect** (a marketing term for someone who is a potential buyer of your product) should respond well to a brochure that stresses such hot-button themes as "life-long learning," "personal development," and "cultural encounters." (A **hot button** is anything that powerfully entices a buyer.) That same brochure would show people visiting famous attractions, attending port lectures, and reading in the ship's library. It would use advertising copy that's intelligent, eloquent, and plentiful. (Educated people like to read.) It might even look more like a well-illustrated guidebook than a brochure.

5. Distribution

How will you get your product out to consumers? With tangible products, the distribution channels are easy to identify. A **tangible product** is one that has physical form, like a TV set, a toaster, or a tire. You make it, load it on a truck, ship it to a store, and help them sell it.

For **intangibles**—products or services that have no physical form, that are more experiential—distribution is less obvious. Some examples: insurance, stocks and, yes, travel.

How, then, will you "distribute" your cruises? As with most cruise lines, you'll rely most heavily on travel agencies to move your product. It works for them, and you're convinced it'll work for you. Of course you'll have to identify those agencies or even some specialty tour operators who—because of their client base—are especially motivated to sell educational travel experiences. (How you do that would be a chapter unto itself.) You might also sell some of your cruises via toll-free numbers and the Internet. (There are some people who have never and will never contact an agency or tour company. There has to be a way for you to reach them.) And you might wish to approach certain educational publications as vehicles for getting your product to those they serve.

At the end of distribution is the sale itself. Sell as many or more cruises than you expected and you have reason to celebrate. Your marketing efforts worked. Sell fewer, and it's time, perhaps, to reconsider some of your assumptions.

6. Follow-Up

To follow up on all sales—a step once neglected in marketing—has become highly important. Whether sales are doing better, worse, or as expected, it's important to know *why*. That way you can recommit to what you've done right and readjust what you've done wrong.

Many mechanisms for follow-up exist: satisfaction surveys, thank-you letters, newsletters, membership in "cruise alumni" clubs, responses to complaints, etc. Remember, too, that follow-up marks the start of the next marketing cycle. It's an opportunity for you to start your customers thinking about their *next* trip with you.

Marketing Plans

Marketing strategies don't just happen. They're well thought out and articulated. The vehicle for those thoughts is usually a marketing plan.

A *marketing plan* is a blueprint for action, a map to success. It explains who you are, what your business is, where you're going, and how you'll get there. Cruise lines certainly have them and many travel agencies do, too. Here are the steps that typically constitute a marketing plan:

1. An *executive summary*. On a single page or even a single paragraph, you summarize what's to follow.

2. A *mission statement*. In a few sentences, you explain your goals: how much net profit you intend to make and why you're in business doing what you're doing.

3. *An analysis of market research*. This summarizes what you've discovered through your studies and to what conclusions they've led you.

4. *An analysis of market attractiveness*. Here you project the size of your market (how many prospects there are), the potential for market growth, ease of getting to your clients, etc.

Large onboard groups sometimes use the main showroom to stage their own events.
Courtesy of Premier Cruises

5. *An analysis of your product's life cycle.* Like people, products have a "life," usually expressed as four stages:

   - *Introduction,* when the product or service is so new there are few, if any, competitors. Cruising was in this stage about 30 years ago.

   - *Growth,* when the public is aware and becoming excited about what you offer. Cruising is still in this stage.

   - *Maturity,* when competition has fully formed, excitement is still high, and profit potential is stable for those who do things best. Cruising may eventually enter this stage, but not for a long while.

   - *Decline,* when demand is dwindling. Still a long, long way off for cruising—assuming decline ever happens.

6. *A SWOT analysis.* This is an acronym for one of the most valuable marketing tools there is. You must determine your . . . .

   - *Strengths:* what you do well

   - *Weaknesses:* what you can't or don't do well

   - *Opportunities:* what can or will benefit you most

   - *Threats:* what could reduce the demand for what you offer

7. *An analysis of your competitors.* What do they do well? What do they do poorly? How can they affect your success? And what must you do to counter their efforts?

8. *An analysis of your customers.* This marshals the demographic (statistical) and psychographic (attitudinal) data about the people to whom you sell. The resulting profile gives a "face" to the type of person who is your best possible customer. It's dependent on something called **database** marketing. A *database* is an organized collection of customer profiles. From this database you can quickly break down your list into specific, targeted customers (for example, all singles, everyone who makes over $50,000 a year, those of your customers who have only taken a 3-day cruise).

9. *An analysis of your cooperators.* Who can *help* you succeed? Among the cooperators that, say, a travel agency might count on: suppliers, vendors, front-line agents, outside sales agents, clients who refer customers to you, clubs, associations, and other companies (for example, a luggage store) with whom you might have a co-marketing agreement.

10. *An analysis of your products and services.* Here you examine what you sell now and, based on previous analysis, what you might sell in the future.

11. *Your marketing mix.* This section nicely ties together much of what you've covered in your marketing plan and, more importantly, how they interrelate. They're often referred to as the eight "P's":

    - *Product:* what you sell

    - *Price:* what it costs the buyer

    - *Profit:* what you plan to make

    - *Place:* where it's sold. Usually you'll be selling from a distinct office and the geographic community it serves. But remember: With the Internet, your "community" can be the whole world.

    - *People:* who works for you and how

    - *Politics:* how laws, regulations, and industry practice affect you

    - *Position:* how you're perceived with regard to the rest of the marketplace

    - *Promotion:* how you communicate your message

12. *Your promotional mix:* This final section explains how you intend to persuade the public to buy and where you intend to allocate your promotional resources.

Groups

"Cheaper by the dozen." That's an old saying that expresses an important truth in cruising. But that truth can vary. To travel agents, it means that you save time and make money more efficiently by selling to a group of people, rather than to many separate individuals or couples. To a cruise line, it means that you're more or less dealing with only one "client" who occupies many staterooms. And to the consumer, it means that by traveling with other people like yourself, you enjoy your cruise vacation more and almost surely pay less for it.

Pre-Formed Groups

There are three types of groups. The first is called a pre-formed group. A **pre-formed group** is one made up of people who belong to a club, association, or other pre-existing organization. These organizations communicate regularly with their members and schedule fairly regular events that the members attend together. Usually the prospects know each other. Some examples: church groups, professional associations, sports groups, fraternal organizations, alumni societies, labor unions, country clubs, college departments, or even families. Travel agencies and cruise lines love proposing group departures to pre-formed groups. Since their members know each other and already do things together, pre-formed groups promise a high probability of success.

For that success to occur, however, three factors must be present:

1. *A clear match must exist* between the group's profile and the line, ship, destination, and departure date. What would appeal to a church group might be very different from what would attract a country club.

2. *The promotion to the group must be well conceived.* In the same way that regular promotions should hit the right hot buttons, so, too, should a group promotion be tailored to the group's buying style. Brochures, flyers, correspondence, ads, presentations at meetings, and cruise nights should all reinforce the group's identity and the product's suitability. (For an explanation of a cruise night, see Figure 10-3.)

3. A pied piper should *anchor the cruise promotion.* A **pied piper** is a member of the organization you're targeting who is especially respected and admired by its members. The pied piper may or may not be one of the group's official officers. He or she *is* someone with strong leadership skills. The group fiercely respects this person's ideas and suggestions. A pied piper leads. The group *wants* to follow.

Pied pipers may assist you in mailings, cruise nights, and planning some or all of the group cruise event. They may even serve as your tour conductor—in exchange for a free cruise.

Speculative Groups

The second kind of group is a **speculative** or **promotional group**. To create such a departure, you must attract a group of individuals who probably do not know each other—at least not until they take the cruise. All they have in common is the desire to buy a certain, special cruise. For example, a travel agency might block space on a specific cruise departure, obtain a special price, then promote that cruise in its newsletter, through a flyer, or even in a newspaper ad.

A cruise night is a special event where the travel agency and/or the cruise line previews the proposed group cruise for the organization's members. It can be part of the group's regularly scheduled meeting. Ideally, though, it should be an event unto itself.

To maximize its attraction, you should give your cruise night a clever name and theme. The room where you'll be staging it is important, too. Can you decorate it? Which audio-visuals should you use and will they work well in this environment? Is there enough room for registration, display, and bookings tables?

Another key question: How much will this cost and who pays? Hopefully the cruise line will be supportive here. Remember that a cruise night may cost more than you think. Among the possible costs: AV equipment rental, invitations, postage, and refreshments.

Staffing—both to organize and to operate the event—is crucial, too. Someone has to coordinate things with the line's district sales manager, order support materials, order and install equipment, refreshments and decorations, and perhaps call all invitees who have RSVP'd—usually a day or two before the event.

And what of the cruise night itself? Think of it as an entertainment event. It should be energetic, lively, informative, and convincing. Have your brochures ready. Invite any of your other clients who have cruised before to share their enthusiasm with the group. Above all, provide the opportunity for attendees to place their deposits then and there. If you do the job right, there will be no better time to convert their enthusiasm into cash.

For those who don't sign up, send follow-up literature as a reminder or even place phone calls.

FIGURE 10-3   Cruise nights

Speculative groups are more challenging to sell than pre-formed ones. They require more time, money, and promotion. One way to facilitate the process: Narrow your focus to people who have some psychographic trait in common (e.g., a love of cultural exploration). Such a speculative group is sometimes called an **affinity group**. Another way: Find a pied piper who is well-known to the public, such as a radio or TV personality. It's also vital to tap into a cruise line's advice and resources to help guarantee the trip's success. (For a list of what cruise lines will provide to an agency to help a group promotion, see Figure 10-4.)

Note that the line between a speculative and a pre-formed group is sometimes blurred. For example, suppose you marketed an adventure cruise to all the members of a large health club.

It's *sort of* a pre-formed group—they all belong to the same club—but only a few of them know each other. In some ways, therefore, they're a *speculative* group, an affinity one with at least two things in common: where they work out and a commitment to health.

Or imagine that you're promoting a special cruise for the alumni of a university. In the loosest sense of the word, they're a pre-formed group. But they're much closer to being a speculative group. They almost surely don't know one another, and there could be tens of thousands of them with whom to make the offer.

Creating and Marketing a Group Cruise Departure

Selling a cruise to a group may be easier than selling to individuals, but it's still a complex process. Here are the 15 steps you might follow to create, market, and operate your own group departure:

Here's what a cruise line can provide an agency to support a group departure:

- A video for a cruise night

- A speech by a district sales manager at the cruise night

- Free *shells* (a shell is a slick color brochure with empty space for the agency to print its message) and other promotional material or "collateral," often assembled in a group marketing kit

- Promotional dollars (for a mailing, to stage the cruise night, to create flyers, etc.)

- Onboard amenities (e.g., reception cocktail party) at low or no cost

- Onboard service assistance (larger ships often have a group coordinator onboard)

- A free tour conductor berth, typically for 15 berths (or eight cabins) sold. The 16th berth is therefore free. (Note: The tour conductor—or TC—berth can go to the tour conductor, pied piper, or even to a client.)

- Free air for the tour conductor, if air is booked through the cruise line.

FIGURE 10-4 Cruise line support

1. **Select your group.** If it's a pre-formed group departure, you're targeting a group that will probably like the idea of a group departure, but which hasn't yet done one. If it's speculative, then it might be selecting a niche that's been underserved in your area, such as adventure travelers.

2. **Research by qualifying the group.** Just as you qualify individual clients to determine what they desire, so, too, must you probe a group's needs and wants. This is especially true for pre-formed groups. Among the things you must determine: previous travel, if any; membership size; organization and leadership; special interests; what they read; how they communicate; how frequently they meet. Ideally, this should be done nine months to a year in advance.

3. **Project what percentage of the "audience" will book.** For speculative groups, this is a real challenge. If you do a direct mailing to all your clients, and if your promotional piece is perfectly conceived, then you may get a 1% response rate. If the mailing is targeted (e.g., an adventure cruise to a mailing list of adventure-seekers), that percentage might be higher. If it's to the general public, it'll be much less than 1%. Often it's a matter of trial and error. But that's why it's called *speculative.*

   Your projection may be somewhat easier with a pre-formed group. Participation in past travel or other events will provide a valuable clue to future behavior. Don't forget that for each person who responds, there probably will be another going. A club member, in effect, "sells" the cruise to their companion for you. Remember, too, that no matter how many people say they're going, *you don't have a booking until you have a deposit.*

4. **Determine the purpose of their trip.** Why will they travel? How will they benefit from a cruise? Answer these questions, and you'll know better which hot buttons to push when you promote to them.

5. **Establish the flexibility of their time.** The more flexible they are, the more leverage you'll have for prices, times, and deadlines as you negotiate with your cruise supplier.

6. **Determine their value range.** What would be an acceptable price for this cruise? The price they're willing to pay will determine which cruise you'll ultimately propose to them. If you're doing a speculative group, you'll need to do some demographic research or rely on your experience. For a pre-formed group, the organization's leadership will be the best source for insights.

7. **Determine the itinerary, destination, and cruise line recommendation.** This will flow naturally from the value range, your knowledge of the business, and input from the district sales representative.

8. **Contact and negotiate with the cruise line.** Just as with an individual, you should have a number one choice and a backup just in case. You should probably set things up through your sales representative, though some choose to go directly to the line's group desk. For what's typically negotiable, see Figure 10-5. The cruise line will ask how many cabins you wish to reserve (i.e., blocked space).

FIGURE 10-5 Negotiating groups

Here's what is generally open to negotiation with the cruise line:

- Cruise price. (Typically 10-30% off the brochure rate, though this very much varies, depending on the cruise line. Season, itinerary, group size, performance record on previous trips, and many other factors strongly affect what group rate will be offered.) Most often quoted as a non-commissionable, "net" rate.

- Free tour conductor berth(s). (Usually the tour conductor, however, must pay port charges and taxes.) The majority of cruise lines give one free cruise for every 15 full-fare adult passengers (that's one berth in a cabin). Several require 16, others require fewer (especially for longer or more expensive cruises).

- Airfare, if obtained from the cruise line. Note: "Deviations" from the usual patterns to and from the port (e.g., on days that aren't the ones when passengers typically arrive and depart) will often lead to extra charges.

- Free airfare for the tour conductor(s)

- Transfers

- Onboard functions

- Special onboard amenities

- Insurance

- Pre- or post-cruise packages (e.g., tours, hotel stays, etc.)

- Shore excursions

- Promotional support

- Deposit and final payment dates

Depending on the cruise line, any one or all of the items listed above may be very negotiable, not very negotiable—or not at all negotiable. You'll quickly find out which ones are and which ones aren't.

Each cruise has different criteria for how many persons constitute a group. Most require between 10 and 16 passengers (five to eight cabins). A few require less.

9. **Review the contract.** The line will send you a detailed, written confirmation of what you have agreed upon, plus plenty of fine-printed terms and conditions. (For an example, see Figure 10-6.) *Read it all — and carefully.* Contact the line on anything that's unclear. Don't be prepared to sign until you're sure of every detail. The contract, or the correspondence that accompanies it, should also stipulate the contact person at the cruise line.

10. **If doing a pre-formed group, present your recommendation to the group's leadership.** You should outline it first in a brief written proposal. Then schedule an in-person meeting with them. Clarify all issues up front, including how the TC ticket will be used. This all should be done six to nine months before departure.

    If you receive the group's commitment, inform the cruise line. Send in the signed contract. At this stage the cruise line may request a first deposit (refundable or non-refundable) and ask which dinner seating your group will prefer.

11. **Plan your promotion.** Select and design your promotional materials and media. Schedule a cruise night. Make sure you know exactly what to say to the group to build maximum enthusiasm. Make sure the "who, what, when, where, why, how much, and how long" questions are all covered. Most important: Your promotional materials should clearly state deposit and final payment policies. The dates that clients should pay you should precede by about two weeks the dates when you must pay the cruise line. Your deposit—determined by cruise line policy—is typically about 10 to 20 percent of the cruise price, non-refundable in the event of client cancellation.

12. **Establish your "fulfillment center."** Who will answer inquiries, send out materials, and track bookings? Determine your staffing needs and responsibilities before the first bit of promotion occurs. (Responding to client queries and requests is called *fulfillment.*)

13. **Plot your timeline.** Here's a rough guideline:

    - 5 - 8 months prior to departure: Operate your promotional campaign, including a second wave of promotion, if necessary.
    - 4 - 7 months prior: Review results and deposits received. Send additional deposits to cruise line, if required.
    - 3 months prior: Review current space. Make a go/no-go decision. Release majority of unsold space. Invoice clients for final payments.
    - 2 months prior: Send final payment, along with passenger list, to cruise line.
    - 1 - 2 months prior: Send special service requests (*e.g.,* vegetarian meals, medical needs, etc.).
    - 1 month prior: Reconfirm special service requests. Finalize meeting space, private receptions and AV requirements, if needed. Receive documents from cruise lines, check for accuracy.
    - 1 month to 2 weeks prior: Distribute documents, either by mail (preferably registered) or in person at a pre-cruise meeting.

14. **Operate the group cruise departure.** This easily could constitute an entire chapter. For more details, consult Appendix C.

15. **Stage a post-cruise party.** It's a great time to exchange photos and also to promote next year's cruise!

NORWEGIAN
CRUISE LINE

GROUP AGREEMENT

P.O. Box 025403, Miami, Florida 33102-5403
1-800-327-7030

VOYAGE: 069

REQUEST #:   ISSUE DATE: 5/ 9/98

TRAVEL AGENT INFORMATION

GROUP INFORMATION   PAGE 1 OF 1

SHIP: NORWEGIAN SEA   SAILING DATE: 8/ 8/98

GROUP CONFIRMATION NO: 36

TOURS INC
CONTACT: ROB
***INT'L INBOUND OPERATOR

GROUP NAME:

SALES MANAGER:

ALL RATES QUOTED ARE IN U.S. DOLLARS. ALL CABIN RATES ARE PER PERSON BASED ON DOUBLE OCCUPANCY; TRIPLE AND QUAD
CABINS ARE ON A REQUEST BASIS. ALL PACKAGE RATES ARE PER PERSON.   NOTE: AIR ADD-ON MUST BE APPLIED WHERE APPLICABLE.
PLEASE REVIEW THE BACK OF THIS CONTRACT FOR ADDITIONAL TERMS AND CONDITIONS.

GROUP CABIN SPACE:

CATEGORY	NO. OF CABINS	QUOTED FARE	DISC PCT	DISC FARE	COMM PCT	PORT CHARGE	GOVT TAX	BOOKNG TYPE
A	1	1389.00	0.00	1389.00	10.00	108.00	0.00	C/O
H	18	1249.00	0.00	1249.00	10.00	108.00	0.00	C/O

A/S=AIR/SEA C/O=CRUISE ONLY I/R=INDUSTRY RATE BUS=BUS RIDE

3/4 FARES C/O   TOUR CONDUCTOR
ADULT   CHILD   PAX   ADD-ON

199.00   199.00   2   0.00

* AIR DEVIATION FEE PLUS ANY DIFFERENCE IN AIR COST WILL APPLY

PAYMENT/REVIEW SCHEDULE:

  OPTION: 06/09/98 10000.00   FINAL DUE: 06/09/98

CABINS: 19   DINING: WAITLISTED

CONFIRMATION REMARKS:

CABINS ASSIGNED W/NAMES REQUIRE DEPOSIT
IN 7 DAYS. CABINS ASSIGNED WITHOUT
NAMES REQUIRE IMMEDIATE PAYMENT.
CABIN ASSIGNMENTS WITH NAMES REQUIRE FULL DEPOSIT WITHIN SEVEN DAYS.
CHILD TRAVELING AS 2ND PAX IN CABIN PAYS ADULT FARE.
ONLY SNGLS PAYING DBL FARE ELIGIBLE FOR GRP RATE & TC.

FIGURE 10-6 Confirmation/contract
Source: Courtesy of Norwegian Cruise Line

Group Terms & Conditions

GROUP SIZE REQUIREMENTS
For 3,4, and 7 day cruises, Norwegian Cruise Line (NCL) requires that a group consist of at least 15 full adult fare paying passengers, occupying a minimum of 8 cabins. For special and longer cruises, minimum requirements may vary. Groups of 100 passengers or more and incentive groups are non-standard groups and as such are subject to other Terms and Conditions.

TOUR CONDUCTORS
Standard group policy allows one complimentary Tour Conductor for every 15 full adult fare paying passengers. The 16th passenger will be the complimentary Tour Conductor berth. For special and longer cruises the Tour Conductor allowance may vary. The Tour Conductor allowance will be credited in the category in which the majority of the group space has been sold subject to availability, but at all times subject to NCL's discretion. As long as the majority of the group is on the Air/Sea program, Tour Conductors are awarded complimentary air from the air city that is holding the most space in the group. Third and fourth passengers do not count towards the Tour Conductor. Singles paying a minimum of 150% of the full fare will count as one passenger for Tour Conductor purposes. Singles paying 200% of the full fare count as two passengers for Tour Conductor purposes. Tour Conductors are non-discountable and non-commissionable.

DISCOUNTS
Group fares are already discounted. Fares exclude port charges, government taxes, fees and gratuities. Singles within the group must pay 200% of the adult group fare. A child traveling as the second passenger pays the adult group fare. Should the number of full fare paying adult passengers in the group fall below the size requirement, tour conductor allowances and any other consideration will be withdrawn. Tour packages, passenger insurance, and Air/Sea add-on's are non-discountable. All charges are subject to change.

COMMISSION
Standard travel agent commission will apply to group bookings. It is based on the discounted fare and does not apply to port charges, cocktail parties, other onboard amenities, prepaid gratuities, government taxes and fees, or any other purchases. Tour Packages, passenger insurance and Air/Sea add-ons are commissionable at 10%. Payment of commissions due hereunder is conditioned upon NCL's receipt of the full payment for the cruise booking.

PROMOTIONAL MATERIAL
A variety of collateral and promotional items are available to assist you in your group marketing activities. Please contact our distribution center through our main telephone number. NOTE: Discounted group rates may not be included in any way in the advertising or promotion of group space to the general public through public media, nor may group space be resold to other travel agencies. NCL reserves the right to cancel all group space whether sold or unsold should either situation occur.

PAYMENTS AND SPACE REQUESTS
It is very important to understand that by confirming a request for space, as opposed to a request for a cabin assignment, which is described below, NCL guarantees confirmation by category, not by cabin location. The following payment schedule applies to all standard groups.

Payment Dates
The initial Deposit of $25 per person is due 30 days after booking. Second Deposit is due no later than 4 months prior to sailing, subject to seasonality. Final payment schedules, by which time NCL must receive full payment, are listed below based on cruise type. Groups that book between 5 months and 60 days prior to sailing must pay cabin deposit within two weeks of the booking date. Groups that book less than 60 days before sailing must pay in full within 48 hours.

Cruise Type	Initial Deposit	Second Deposit	Cabin Deposit	Final Payment/Rooming List
Three and Four Days	$25 Per Person	$75 Per Person	$100 Per Person	Due 45 Days Prior to Sailing
Five through Nine Days	$25 Per Person	$225 Per Person	$250 Per Person	Due 60 Days Prior to Sailing
Ten plus Days (To and From North America and Caribbean)	$25 Per Person	$375 Per Person	$400 Per Person	Due 90 Days Prior to Sailing
Europe, South America, Asia, other international Destinations plus Holidays, Themes and Special Sailings	$25 Per Person	$375 Per Person	$400 Per Person	Due 90 Days Prior to Sailing

Cabin Assignments
Cabin assignments require a deposit within 7 days of booking if done before the second deposit is required. The amount due for cabin assignments is the cabin deposit, which is the sum of the initial and second deposits. If cabin deposit has already been received, cabin assignment will be done without additional deposit requirements. NCL reserves the right to require cabin assignments at any time. If NCL requires cabin assignment, cabin deposit is required and must be received within seven days. Triple/quad cabins are limited and are available on a request basis only. Third and fourth passengers cannot be guaranteed by the travel agent to their client until prior confirmation has been obtained from NCL. Cabin upgrades are subject to availability at current rates, not contracted, if different.

SPACE REVIEW/ADJUSTMENT
NCL reserves the right to reclaim any or all unsold space at any time; that is, cabin allocations or assignments for which any of the scheduled payments and names, when required, have not been received. Groups will automatically be canceled should NCL not receive any of the scheduled payments by the due date. It is your responsibility to advise NCL of your sales progress, to provide the required deposits and names in a timely manner, and to submit sample copies of applicable promotional material. Beginning at 8 months before sailing, NCL may contact you every 30 days to review the progress of your sales. While NCL may recall any or all unsold space at any time, you may add to your allocation upon review if space is available so that you may achieve the greatest possible success from your efforts.

NAME CHANGES
Name changes are not permitted without the approval of NCL. Name changes will be assessed a cancellation charge according to the "Cancellation Policy" provision set forth below if they are made within the applicable relevant period. If a name change is made to modify the spelling of an existing passenger that requires reprinting of documents, a service fee of $25 per person will be assessed for each such change. If a prepaid air ticket is required, additional charges apply.

FINAL PAYMENT AND CANCELLATION POLICY
NCL must receive the full and final payment and rooming list in house no later than 45 days before the sailing for cruises of 3 and 4 days, 60 days before the sailing for cruises of 5+ days. NCL may require final payment and rooming lists at 90 days prior to sailing for certain cruises, including international, holiday cruises, theme cruises and special sailings. Cabins canceled after the final payment date will be assessed the following charges:

Cruise Type	Before Sailing	Cancellation Charge	Cruise Type	Before Sailing	Cancellation Charge
Three and Four Days	45 - 30 Days	$ 50 Per Person	Five through Nine Days	60 - 30 Days	$100 Per Person
	29 - 04 Days	$100 Per Person		29 - 04 Days	$200 Per Person
Ten or More Days (To or From North America and the Caribbean)	60 - 30 Days	$400 Per Person	Europe, South America, Asia, and other International Destinations; Holidays, Themes and Special Sailings	90 - 60 Days	$200 Per Person
	29 - 04 Days	$800 Per Person		59 - 30 Days	$400 Per Person
				29 - 15 Days	50% of Total Fare
				14 - 04 Days	75% of Total Fare

In addition to the above charges, there will be no refund for "no-show" or cancellations that occur less than 4 days prior to sailing day.
Refund requests must be in writing and accompanied by all documents. Refund processing time is approximately 4 to 6 weeks after sailing. Credit card payments must be refunded to the card received.

INSURANCE
NCL Trip Cancellation, Baggage, and Medical Protection Plan is available to all U.S. and Canadian Residents who are part of the group. Payment must be made no later than the group's final payment due date. Insurance payments are paid separately and mailed to NCL's accounting department with enrollment forms to: - ATTN. - Insurance Desk, P.O. Box 025403, Miami, Florida 33102-5403.

AIR/SEA
All group air space is on a request basis. Airline seat availability may be limited on certain sailing dates and is subject to capacity control. NCL may not be able to confirm requested gateways. For Air/Sea passengers, NCL will only block air space upon receipt of cabin deposit, Air/Sea cities, and passenger names. Confirmation of air space is subject to carrier availability and NCL reserves the right to withdraw air space at anytime. NCL will only assign flight itineraries upon receipt of full payment. This is to prevent any untimely release or non-use of air space close to the sailing date. Late submission of rooming lists and final payment may result in air allocations being revoked by the airlines. NCL reserves the right to choose air carriers and routings; therefore, flights may not be non-stop or direct. Should passengers require specific air arrangements (i.e.. Non-stop flights or flights at specific hours; a particular airline; etc.), please contact NCL's Premium Air Desk. Service fees, other charges and restrictions may apply. NCL reserves the right to substitute any previously designated airline or scheduled flights without incurring any liability to passengers or the travel agent on account thereof.

FIGURE 10-6 *(continued)*

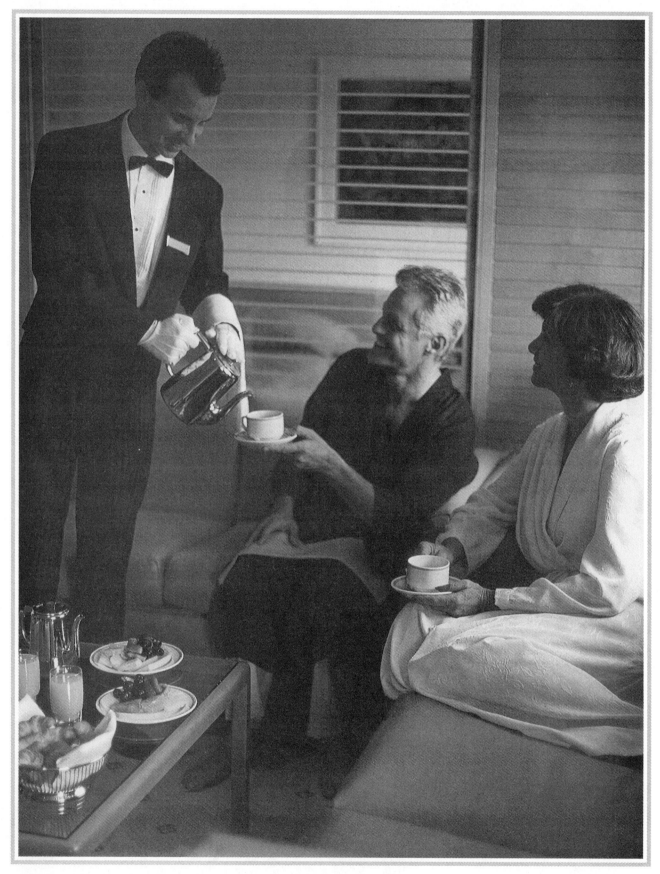

Incentive clients love the high level of attention they receive on a cruise.
Courtesy of Celebrity Cruises

Incentives

Earlier we said that there were *three* kinds of groups. The third is a very specialized kind called an **incentive group**.

The incentive business is a unique segment of the travel industry. (It also spans other industries, as well.) A **travel incentive** is a program to motivate people to perform better through the potential award of an exceptional travel experience.

Here's how it works. Let's say you approach a large chain of car dealerships in your state. You propose that every salesperson who sells 40 cars or more in a given year will be awarded a free 7-day cruise in the Caribbean. (Their average is 25 per salesperson per year.) All the awardees will be on the same cruise departure, each with an outside, "ocean-view" superior cabin, and will enjoy special onboard and shore-side events. They'll be pampered as never before, have fun, and be treated as VIPs. They can even bring along a guest.

What's the catch? *There's none.* The cost of the cruise will be paid from part of the increased sales and profits that result from the incentive offer. If sales don't increase, the trip won't happen. But it will. Incentives have an astonishing power to work.

What's amazing is that, with incentive groups, everyone wins:

- The client-company makes more money with minimal risk. Morale is improved and goodwill is created.
- The employees get travel and prestige.
- The cruise line fills prime cabins.
- The incentive company or travel agency makes a handsome profit.

Incentives constitute a complex and unique business. For more information, consult the texts cited in Appendix C.

A Final Note

Never thought there was so much to the cruise business, did you? Neither did I when I took my first cruise a decade ago. Since then I've taken dozens. And each time my respect, delight, and love for the cruise vacation experience grows.

If you've never cruised, then a remarkable adventure awaits you. And if you have already taken a cruise vacation, I hope that your next one brings you even richer insights into this significant, exciting, and wondrous segment of the travel industry.

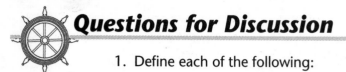

Questions for Discussion

1. Define each of the following:

   • marketing

   • hot button

   • distribution

   • mission statement

   • SWOT analysis

   • database

   • fulfillment

   • incentive

2. What are the six steps of marketing?

3. What's the difference between product research and consumer research? Between advertising and publicity? Between a tangible product and an intangible product? Between a pre-formed group and a speculative group?

4. Give the twelve steps to a marketing plan.

5. Name at least six things a cruise line can provide an agency to support a group departure.

6. Give ten items that are potentially negotiable with a cruise line.

7. How do each of the following "win" on an incentive cruise—the client-company, its employees, the cruise line, the travel agency or incentive company?

⚓ *Activity*

Are there groups in your community who might be prime prospects for a group cruise?

Using every means at your disposal, identify three specific groups in your community to whom you think you could sell a group cruise. Explain why you think they would respond favorably to a cruise and what kind of cruise (or even specific cruise) you would pitch to them.

Group #1: _____

- What kind of cruise?

- Why?

Group #2: _____

- What kind of cruise?

- Why?

Group #3: _____

- What kind of cruise?

- Why?

APPENDIX A

KEY ADDRESSES: CLIA MEMBER CRUISE LINES

Please note that the internet resources are of a time sensitive nature and URL sites and addresses may often be modified or deleted.

American Hawaii Cruises
Robin Street Wharf
1380 Port of New Orleans Pl.
New Orleans, LA 70130-1890
(504) 586-0631
http://www.cruisehawaii.com

Bergen Line, Inc.
405 Park Ave.
New York, NY 10022
(212) 319-1300
http://www.bergenline.com

Carnival Cruise Lines
3655 NW 87th Ave.
Miami, FL 33178
(305) 599-2600
http://www.carnival.com

Celebrity Cruises, Inc.
1050 Caribbean Way
Miami, FL 33132
(305) 530-6000
http://www.celebrity-cruises.com

Commodore Cruise Line
4000 Hollywood Blvd.
Ste. 385 South Tower
Hollywood, FL 33021
(954) 967-2100
http://www.commodorecruise.com

Costa Cruise Lines
80 SW 8th St.
Miami, FL 33130-3097
(305) 358-7325
http://www.costacruises.com

Crystal Cruises
2121 Ave. of the Stars, Ste. 200
Los Angeles, CA 90067
(310) 785-9300

Cunard
6100 Blue Lagoon Dr., Ste. 400
Miami, FL 33126
(305) 463-3000
http://www.cunardline.com

Disney Cruise Line
210 Celebration Pl., Ste. 400
Celebration, FL 34747-4600
(407) 566-3500
http://www.disneycruise.com

First European Cruises
95 Madison Ave., Ste. 1203
New York, NY 10016
(212) 779-7168
http://www.first–european.com

Holland America Line
300 Elliott Ave. W.
Seattle, WA 98119
(206) 281-3535
http://www.hollandamerica.com

Mediterranean Shipping Cruises
420 Fifth Ave.
New York, NY 10018-2702
(212) 764-4800
http://www.crucerosmsc–arg.com

Norwegian Cruise Line
7665 Corporate Center Dr.
Miami, FL 33126-1201
(305) 436-4000
http://www.ncl.com

Orient Lines, Inc.
1510 SE 17th St., Ste. 400
Fort Lauderdale, FL 33316
(954) 527-6660
http://www.orientlines.com

Premier Cruises
901 South America Way
Miami, FL 33132-2073
(305) 358-5122
http://www.premiercruises.com

Princess Cruises
10100 Santa Monica Blvd.
Los Angeles, CA 90067
(310) 553-1770
http://www.princesscruises.com

Radisson Seven Seas Cruises
600 Corporate Dr., Ste. 410
Fort Lauderdale, FL 33334
(954) 776-6123
http://www.rssc.com

Regal Cruises
300 Regal Cruises Way
PO Box 1329
Palmetto, FL 34220
(941) 721-7300
http://www.regalcruises.com

Royal Caribbean International
1050 Caribbean Way
Miami, FL 33132
(305) 539-6000
http://www.royalcaribbean.com

Royal Olympic Cruises
1 Rockefeller Plaza, Ste. 315
New York, NY 10020
(212) 397-6400
http://www.royalolympiccruises.com

Seabourn Cruise Line
6100 Blue Lagoon Dr., Ste 400
Miami, FL 33126
(305) 463-3000
http://www.seabourn.com

Silversea Cruises
110 E. Broward Blvd.
Fort Lauderdale, FL 33301
(954) 522-4477
http://www.silversea.com

Windstar Cruises
300 Elliott Ave. W.
Seattle, WA 98119
(206) 281-3535
http://www.windstarcruises.com

APPENDIX B

KEY ADDRESSES: ASSOCIATIONS

American Society of Travel Agents (ASTA)
1101 King St.
Alexandria, VA 22314
(703) 739-2782

Association of Canadian Travel Agents (ACTA)
201-1729 Rue Bank St.
Ottawa, ON K1V 7Z5
(613) 521-0474

Association of Retail Travel Agents (ARTA)
501 Darby Creek Rd., Ste. 47
Lexington, KY 40509
(606) 263-1194

Canadian Institute of Travel Counsellors (CITC)
41 Richmond Dr.
Markham, ON L3P 3Y7
(905) 472-8533

Cruise Lines International Association (CLIA)
500 Fifth Ave., Ste. 1407
New York, NY 10110
(212) 921-0066

Institute of Certified Travel Agents (ICTA)
148 Linden St.
PO Box 812059
Wellesley, MA 02181-0012
(781) 237-0280

Intl. Airlines Travel Agent Network (IATAN)
300 Garden City Plaza, Ste. 342
Garden City, NY 11530
(516) 747-4716

Natl. Association of Commissioned Travel Agents (NACTA)
PO Box 2398
Valley Center, CA 92082-2398
(760) 751-1197

Natl. Association of Cruise Only Agencies (NACOA)
7600 Red Rd., Ste. 128
S. Miami, FL 33143
(305) 663-5626

Natl. Tour Association (NTA)
546 E. Main St.
PO Box 3071
Lexington, KY 40596-3071
(606) 226-4444

Outside Sales Support Network (OSSN)
1061 E. Indiantown Rd.
Jupiter, FL 33477
(561) 743-1900

Pacific Asia Travel Association (PATA)
1 Montgomery St., Ste. 1000
San Francisco, CA 94104
(415) 986-4646

Society of Incentive and Travel Executives (SITE)
21 W. 38th St., 10th Fl.
New York, NY 10018-5584
(212) 575-0910

United States Tour Operators Association (USTOA)
342 Madison Ave., Ste. 1522
New York, NY 10173
(212) 599-6599

APPENDIX C

BIBLIOGRAPHY

Trade Publications on Cruising: Books

CLIA Cruise Manual, CLIA

Cruise Hosting: A Step-by-Step Guide for Beginners and Professionals, Brooke Shannon Bravos, CTP, Travel Time Pub

Cruises: Selecting, Selling, and Booking, Juls Zvoncheck, CTC, Regents/Prentice Hall

Official Cruise Guide, Cahners Travel Group

Official Steamship Guide International, Transportation Guides Inc.

Ports of Call, Arnie Weissmann, Weissmann Travel Reports

Sails for Profit, Jeanne Semer-Purzycki and Robert H. Purzycki, Prentice Hall

Sea Travel: The Book, Douglas Shachnow, MCC, Right Track Publications

Selling Cruises, Claudine Dervaes, Solitaire Publishing

Selling Cruises, Tom Ogg and Joanie Ogg, MCC, Tom Ogg & Associates

Trade Publications on Cruising: Periodicals

Agents Cruise Monthly, PO Box 92, Stamford, CT 06904

Cruise & Vacation Views, 25 Washington St., Morristown, NJ 07960

Cruise Industry News, 441 Lexington Ave., Ste. 1209, New York, NY 10017

Cruise Reports, 88 Main St., Ste. 453, Mendham, NJ 07945

Cruise Week, 910 Deer Spring Ln., Wilmington, NC 28409

Ocean and Cruise News, PO Box 92, Stamford, CT 06904

Trade Publications with Cruise-Related Features and/or Supplements

ASTA Agency Management, One Penn Plaza, New York, NY 10119

Tour and Travel News, 600 Harrison St., San Francisco, CA 94107

Travel Agent Magazine, 801 Second Ave., New York, NY 10017

Travel Counselor Magazine, 600 Harrison St., San Francisco, CA 94107

Travel Courier, 310 Dupont St., Toronto, ON M5R 1V9

Travel Trade, 15 W. 44th St., New York, NY 10036

Travel Weekly, 500 Plaza Dr., Secaucus, NJ 07094

Travel World News, 1 Morgan Ave., Norwalk, CT 06851

TravelAge West, 49 Stevenson St. #460, San Francisco, CA 94105

Consumer Publications on Cruising: Books and On-Line

Berlitz Complete Guide to Cruising, Douglas Ward, Globe Pequot Press

Bon-Voyage—The Cruise Traveler's Handbook, Gary Bannerman, National Textbook Co.

Cruise Critic, America Online

The Essential Little Cruise Book, Jim West, Globe Pequot Press

Fielding's Worldwide Cruises, Shirley Slater and Harry Basch, Fieldings Worldwide, Inc.

Fodor's Worldwide Cruises and Ports of Call, M. T. Schwartzman, editor, Fodors Travel Publications

Frommer's Cruises, Frommer

Garth's Profile of Ships, Garth Peterson, Cruising with Garth

How to Get a Job with a Cruise Line, Mary Fallon Miller, Ticket to Adventure

Selling the Sea, Bob Dickinson and Andy Vladimir, John Wiley & Sons

Stern's Guide to the Cruise Vacation, Steven Stern, Pelican

The Total Traveler Guide to Worldwide Cruising, Ethel Blum, Onboard Media

The Unofficial Guide to Cruises, Kay Showker with Bob Sehlinger, Macmillan Travel

Consumer Periodicals That Feature Major Articles on Cruising

Arthur Frommer's Budget Travel, The Empire State Bldg., Ste. 2701, New York, NY 10118

Conde Nast Traveler, 360 Madison Ave., New York, NY 10017

Consumer Reports Travel Letter, 101 Truman Ave., Yonkers, NY 10703

Cruise Travel, 990 Grove St., Evanston, IL 60201

Porthole, 7100 W. Commercial Blvd., Fort Lauderdale, FL 33319

Travel and Leisure, 1120 Ave. of the Americas, New York, NY 10036

Travel Holiday, 28 W. 23rd St., New York, NY 10010

Miscellaneous Trade and Consumer Resources

Conducting Tours, Marc Mancini, Delmar Publishers

Guerrilla Marketing, Jay Conrad Levinson, Houghton Mifflin

Incentive Travel: The Complete Guide, Bruce Tepper

Selling Destinations, Marc Mancini, Delmar Publishers

The Star Service, Cahners Travel Group

The Travel Dictionary, Claudine Dervaes, Solitaire Publishing

Travel Sales and Customer Service, ICTA

Ultimate Marketing Plan, Daniel S. Kennedy, Bob Adams Inc.

GLOSSARY

A

Advertising Promotion that costs money.

Affinity group A group of people who have some psychographic trait in common.

Air/sea package A package that includes airfare, the airport-to-dock transfer, and perhaps lodging.

Alumni rate See **Past passenger rate**

Atrium A multi-story space on newer ships.

At-sea day A day when the ship is traveling a long distance and doesn't stop at a port-of-call.

B

Bare boat charter A yacht charter without a crew.

Basis two (also called **Double occupancy**) Pricing per person, based on two passengers sharing a stateroom designed to accommodate two or more.

Berth A bed on a ship; also can refer to the docking space of a ship.

Bow The front of the ship.

Bridge Place on the ship from where it's controlled.

C

Cabin See **Stateroom**

Cabin steward The person who maintains staterooms.

Circle itinerary (also called **Round-trip itinerary**) Itinerary with the ship leaving from and returning to the same port.

Closed-ended question Question that requires simple, factual responses.

Closed-jaw itinerary (also called **Round-trip itinerary**) A flight to and from the same city.

Consumer research (also called **Market research**) Research that tries to discover who the public is, how they think, and what they like to buy.

Cross-selling Offering the client something in addition to the cruise itself, but related to it.

Cruise-only trip Cruise with no need for air transportation.

D

Database An organized collection of customer profiles.

Debarkation See **Disembarkation**

Deck The equivalent of a story in a building.

Deck plan Ship's floor plan, showing cabins and public spaces.

Disembarkation (also called **Debarkation**) Exiting the ship.

Double occupancy See **Basis two**

Draft Measurement from waterline to lowest part of the ship's frame.

E

Embarkation Boarding the ship.

F

Fam See **Familiarization cruise**

Familiarization cruise (also called a **Fam**) A cruise offered at a very reduced price to travel agents by a cruise line.

First seating (or **sitting**) The earlier of two meal times in the ship's dining room.

Front desk See **Purser's office**

G

Galley Area on ship where food is prepared (the kitchen).

Gangway Walkway that connects the ship with the dock.

Gross registered tonnage (GRT) Size determined by a formula that gauges the volume of the public spaces on a ship.

GRT See **Gross registered tonnage**

Guaranteed share A single passenger who is willing to share a cabin with a stranger (of the same sex) may book at the per-person double occupancy rate. Offered by some cruise lines.

H

High season The time of year with the highest demand and the highest prices.

Hot button Anything that powerfully entices a buyer.

Hotel desk See **Purser's office**

I

Incentive program A program to motivate people to perform better through the potential award of an exceptional travel experience.

Information desk See **Purser's office**

Inside stateroom (also called **Interior stateroom**) Stateroom which has no windows.

Intangible product Product or service that has no physical form.

Interior staterooms See **Inside stateroom**

L

Lido deck Pool deck area that offers informal, buffet-like dining, both indoors and outdoors.

Lower bed A bed that's on the stateroom's floor.

Low season The time of year with the lowest demand and the lowest prices.

M

Magrodome A glass skylight that can slide to cover the pool area in cold weather.

Market research See **Consumer research**

Meet-and-greet A company representative meets cruise passengers at their airport arrival gate.

Megaship Giant-sized ships, 70,000 GRT and above, that can accommodate at least 2,000 passengers.

N

Niche A narrow segment of consumers who have something in common.

O

One-way itinerary Itinerary with the ship starting at one port and finishing at another.

Open-ended question Question that elicits complex and telling responses.

Open-jaw itinerary An air itinerary featuring a return from a different city than from the one first flown to.

Open seating (or **sitting**) Passengers may sit anywhere in the dining room; tables are not assigned.

Outside stateroom Stateroom which has windows.

Override commission A commission over and above the standard commission rate.

P

Past passenger rate (also called **Alumni rate**) Discounted rate given to people who have sailed a cruise line before.

Pax Industry abbreviation for "passengers."

Pied piper A member of an organization who is especially respected and admired by its members.

Port Facing forward, the left side of the ship.

Port day A day when the ship stops at a port-of-call.

Port charge What ports charge the cruise lines to dock their ships.

Post-cruise package Package that includes lodging at the cruise arrival port after the cruise.

Pre-cruise package Package that includes lodging at the cruise departure port before the cruise.

Pre-formed group A group of people who belong to a club, association, or other pre-existing organization.

Product research Research that focuses on the elements of what is to be sold.

Promotional group See **Speculative group**

Prospect A potential buyer of a product.

Publicity Promotion that is nearly or completely cost-free.

Purser's office (also called **front desk, hotel desk, reception desk,** or **information desk**) The direct equivalent of a hotel's front desk.

R

Reception desk See **Purser's office.**

Repositioning cruise A cruise where the ship moves from one general cruise area to another.

Round-trip itinerary See **Circle itinerary** or **Closed-jaw itinerary**

S

Second seating (or **sitting)** The later of two meal times in the ship's dining room.

Shore excursion A port-based tour or activity.

Shoulder season The time of year between high season and low season, when prices are somewhat lower than in the high season.

Single occupancy One passenger booking a stateroom designed to accommodate two or more.

Single supplement The additional price one passenger must pay for single occupancy.

Spa Facility on the ship which offers massages, facials, saunas, whirlpools, aromatherapy, and other beauty or relaxation-related services.

Space ratio Figure determined by dividing GRT by passenger capacity.

Speculative group (also called **Promotional group**) A group of individuals who probably do not know each other.

Stabilizers Underwater wing-like devices that reduce a ship's roll.

Starboard Facing forward, the right side of the ship.

Stateroom (also called **Cabin**) A guest room on a ship.

Stateroom category The price that a certain kind or level of stateroom represents.

Stern The back of the ship.

Suite The most expensive accommodation on a ship, typically featuring, in the same rectangular space, both a sitting area and a sleeping area, often divided by a curtain.

T

Tangible product Product that has physical form.

Tender A small boat that ferries passengers between port and ship.

Travel incentive A program to motivate people to perform better through the potential award of an exceptional travel experience.

U

Upper bed Similar to an upper bed in a bunk bed. It's recessed into the wall or ceiling during the day and is pulled out for bedtime, above floor level.

Upselling Offering the client something that costs a little more than they expected to pay.

Y

Yield management The practice of adjusting price to supply and demand.

Z

Zodiac boat A large rubber boat, mainly used on adventure cruises.

INDEX

NOTE: Italicized page numbers refer to figures.

Great Britain, 103
   map, *103*
gross registered tonnage (GRT),
   27-30
groups
   contracts, 183, *184-185*
   negotiating, *182*
   promotion, *180*, 183
   rates, 19
   sales, 179-185, 187
   support from cruise line, *181*
   types, 179-180, 183
GRT, 27-28
Guadeloupe, 96
guaranteed shares, *163*
gyms, *8*, 32

H

Haiti, 98
Halifax (Nova Scotia), 91
handicapped cruisers, 81-82
Hawaii, 108, 122
head housekeeper, 59
health clubs, *8*, 32
high season, 19
history of cruising, 3-6, 8
Holland America Line, 4, 131
home-based agents, 66
hot buttons, 176
hotel desk, 30
hotel director, 59
hotel manager, 59
hotel operations, 59
hotel purser, 59

I

immigration, 4
incentive programs, 183, 187
inclusiveness, 18
independent travel agencies, 63
informational sources, 116-119
information desk, 30
Inside Passage, The, 88-90
inside salespersons, 66
inside staterooms, 19, 33
inspections, *67-68*, 116
Institute of Certified Travel
   Agents, The (ICTA), 70
intangible products, 176
interior staterooms, 33
International Airlines Travel
   Agent Network, The
   (IATAN), 70
Internet
   as source of information,
     118-119
   use in booking, *64*, 162

Ireland, 103
   map, *103*
itineraries
   example, *10*
   types, *9*

J

Jamaica, 98
Juneau, 89

K

Ketchikan, 89
knowledge, lack of
   as an objection to cruise pur-
     chase, 22, *160*

L

land-based operations, 60-62, *61*
last night, 50
leisure sailing, 3-4
Lido deck, 32, 48
lifeboat drills, 46
lifestyle questions, 154-155
Love Boat, The, 137
lower beds, 33
low season, 19
luggage, 43, 50
Luxury Cruisers, 148

M

magazines, use in advertising, *174*
magrodomes, 32
management (land-based operations), organization, 60, *61*
market
   potential, 8, *151*
   types who have cruised, 148
   types who have not yet
     cruised, *152*
marketing, 170-187
   definition, 170
   elements, 170, 172-177
   plans, 177-179
   research, 172
   to groups, 180-183
   see also sales
marrying aboard ship, *75*
masted sailing ships, 26
mature cruisers, as an objection
   to cruise purchase, 20, *159*
Mazatlan, 94
media, comparison, *173-175*
medical facilities, 32
Mediterranean Shipping Cruises,
   132

Mediterranean, The, 3
   Eastern, 101
     map, *101*
   Western, 100
     map, *99*
meet-and-greet staff, 43, 74
megaships, 8, 26, 27, 28
menus, 46
   alternative, 52
   examples, *47*, *53*
   see also dining; food
Mexico
   Pacific Coast of, 93-94
     map, *93*
Miami, embarkation port map of,
   44
Middle East, ports, *100*
Mississippi River, 92-93
   map, *92*
motion sickness, as an objection
   to cruise purchase, 22, *160*
motives
   for cruising, 15-16, 18
   for not cruising, 19-22, *159-160*
multi-line reps, 62
multi-purpose ships, 27

N

Nassau, 95
National Association of
   Commissioned Travel
   Agents, The (NACTA), 70
National Association of Cruise-
   Oriented Agencies, The
   (NACOA), 70
National Geographic's Cruise
   Finder, 119
National Tour Association, The
   (NTA), 70
Navy experience, as an objection
   to cruise purchase, 21, *160*
Newport, 91
newspaper inserts, use in adver-
   tising, *174*
newspapers, use in advertising,
   173
niche cruise lines, 120
Nile River, 110
North America, 88-98
   maps, *89*, *91-97*
Northeast (U.S.), 90-92
   map, *91*
North Sea, 103
   map, *103*
Norwegian Coastal Voyages, Inc.,
   133
Norwegian Cruise Line, 134

O

objections to cruise purchase, 19-22
  responses, 158, *159-160*
ocean liners, 4, 26
officers, 58-59
Official Cruise Guide, The, 117
Official Steamship Guide International, The, 117
one-way itineraries, 9, *10*
open-ended questions, 154
opening the sale, 149, 151
open-jaw itineraries, 11
open seating, *46*, 48
operations
  hotel, 59
  land-based, 60-62
  sailing, 58-59
  sea-based, 58-60
organizational chart (land-based operations), *61*
Orient Lines, 135
outside salespersons, 66
Outside Sales Support Network, The (OSSN), 70
outside staterooms, 19, 33
override commission, 65

P

P&O, 4, 137
Pacific Ocean, 108
  map, *108*
  Mexican coast, 93-94
    map, *93*
Panama Canal, 94
passengers, *see* cruisers
past passenger rates, 19
pax, 28
payments, 163-164
phone sales, 149, 151, 153, 162
photographs, 32, 43, 45
physically challenged cruisers, 81-82
pied pipers, 179, 180
pools, 32
popularity of cruising, 2, 16, 18
port (side of ship), 36
port charges, 18
port days, 9-10
  activities, 75-76
  example, 49-50
  see also shore excursions; port experiences; pre-cruise packages; post-cruise packages
port experiences, 74-82
  and cruiser profiles, 80-82

for families, 81
for the physically challenged, 82
see also shore excursions; port days; pre-cruise packages; post-cruise packages
port time, limited
  as an objection to cruise purchase, 21, *159*
post-cruise packages, 10, 21, 80
pre-cruise packages, 10, 21, 43, 74
preferred agencies, 65
pre-formed groups, 179
Premier Cruises, 136
president, 60
price, 18-19, 65, 74, *163*
  as an objection to cruise purchase, 19-20, *159*
  compared with land-based vacation, *20*
  determining, 173
  factors affecting, 19
  negotiating for group, *182*
  of staterooms, 36
Princess Cruises, 137
product design and research, 172
profiles of cruisers, 14, 80-82, 83-85, 120, 148
profit, 65, 173
Prohibition, cruising during, 4
promotion, 173, *173-175*, 176
  creating campaigns, 176
  to groups, 183
promotional groups, 179-180
promotional information, 116
prospects, 176
publications, 117-118
publicity, 173
public spaces, 30, 32
Puerto Vallarta, 94
purser, 59
purser's office, 30

Q

qualifying, 151-154, 156
  clients with definite ideas, 153-154
  clients with rough ideas, 152
  clients with vague ideas, 151-152
  groups, 181
  questions, 154, 156
Quebec City, 91
Quick-Getaway Vacationers, 84

R

radio, use in advertising, *174*
Radisson Seven Seas Cruises, 138

rates, *see* price
reasons for cruising/not cruising, *see* motives
reception desk, 30
recommendations, 156-157
Regal Cruises, 139
regimentation, as an objection to cruise purchase, 21, *159*
registry, 37
repositioning cruises, 19, 91, 102, 110-112
reservations, *see* booking
reservation sheet, 154
  example, *155*
response rates, 181
Restless Baby Boomers, 148
riverboats, 26, 92-93
  cruiser profile, 93
river cruises
  in Europe, 104
  on Mississippi, 92-93
Romantic Vacationers, 84
roominess, *see* space ratio
room stewards, 59
round-trip itineraries, 9, *10*, 11
Royal Caribbean International, 140
Royal Olympic Cruises, 141

S

safety, 16, 46
  as an objection to cruise purchase, 21, *160*
sailing operations, 58-59
Saint John's (New Brunswick), 91
sales, 148-164
  closing, 161-162
  distribution channels, 63-66, *64*
  following up, 164
  in person, 149, 153
  opening, 149, 151
  process, 42, 149-164
  publications, 164
  telephone, 149, 151
  training, 119
  see also marketing
sea-based operations, 58-60
Seabourn Cruise Line, 128, 142
Seabourn Goddess, 39
seasickness, as an objection to cruise purchase, 22, *160*
seasons, 19, *111*
seatings, 46
second class, 4
second seating, 46
seminars, 116, 117
Seven Ancient Wonders of the World, 3, *3*